IDIOT'S
GUIDE

AS EASY AS IT GETS!

P9-APX-203

Beginning Programming

by Matt Telles

ALPHA

A member of Penguin Group (USA) Inc.

This book is dedicated to my wife, Teresa, without whom it would have been done a lot sooner, but life would be a lot less fun.

ALPHA BOOKS

Published by Penguin Group (USA) Inc.

Penguin Group (USA) Inc., 375 Hudson Street, New York, New York 10014, USA • Penguin Group (Canada), 90 Eglinton Avenue East, Suite 700, Toronto, Ontario M4P 2Y3, Canada (a division of Pearson Penguin Canada Inc.) • Penguin Books Ltd., 80 Strand, London WC2R 0RL, England • Penguin Ireland, 25 St. Stephen's Green, Dublin 2, Ireland (a division of Penguin Books Ltd.) • Penguin Group (Australia), 250 Camberwell Road, Camberwell, Victoria 3124, Australia (a division of Pearson Australia Group Pty. Ltd.) • Penguin Books India Pvt. Ltd., 11 Community Centre, Panchsheel Park, New Delhi—110 017, India • Penguin Group (NZ), 67 Apollo Drive, Rosedale, North Shore, Auckland 1311, New Zealand (a division of Pearson New Zealand Ltd.) • Penguin Books (South Africa) (Pty.) Ltd., 24 Sturdee Avenue, Rosebank, Johannesburg 2196, South Africa • Penguin Books Ltd., Registered Offices: 80 Strand, London WC2R 0RL, England

International Standard Book Number: 978-1-61564-505-3
Library of Congress Catalog Card Number: 2014930955

16   15   14   8   7   6   5   4   3   2   1

Interpretation of the printing code: The rightmost number of the first series of numbers is the year of the book's printing; the rightmost number of the second series of numbers is the number of the book's printing. For example, a printing code of 14-1 shows that the first printing occurred in 2014.

Printed in the United States of America

Note: This publication contains the opinions and ideas of its author. It is intended to provide helpful and informative material on the subject matter covered. It is sold with the understanding that the author and publisher are not engaged in rendering professional services in the book. If the reader requires personal assistance or advice, a competent professional should be consulted. The author and publisher specifically disclaim any responsibility for any liability, loss, or risk, personal or otherwise, which is incurred as a consequence, directly or indirectly, of the use and application of any of the contents of this book.

Most Alpha books are available at special quantity discounts for bulk purchases for sales promotions, premiums, fundraising, or educational use. Special books, or book excerpts, can also be created to fit specific needs. For details, write: Special Markets, Alpha Books, 375 Hudson Street, New York, NY 10014.

3 9547 00397 5708

Publisher: *Mike Sanders*
Executive Managing Editor: *Billy Fields*
Senior Acquisitions Editor: *Brook Farling*
Development Editor: *Kayla Dugger*
Senior Production Editor: *Janette Lynn*

Cover Designer: *William Thomas*
Book Designer: *William Thomas*
Indexer: *Tonya Heard*
Layout: *Ayanna Lacey*
Proofreader: *Amy Borrelli*

Contents

Appendixes

Introduction

Computer programming has become a necessity in today's business world. Programmers, analysts, and designers are in more demand than ever before in history. Whether your goal is to become a professional computer programmer or just to learn how this industry works, this book is for you. It isn't designed for experts and assumes no previous programming experience. Therefore, I make sure to explain to you all those mystical words that computer folks use (such as ROM, RAM, preload, and so forth) and show you how to use that information.

The language I provide you with instructions to use is called *Python,* like the snake. I chose it because it is easy to write code in and doesn't require an advanced degree to understand. Using this programming language along with the book, you learn how to write little programs to accomplish tasks, as well as how to use the functionality of the language to create reusable components that you—or anyone else—can use in the future.

I wish you the best of luck on your journey into programming!

How This Book Is Organized

I've divided the book into four major parts:

Part 1, Background on Computers and Terminology, teaches you the words, phrases, and concepts you need to be able to write computer programs. This part also includes an introduction on Python and how to get it up and running.

Part 2, Learning Python, teaches you the basic syntax of the Python programming language, as well as how to put together lines of code into a single script that accomplishes something. You won't be an expert after going through this part, but you will have the background to understand and learn from those that have been using the language for years.

Part 3, Basic Programming Concepts, shows you how to put together what you've learned into real programs that accomplish something. You'll also read about some of the more esoteric subjects in programming, such as graphics.

Part 4, Working with the Python Environment, shows you how to use the Python environment to produce high-quality software, as well as how to track down problems in your code.

Extras

Throughout the book, you'll find bits of extra information to help you along your journey to a career or hobby in computer programming.

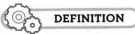

DEFINITION

These sidebars explain programming subjects and terms that might not be clear.

PROGRAMMING TIP

In these sidebars, you get shortcuts and advice to make you a better programmer.

ERROR MESSAGE

These tell you things to watch out for in your own programs.

Acknowledgments

This book was difficult to write for a variety of reasons, from personal health to trying to really explain things to people I do not work with every day. A special thank you to my editor, Brook Farling, as well as all of the people at Alpha Books for helping me along to fit into their system. In addition, I'd like to thank my agents at Waterside Productions for making the finishing and publishing of this book such a smooth process—I couldn't have done it without you guys.

Finally, I'd like to dedicate this book to all the women in my life—Jenny, Rachel, Sarah, and Teresa—without whom it wouldn't be nearly as stressful to live, nor half as much fun.

Special Thanks to the Technical Reviewer

Idiot's Guides: Beginning Programming was reviewed by an expert who double-checked the accuracy of what you'll learn here, to help us ensure this book gives you everything you need to know about programming. Special thanks are extended to Al Sweigart.

Trademarks

All terms mentioned in this book that are known to be or are suspected of being trademarks or service marks have been appropriately capitalized. Alpha Books and Penguin Group (USA) Inc. cannot attest to the accuracy of this information. Use of a term in this book should not be regarded as affecting the validity of any trademark or service mark.

Background on Computers and Terminology

Before you get started, you need to know some basic information about computers and the programming language you'll be using (Python). This part gives you the backstory of programming from the perspective of professional programmers. You also learn the terminology you need to understand the remainder of the book, as well as any technical articles or other books you might pick up. You even write your very first program and see it run!

So You Want to Program Computers

If you have picked up this book, the chances are pretty good you are considering writing computer programs. Okay, it isn't an absolute given—perhaps you simply want to know what programmers do, so you can laugh at them. (It wouldn't be the first time.) Still, you and I both know you really want to understand what programmers are doing all day behind closed doors. Whatever the case, you picked the right place to start.

Before you can determine how to program a computer, though, you should know what it is you are programming. In this chapter, I help you take a look under that shiny cover of your computer.

In This Chapter

- The parts of a computer
- The function of a program
- Getting into the programming mindset

What Is a Computer, Really?

We've all seen those scary movies of the future, where computers take over the world. You have probably felt that way about your PC (personal computer) when you first turned it on. Really, though, a computer isn't a very complicated piece of equipment. It is made up of a few big pieces, and those big pieces are made up of smaller pieces. Your car is considerably more complicated inside, and you drive it all the time.

There are lots of parts to a computer. Most of them, people really don't care about until they break. From the perspective of a programmer, however, they are important.

Hardware

Let's begin with the hardware in the system. There are certainly lots of other kinds of hardware and many other devices you will run into when you are working with computers. From the perspective of a programmer, however, the following are the big ones.

Central Processing Unit (CPU): The CPU is the "brain" of the computer. Unfortunately, unlike our brains, computer CPUs are pretty dumb. They know how to add and subtract, save little bits of memory, and retrieve information. For now, though, think of the CPU as the part of the computer that does all the real work.

Monitor (or display): A computer isn't much use unless you can see what it is doing, and the monitor is the part of the computer that is used to show things to the user. Monitors can be big CRTs (Cathode Ray Tubes) like you've seen for older computers, flat-screen plasma devices like your HDTV, or even tiny flip screens like your phone. Most of the time, monitors are purely there to show you stuff; they don't interact with anyone or anything.

Keyboard: If you can't get information into your computer, it isn't very useful to you. The keyboard is a big part of adding that stuff to your computer. Keyboards are *input devices* that not only allow you to type names, addresses, computer programs, and other information, but also provide a way to change the language in which the computer is "talked to."

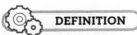 **DEFINITION**

> **Input devices** provide information to the computer from the user. Other examples of input devices are scanners and card readers, which are common add-ons to computers these days.

The mouse: Like the keyboard, the mouse provides the user with a way to talk to the computer. Clicking on things with a left or right button and dragging things around the screen provide a very intuitive method (at least for some) to accomplish tasks.

Memory: A computer has little chips inside of it that are called *memory chips.* These memory chips provide transient storage of information, as in the information goes away when your computer is turned off (most of the time). However, there are forms of memory chips that do not lose their information when power is turned off, called *nonvolatile memory chips.* It is easier, though, to think of memory as something that only holds onto information when the computer is running.

Disk drives: Also called *hard drives* because they have hard cases, disk drives are a form of storage that computers use to maintain your data persistently. Unlike memory, disk drives hold onto information whether the computer is on or off.

 PROGRAMMING TIP

The reason that disk drives are called *hard drives* is that once upon a time, there were also floppy drives in which you put floppy disks. They were "floppy" because, well, they bent when you shook them, like a floppy hat.

Networks: Where would you be these days without the internet? Networks work using a little card within the computer that knows how to "talk" to other computers and devices. In the good old days, that card was called a *Network Interface Card (NIC),* and it attached to other network devices via a really long cord, like a phone cord. Nowadays, people mostly use wireless network cards that "talk" to other devices via radio frequencies. Yes, that's right—your computer is really using a walkie-talkie to communicate with networks.

Firmware

If a computer was only made of hardware, things would be very disappointing for users. For one thing, it would just have little lights that turned on and off, and it wouldn't run any applications.

Firmware is the software that runs the actual computer provided by the computer manufacturer. It is called *firmware* because it really doesn't change. While it is possible to change your firmware, it is a very rare occurrence. And when compared to updating your software, which seems to happen every other day, it is definitely a bit more "firm."

Firmware operates at a higher level than hardware. The firmware level takes care of things like writing to disk drives, displaying things on monitors, and getting input from the hardware devices, such as the keyboard and monitor. You will rarely directly interact with the firmware, but it is important to know it is there.

Part of the firmware level is the Basic Input Output System, or BIOS. This is the level that implements the functionality of the keyboard, mouse, touch screens, and card readers.

The Operating System

The heart of what users think of as the computer is the operating system. The operating system is just a program or series of programs that runs when the computer starts up. You will often hear people refer to "booting up" or "booting into" some operating system, such as Windows, Linux, or the Mac's OSX.

Operating systems run in what is known as *kernel mode.* That is, they form the kernel (like a kernel of corn) that holds all of the rest of the computer system together. When you run an application, such as Microsoft Word, the Chrome Browser, or even a game like Solitaire, you are loading that program into the operating system.

The operating system is made up of many small, complex components, most of which you will never need to know anything about. However, you do need to know something about how the operating system loads and runs your programs. I am not going to get into great detail here, since that's a major part of writing computer programs, but it is important to know that your program isn't doing things in complete isolation. Other programs run at the same time, which is known as *multi-processing.* So you can't "hog" the whole machine; the operating system won't let you. You have to be a good computer citizen and share resources, including processing time (the time the computer spends executing your commands), memory (the space that programs can occupy on the computer), and hardware.

Application Programs

The top layer of the computer hierarchy is the application program. Application programs, often called *apps,* are the bread and butter of the computer software world. Users use apps to accomplish tasks, such as writing books, balancing their checkbooks, and checking their email on the internet. Apps have no real set of standards as to what they do; the ability to create an app to do something new is what computer programming is all about.

In this book, I will focus on application development. Applications can be written in a wide variety of ways, from Microsoft Excel macros all the way down to system commands that extend the operating system.

PROGRAMMING TIP

What all applications share in common is a programming language. A language is simply a medium for communication. For example, you and I agree that the word *wombat* describes a small furry mammal from Australia. That agreement means that when I say, "I shot a wombat in my pajamas yesterday," you don't have to ask what a wombat is, or what pajamas are. You might ask what the wombat was doing in my pajamas, but that would be a conversation for another time.

What Do Programs Do?

Anything that a computer is capable of doing, a computer program can do. Now, sometimes that capability is strained, such as animating graphics on a very old computer. That doesn't mean it can't be done; it simply means things happen too slowly for the user to tolerate or at a snail-like performance. In time, hardware always catches up with performance needs, which is why today's computers are so much faster than the ones just a decade or so ago. You could never have played realistic 3D games or watched videos on a computer in 1988; it would have been painful to do. Today, however, people take those capabilities for granted. The question is, how does a program do what it does?

Types of Programs

As you've seen, there are various kinds of programs. They can be classified into two types:

- **Executable programs:** These are comprised of self-contained files called *executables* that live on your hard drive and are written directly in instructions the computer can run. There is really only one sort of executable program.

- **Interpreted programs:** These are loaded into the computer from a hard drive and then parsed, line by line, and made into computer-readable instructions. There are thousands of interpreted programs, from writing a macro in Excel all the way to creating programs in high-level languages like Python (as you will do in this book). An add-on program is required to convert them to machine-readable form.

You can think of executable versus interpreted as the difference between writing something in the native language of someone reading it and writing it in a different language that needs to be read by a third party and translated into your reader's native language.

How Does a Computer Program Work?

How do programs work? First, a computer programmer (you!) creates a set of instructions that tell the computer what to do. So computer programs are nothing more or less than instructions to the computer—recipes, if you will. When you cook following a recipe, you do the instructions in order, and the result is an edible meal. (Well, at least most of the time; there was that one experiment with eggplant Parmesan ….)

Most computer programs have users, or the people who run the program on their computer and interact with it. The users expect the program to do what it is supposed to do and to make their lives easier—the programmer has to make sure the program does just that.

Unfortunately, computers are very dumb. They can't make value judgments, of course, but neither can they do anything you don't tell them to do. For example, suppose you told your teenage child to take out the trash. There are all kinds of implied things to do in that statement. Let's take a look at what is really involved:

- Take the bag out of the trash container.
- Tie the top of the bag.
- Carry the bag out to wherever the garbage goes.
- Cover the container that holds the bag.
- Put a new bag into the trash container.

Now, assumedly, you have shown the teenager several times what you mean when you say "take out the trash," so he understands the implicit steps involved and does them all. A computer doesn't understand implicit steps. If you want it to take out the trash, you need to give it all five steps every time you give it the command, "take out the trash."

 ERROR MESSAGE

Always remember that computers only do what you tell them to do, and never anything else. It is never the computer's fault when something goes wrong—it is always the programmer's fault!

Once upon a time, that meant the laborious task of writing machine code, which is a very low-level set of code the computer understands. Machine code was written in the only thing the computer understood: zeroes and ones, also known as *binary*. Later, that task got somewhat easier with the introduction of a programming language called *assembler code*. Assembler code looks something like Listing 1.1.

```
        global  _start

        section .text
_start:
        ; write(1, message, 13)
        mov     eax, 4_____; system call 4 is write
        mov     ebx, 1_____; file handle 1 is stdout
        mov     ecx, message_____; address of string to output
        mov     edx, 13_____; number of bytes
        int     80h

        ; exit(0)
        mov     eax, 1_____; system call 1 is exit
        mov     ebx, 0_____; we want return code 0
        int     80h
message:
        db      "Hello, World", 10
```

Listing 1.1

An assembly programming listing.

Believe it or not, all these strange lines do is print the text "Hello, World" on the screen! For many years, this was how computer programs were written. However, it became clear that writing and maintaining this kind of low-level interface to the computer was difficult. For one thing, if you moved to a different computer or a different version of the operating system, it normally meant completely rewriting the program. That was hardly optimal.

Later, new programming languages allowed programmers to write more like people think, in languages closer to English than to machine code. Just a few of the languages in use today are C, C++, C#, Java, JavaScript, PHP, and Python.

In Python, the language I will be using in this book, Python code, is very simple. Listing 1.2 shows you some Python code that does the same thing as Listing 1.1.

```
print("Hello, World")
```

Listing 1.2

The same program in Python.

Much easier, isn't it? There are many, many more languages out there, but once you learn one, you are well on your way to writing in any of them because, as you will see, the concepts are the same in all programming languages.

The Lifetime of a Program

Programs live, and programs die. The lifetime of a program is from the point at which the program starts up to the point where the operating system terminates it and it is no longer usable by the user. What is important to understand as a programmer is that programs aren't just "there." They start up, they run for some period of time, and then they eventually end. What happens in between is key to the application itself. It might be a word processor that allows the user to create a new document. It might be an email program that retrieves the latest important missives for the user from the internet. Whatever it does, it does it during the "run" part of the program.

When you think about writing a computer program, it is important to consider the lifetime of that program. For example, when the program starts, there are things you might do to initialize your world. If you were writing a word processor, you might want to display the last few documents that the user has worked on (called the *recent file list*) for them to select from. If you were writing a game, the first step might be to load something telling you where the user was in the game when he last played (this is called the *state* of the program).

Equally important, aside from the running of the program, is what happens when the application ends (closes). For example, your word processor might want to check if the user has saved their file before it ends.

Thinking Like a Programmer

The hardest part of any new profession is learning how to get in that profession's mindset. There is the jargon, the acronyms, and all of the "in words" the profession has. But what is really difficult is learning how to think like someone who has been doing the tasks for years.

In the programming world, thinking like a programmer is the single-most-important aspect to writing computer programs. Programmers don't think in big-picture terms—they think in terms of processes and steps.

Computers only understand a single instruction at a time. You and I, however, understand groups of instructions. In the programming world, these groups of instructions are called *modules* or *functions*. A module is simply a set of related instructions that accomplish a single goal. For example, if you were doing laundry, the modules would be sorting the clothing, putting the clothes in the machine, and setting the machine to the right level.

Working with computer programs is the same way. By the time you finish doing this kind of breakdown for your computer, you may feel like it's easier to just do the job by hand. Computer programming is a lot like that sometimes. A computer doesn't know how to solve any kind of problem; it only knows how to follow very direct instructions.

The process of breaking down a problem into smaller pieces is called *decomposition*. You can think of it this way: if a composer creates a grand opus by composition, then decomposition is tearing apart his grand opus into individual notes you know how to play on the kazoo. (Just don't tell the composer, okay?) Learning how to decompose a problem will lead you to think like a programmer.

 PROGRAMMING TIP

My favorite quote about programming came from Henry Ford, the automaker and creator of the assembly line: "There are no big problems. There are only a lot of little problems." Oh, he wasn't thinking of programming when he said it, but it sums up the entire programming world quite succinctly.

Imagine, for example, that you want to create a massive program that allows everyone in the world to see every issue facing them and offer commentary on how to fix it. That's a pretty big problem, don't you think? Yet by decomposing the problem into smaller pieces, you can see that it is a lot of little problems. Those little problems may not be easy to solve, but they are considerably smaller than the massive problem you started with. You might come up with a list like this:

- Allow people to show new issues.

- Allow people to read new issues.

- Allow people to comment on issues.

That doesn't seem as complicated, does it? The actual implementation might be a bit harder, but now that you've broken down the problem, it seems solvable. This is the core to programming: breaking down big problems into small tasks that can be accomplished.

The Least You Need to Know

- Before you begin learning how to write programs, you should be familiar with the different parts of your computer.

- Programs are merely instructions you provide to the computer to get a certain result.

- Get into the programming mindset by thinking about how big problems can be broken down into smaller issues.

Programming with Python

In order to write computer programs, you have to work in a programming language. There are hundreds of programming languages available to you, from the simple to the fiendishly complex. Because the purpose of this book is to focus on the fundamentals of programming and not on the arcane syntax of strange languages, you will be using a language called *Python* to write your programs.

This chapter goes over what Python is, how to install it, and other important information related to what you'll use for creating computer programs.

In This Chapter

- Understanding Python
- How to install Python
- How IDLE helps you create the text for a program
- Packages: how programmers share functionality fixes
- Miscellaneous programming tools

What Is Python?

As I mentioned in Chapter 1, Python is a programming language. Python was created by a man named Guido van Rossum, a Dutch computer programmer who developed the language while working for Google.

PROGRAMMING TIP

Python is named after the British comedy show *Monty Python's Flying Circus*. If you don't want to use a programming language named after British folks who liked blowing up cows and doing funny walks, the programming world is probably not going to appeal to you too much. Programmers are many things, but "weird" is definitely one that applies across the board.

When van Rossum created Python, he set out a list of basic tenets for the language. The following are a few I think are important to keep in mind as you learn about Python and programming in general:

Beautiful is better than ugly. When you want to read code, it is easier if the code is formatted in such a way that it tells you a lot about itself. This is code "beauty"—the ability to read and understand code directly, even if you don't honestly know what it is supposed to do.

Explicit is better than implicit. The point of code is not only to accomplish some task (an application), but also to make it possible for someone else to add to, modify, or build from your code. If your code is explicit as to what it is doing and how, this is much easier.

Simple is better than complex. Reading code that is complex can make another programmer's head hurt and force her to dig into the syntax and functionality, instead of simply worrying about what she needs to do. For example, consider the following directions:

1. Get a word from the user

2. Count the number of vowels in the word.

3. Print it out.

Now here are some more-complex directions:

1. Input a word from the user, skipping white space and only permitting keyboard entries.

2. Run the Parson's algorithm (see internal documentation) to parse the word into letters that either fit the set or do not fit the set.

3. Report on all that fit the set.

I don't know about you, but I'm sure the other programmer would rather work with the first set, even though both sets of instructions are for the same thing.

Complex is better than complicated. Complex means there are many moving parts and you have to keep track of them. Complicated means there are hidden parts that you don't necessarily know about and have to keep track of. Clearly, complex beats complicated, although simple surely beats complex.

Readability counts. As I've mentioned before, you aren't the only one who will have to read your code. Someone else will likely have to modify it at some point in any kind of professional programming shop. For that matter, that someone might be you, 3 years down the road. If the code is readable, you can probably pick up right where you left off. If it isn't, a lot of time will be wasted figuring it out.

Python is an interpreted language (see Chapter 1). This means you can run it anywhere an interpreter is available for it, which is a nice thing if you work on multiple operating systems. It also means you have to install the Python interpreter on every computer you want to run your programs on, which isn't always so nice (fortunately, I walk through the process of downloading and installing Python on your computer in this chapter).

Python is free, so you can download and install it as many times as you want without it costing you a dime.

Installing Python on Your Computer

The process of installing Python is more or less the same for every operating system it runs on. You download it, you run the installer, and it does the rest.

Determining Your Operating System Version

For Windows users, it's best to figure out what version or type of Microsoft Windows (32-bit or 64-bit) you are running before you go to the Python page, if you don't already know.

The 32- and 64-bit numbers represent the size of the "computer word" used in the operating system. This doesn't really affect you now, or likely in the future, but some programs need to know. To find out, launch Windows Explorer. You can do this by clicking the right-mouse button on the Start button at the bottom of the screen in Windows 7, or press the Windows key and the **E** key together in Windows 8. You will see the File Explorer (Windows 8) or Windows Explorer (Windows 7). Click the right mouse button on the **Computer** icon as shown in Figure 2.1.

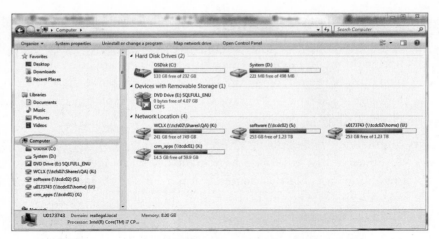

Figure 2.1: *The Windows Explorer window showing the Computer icon.*

When you click on that icon with the right mouse button (meaning, move the mouse over the icon and press the right button on your mouse), a small menu will pop up. Select **Properties** from that menu and you will see a screen similar to the one shown in Figure 2.2.

Figure 2.2: *The computer properties screen.*

The important things to note on this screen are the Windows edition entry at the top, which tells you what operating system you are running, and the System type entry, which tells you whether it is a 32-bit or 64-bit operating system. I know it sounds complicated and a lot to remember, but really, this is the last time you will have to look at it. Python doesn't care what operating system you use or how many bits there are in a word, I promise!

Downloading the Python Installer

To download Python, go to the python.org and click the **Download** button on the left side of the screen, as shown in Figure 2.3.

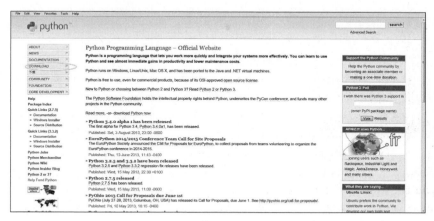

Figure 2.3: *The Python.org main page.*

Once you click on that link, you'll be taken to the Download Python page, where you click on the link for your operating system. For example, if you are using the Microsoft Windows operating system, click on the link that says **Windows X86-64 MSI Installer**, as shown in Figure 2.4. Don't worry if your screen doesn't exactly match mine; as long as you are running Windows and you select the X86-64 mode, you will be fine.

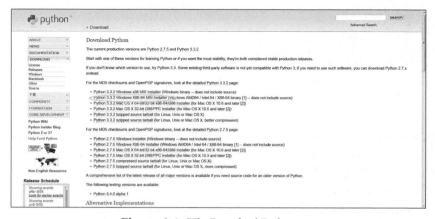

Figure 2.4: *The Download Python page.*

PROGRAMMING TIP

The version numbers may be different on your screen, as Python is always being updated. Fortunately, almost everything is backwardly compatible, which means that newer versions of the language will work the same way that older versions did. Please make sure to download the 3.0 version of the software, since previous versions are not necessarily compatible with the code in this book. No reason to be confused to start out!

If you are using a Mac, select the MacOS version that you need. If you are running Linux, you probably don't need my help figuring it out, but your best choice is the bzipped source tarball; it is a compressed file that contains all the stuff you need to run Python, and it will do all the rest for you when you install it.

Once you click on the link that corresponds to your operating system and version, you will see a little pop-up that asks you if you really want to download a file. What you see will vary slightly depending on which browser and what version of it you are using, but it will likely contain the same basic information that's shown in Figure 2.5. This pop-up, called a *download prompt,* is used to prompt you to allow the Python installer to be downloaded to your computer.

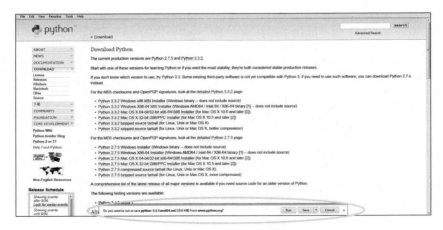

Figure 2.5: *Download prompt for the Python installer.*

There are a number of options here, but the best one for keeping your sanity is to click the little arrow to the right of the Save button on the prompt and select **Save As**. This will bring up a Save As dialog, and you can put the file anywhere you like. For Windows 7 or 8, I like to recommend people put things in the main Downloads library, since it makes them easy to find and you don't have to remember where you put some specific version of a file.

Running the Installer

Once you have the Python installer file downloaded, you have to run it in order to put all the little bits where they belong on your computer. Take heart; this is something you only have to do once, and the process is mostly automated.

PROGRAMMING TIP

These instructions apply to the Windows installation. If you use Linux or Mac, though, just follow the directions the installer gives you once you run the script you downloaded.

First, you need to find the installer file. The file will have an extension of "MSI," which stands for "Microsoft Installer." If you followed my advice previously for Windows, you will find the file in your Downloads library. If you didn't, you may still be in luck. The last thing the download process does is show you the download finished, with a button titled **Open Folder**. Click on that, and you will see your installer file.

Double-click the Python installer file with your left mouse button (or just click on it so it is highlighted and press **Enter**), and the installer will launch. You should see something like the panel shown in Figure 2.6.

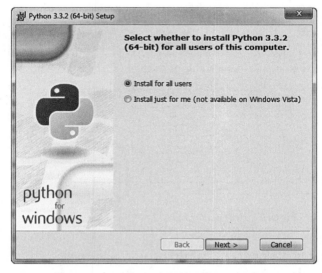

Figure 2.6: *The Python installer setup screen.*

Unless you have a compelling reason to change them, you can leave most of the defaults. Click **Next** to move to the screen shown in Figure 2.7. This screen asks where you want to install Python. If your computer is set up the way most are, just accept the default (c:\ Python33) and click **Next** again.

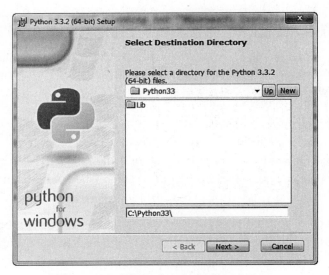

Figure 2.7: *The Python destination directory.*

This brings you to the Customize Python screen, shown in Figure 2.8. This screen allows you to determine what features are installed on your computer. The only change you are going to make here is to click on the little **x** drop-down next to Add python.exe to Path. You should then select the **will be installed on the local hard-drive** option.

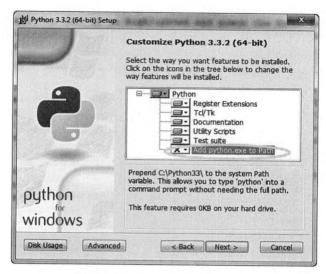

Figure 2.8: *Customize Python options.*

Once you've made those changes, click **Next**. You should see a little progress screen that shows you installer is installing something, like the one shown in Figure 2.9.

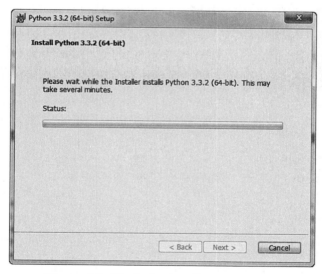

Figure 2.9: *The Python installer progress screen.*

PROGRAMMING TIP

You may get a security warning from Windows asking if you want to allow the installer to make changes to your system. Go ahead and say "yes" to that prompt; the installer is quite safe.

Once the installer has finished its work, you will see one last screen indicating that the installation has gone properly, as shown in Figure 2.10. If there are any errors shown, such as an out of disk space error, you need to free up some space on your hard drive to install Python or place it on another hard drive. Otherwise, you can simply click **Finish**.

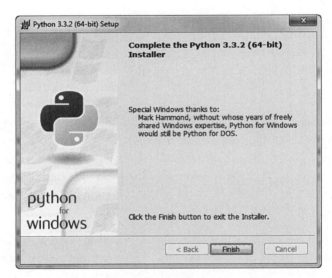

Figure 2.10: *The installation is complete!*

At this point, your Python installation is complete, so feel free to disconnect from the internet. You are now ready to begin using the Python interpreter, which I'll get into in the next chapter, when you write your first program. First, I'd like to discuss exactly what has been installed and what you have available to you.

Finding All the Little Pieces

When a program or set of programs is installed on your computer, you get a lot of stuff. You can see what got installed by looking at the installation directory for Python. If you kept the defaults during the installation process, that would be c:\Python33; otherwise, it would be wherever you told the installer to put Python.

The directory listing for the Python installation directory looks something like this:

```
Volume in drive C is OSDisk
 Volume Serial Number is 3450-71DF

 Directory of C:\Python33

08/26/2013  10:19 AM    <DIR>          .
08/26/2013  10:19 AM    <DIR>          ..
08/26/2013  10:19 AM    <DIR>          DLLs
08/26/2013  10:19 AM    <DIR>          Doc
08/26/2013  10:19 AM    <DIR>          include
08/26/2013  10:19 AM    <DIR>          Lib
08/26/2013  10:19 AM    <DIR>          libs
05/16/2013  12:16 AM            33,326 LICENSE.txt
05/15/2013  10:51 PM           214,554 NEWS.txt
05/16/2013  12:07 AM            40,448 python.exe
05/16/2013  12:07 AM            40,960 pythonw.exe
05/15/2013  10:51 PM             6,701 README.txt
08/26/2013  10:19 AM    <DIR>          tcl
08/26/2013  10:19 AM    <DIR>          Tools
               5 File(s)        335,989 bytes
               9 Dir(s)  142,363,496,448 bytes free
```

The dates and times information on the left side are simply when the files were created. The directories listed, such as DLLs, Doc, and include, contain files the Python interpreter will need to run. I'll show you more about these as they become important. For now, accept that they are necessary and don't delete them!

Two of the files have an .exe extension. These are compiled executable files, the kind I told you about in Chapter 1. These files are capable of being directly understood by the operating system. In fact, python.exe and pythonw.exe are the interpreters for Python.

How did I get the preceding listing? I used what is called a *command prompt*. If you go to the Start button in windows and select **Accessories** in Windows 7, you will see a listing for Command Prompt. If you are as old as I am, this is just an MS-DOS box. (If that means nothing to you, you can feel a lot younger.)

Learning about the command prompt is important, because you will be using it a lot during the writing and executing of Python programs in this book. If you are using Linux or MacOS, then most of this will be second nature to you. If you are a Microsoft Windows user, you probably haven't ever been involved at the command prompt level, so this is a new experience for you.

To accomplish this, run the "cmd.exe" command at the Windows start button (in Linux or Mac, a command prompt is very similar, but consult your documentation for your specific situation). You will see a blank black box. Type **c:\Python33** (or wherever you installed

Python). Next, type **dir**; this command, short for "directory," simply lists the files in the current directory.

The IDLE Programming Editor

Although it is not shown in the directory listing in the previous section, the Python installer gave you one more gift. If you look at the Start program list, you will see a new entry there: IDLE (Python GUI). In some cases, this may be listed under the Python33 entry on your start list.

IDLE, which stands for Interactive DeveLopment Environment, is a *programming editor.*

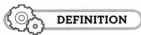

DEFINITION

A **programming editor** is something like a word processor for programmers. The programming editor helps programmers create the text that will make up a program.

When you launch IDLE, you will see something like the display shown in Figure 2.11.

Figure 2.11: *Launching the IDLE programming editor.*

There are a few things to notice here. First of all, IDLE tells you what version you are running and what operating system you are running on. This is nice information, especially if something is not working correctly. Next, you will see a prompt (in this case, ">>>"), followed by a blinking cursor. This is IDLE's way of telling you it is waiting for input. Type **copyright** and hit **Enter**. IDLE responds with the following:

```
>>> copyright
Copyright (c)2001-2013 Python Software Foundation.
All Rights Reserved.

Copyright (c)2000 BeOpen.com.
All Rights Reserved.

Copyright (c)1995-2001 Corporation for National Research Initiatives.
All Rights Reserved.

Copyright (c)1991-1995 Stichting Mathematisch Centrum, Amsterdam.
All Rights Reserved.
```

You will be doing a lot with IDLE throughout this book. For now, feel free to explore the menus and type anything you want into the prompt area. If you end up in a really bad place where IDLE won't respond or shows you very strange results, select the **Restart Shell** option under the Shell menu. This will put the editor back into its default state.

IDLE is truly interactive. This is the biggest difference between working in an interpreted language and a compiled language. Commands in an interpreted language can be immediately processed and the result displayed. With compiled languages, you would need to first run through a cycle of building the application (called *compiling and linking*) before you could run it and get results. Interpretive languages are great for learning for this reason, and the main reason that Python was selected for this book.

Using Packages to Augment Your Programming

One of the biggest advantages to using Python over many other languages, interpreted or compiled, is that Python was built to be *extensible*. In the programming world, we call this "reuse" or "not re-inventing the wheel." Too often, programmers tend to re-create solutions that already exist, which is a waste of time and effort and often leads to confusing webs of programming code. A programmer's best attitude is the willingness to use other people's solutions. It means programmers then end up with a single library of really well-written, well-thought-out solutions rather than a hodgepodge of different solutions that may or may not cover the entire problem.

To aid with this approach, Python provides the notion of packages. Packages put a bunch of related functionality together and allow programmers to share it. They also point out another way in which programmers need to think, in terms of groups of related functionality. When you focus on a problem in programming, you need to learn how to think in terms of different pieces to do different jobs—packages can help with that.

You can find the Python package list at https://pypi.python.org/pypi. Take a moment to point your browser there and look at the wealth of information and functionality that others have provided. The Python community is one of sharing and helping, a good trait for all developers.

Miscellaneous Tools for Programmers

A programmer has many tools in her arsenal for solving problems and making the job easier. While you may not use most of these when you are starting out, it is important to know what programming tools are available, so when you do need them, you know where to look and what to look for.

Code Editor

The first tool most developers use when they start out and move beyond the basic installed system is the *code editor.* Python does come with IDLE, which is a very basic if not flashy code editor. Once you begin to write significant amounts of code, though, you will need something a bit more powerful than IDLE. There are almost as many different code editors as there are programmers, and picking one is definitely a matter of individual taste and style. Most of them make it easier to write good code and harder to create bad code, which is all you really care about.

You can find a list of decent code editors specifically designed for Python on the Python Wiki (http://wiki.python.org/moin/PythonEditors), which is always a good place to start looking for anything Python related. Most of these editors can be used for other languages as well. Outside of Python Wiki, you can find many commercial products that work with numerous languages if you do a search.

Debugger

The second-most-common tool for Python is the *debugger*. You would think from its name that a debugger removes bugs from code. Sadly, this is not the case. A debugger, formally called a *symbolic debugger*, allows you to run your program in an instrumented fashion, stopping at specific points in the code and examining the state of the system at any given point (see Chapter 19). For now, it is enough to know it is available and you will almost certainly learn to love (or loathe) it when writing Python code.

Every language I am aware of has a debugger of some sort, and they all do tend to work the same way. Therefore, learning to use one is a good stepping stone for later programming efforts.

Profilers, Automation, and Extensions

I'll mention just a few more tools in passing, so when you hear others bandying the terms about, you'll know what they are talking about.

Profilers are programs that run with your application and show you information about it. You can find out which parts run slowly, what memory the application uses, where the parts are that need to be fixed, and so forth. Profilers are usually used on production applications to find problems before end users do, but anyone can use them. Python has a built-in profiler.

One of the most important new additions to the software development process is the importance of testing. Testing is simply finding out whether things work or not and where the problems (defects or bugs) are in the system. It is very time consuming and expensive to run the same tests against an application every time, so programmers developed *automation* to solve the problem. Automation allows you to write code to test other code, which is kind of an interesting idea when you think about it. By running the same tests over and over, you find out what broke when you changed the application, which is useful information to have when you are trying to fix things. Testing frameworks provide most of the heavy lifting in automating tests.

The final element you should know about in the Python world is *extensions*. Extensions are parts of the system that allow Python to do things the original developers never imagined or built into the system. Python extensions are written in another language—usually C or C++—and become a part of the system as if they were written into the original application. Some of these are collected into packages (as you learned about earlier in the chapter), but other parts simply look as if they were part of the Python interpreter. You can add commands, new modules, or functions via the extension process.

> **PROGRAMMING TIP**
>
> You may hear the process of writing programs called *coding* and the people who do it *coders*. Some people prefer *software development* and *software engineers*. For myself, I find that whatever it says on my business card is fine, since that means I get paid for it.

The Least You Need to Know

- Python is an interpreted language, meaning you can run it anywhere an interpreter is available for it.
- To download Python, go to python.org's Download page and click on the link based on your operating system.
- To see the Python installation directory, use the command prompt or Windows Explorer.
- When programming, you will use a code editor, a debugger, profilers, automation, and extensions.

Your First Python Program

At this point, you have a basic knowledge of how a computer works, and you've gone through the surprisingly painless process of installing your brand-new interpreter for Python on your computer system.

I can hear you saying, "When do I get to write a program?" out there in reader land. Well, the answer is, right now. In this chapter, you learn how to write your first program and how to troubleshoot a simple program issue.

In This Chapter

- Learning the Hello world program
- Writing code in an editor
- Dealing with program issues

Never Mind All That, I Want to *Do* Something!

Most of programming is about writing code. You will never become a better programmer until you have written lots of programs and learned a bit from each one. So clearly, the first step is to write your first program.

In most programming languages, the prototypical first program is *Hello world*. The reason for this is that it is an extremely simple program that prints out those two words to the console (the output window in an interpreter). You've actually already looked at the Hello world program in Python in Chapter 1, but here it is again:

```
print("Hello world")
```

The following is a breakdown of the parts of the Hello world program:

- **Function:** This is basically a name with a set of parentheses following it. In the preceding program, the function is *print*.

- **Argument:** The data sent to the function to enable it to do its job. There is only one argument in this case for the print function—the Hello world string. (You can learn more about arguments in Chapter 11.)

- **String:** A *data type* that, for the purpose of this example, is made up of a set of quotes with text inside of them. In the preceding, the string is "Hello world."

When writing a string, you can use single quotes (') or double quotes (")—Python doesn't really care. The following are the same thing to Python:

```
"Hello world"
'Hello world'
```

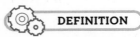 **DEFINITION**

Data types are simply classifications that identify a type or types of data (such as integer), which determines the possible values for that type.

However, you can't do things like this:

```
"Hello world'
```

Or the following:

```
'Hello world"
```

If you don't use the same type of quotation mark at the beginning and end, Python will complain, calling it a "syntax error."

Try out the Hello world program with the two different quote types. Bring up the IDLE editor and type the following (don't type the >>> part; that's IDLE showing you a prompt):

```
>>> print("Hello world")
```

IDLE then displays this:

```
Hello world
```

Good, you wrote some code! Now, try typing the following:

```
>>> print('Hello world')
```

IDLE then displays this:

```
Hello world
```

As you can see, Python doesn't care whether you use single quotes or double quotes; it thinks of them the same way.

But what if you need to use single or double quotation marks within a string? For example, let's say you want to print out a string that contains a single quote, like "Hello world. It's a fine day!" You couldn't put that inside single quotes, because the string itself contains a single quote in "It's." However, you can put it inside double quotes so Python knows to print out the single quote:

```
>>> print("Hello world. It's a fine day!")
Hello world. It's a fine day!
```

Likewise, suppose you want to display the title of *The Great Gatsby* in double quotes in the middle of a string. You could use a single quote around the whole string to tell Python the double quotes are just part of what you want to print out:

```
>>> print('I just got finished reading "The Great Gatsby"')
I just got finished reading "The Great Gatsby"
```

Writing a Script in an Editor

Up to this point, everything I have talked about involves working in "immediate mode." That is, the command you enter is immediately processed by the Python interpreter. This is the real value of an interpreter; you can enter some code very quickly and test it. Unfortunately, it isn't very representative of how programmers work in the real world. Most of the time, they have a whole bunch of code that needs to be processed at the same time to accomplish some task. To do this, you have to create scripts or script files that contain all of the statements you want the interpreter to process. Let's take a look at how this works.

To begin with, you are going to create a very simple piece of code that asks the user to enter a name and then greets that user by name. To see how it works, do it first in immediate mode within the IDLE editor. Make sure you have launched IDLE so it is on your screen, and then type the following (don't worry about what it does yet; I'll dissect this later):

```
>>> input_var = input("What is your name? ")
```

IDLE responds with the following:

```
What is your name?
```

You will notice that IDLE isn't doing anything except blinking the cursor. That is because it is waiting for you to type something. Type your name—in my case, the string "Matt"—without the quotation marks:

```
What is your name? Matt
```

IDLE responds by putting up another prompt (the >>> thing). What has happened here? Well, IDLE processed the command, which in your case was the "input" command. The input command, which is shown as "input('What is your name? ')," is provided by the programmer. It stored the result of the input into a variable called *input_var* (I will discuss variables more in Chapter 4). Now, you want to print out the greeting to the user. Again, at the IDLE prompt, type the following:

```
>>> print("Hello " + input_var)
```

IDLE responds with the following:

```
Hello Matt
>>>
```

Congratulations! You have just written a script in Python. Now, what if you want to run it over and over again? That would be tedious to say the least, having to type in the commands one at a time. This is why programmers create script files, which are just files filled with text that contain commands the Python interpreter understands. There are lots of ways to create a script file, but let's just stick with using IDLE for now.

Before you start, you'll have to do a couple of things. First of all, you are going to start a command prompt to run your scripts in. This sounds hideously complicated, but it really isn't. In Microsoft Windows, click the **Start** button and then select **All Programs**. Find the Accessories entry near the top and open it up; click **Command Prompt**. You should see a command prompt window open up on the screen, as shown in Figure 3.1.

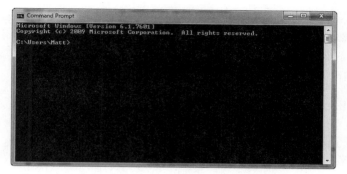

Figure 3.1: *A command prompt window.*

You should now make sure the Python interpreter works properly when in the command prompt. You can test this by typing "python" in the command prompt and hitting **Enter**. If you've done everything properly, you should see the display shown in Figure 3.2.

 ERROR MESSAGE

If the interpreter isn't working, the easiest thing to do is go back and reinstall Python and select the "Add python.exe to Path" option as I discussed in the section "Running the Installer" in Chapter 2.

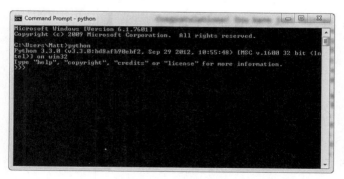

Figure 3.2: *Python running in the command prompt.*

You won't be using the interpreter in immediate mode this time, so you need to exit it. The quit() command is a function in Python to exit interpreter mode. To use it, type **quit()** and hit **Enter**. You should be returned to the command prompt (in my case, C:\users\matt>) on the screen.

Creating a Place to Save Your Files

Before you begin to create an actual script, you need to know just a little bit about the file system, particularly where you want to store things.

When you create a script file, you need to store it somewhere on your computer. By default, the IDLE editor is going to want to store it in the default Python directory (c:\Python33). If you don't mind the script files cluttering things up in there, that's fine—it is entirely up to you. However, one of the things programmers generally do is segregate the code into separate areas, so code associated with one task (such as a business project) is not found in the same place as code for another task (such as a personal project). This makes it easier to save your files for a given purpose to a backup location and looks much more professional.

In order to accomplish this, you need to create a new directory to store your files. Where you do this is up to you, but I've chosen a directory called "Code" to create them. Follow these steps to create a new directory:

1. Use Windows Explorer to navigate to where you want the directory created, like the root of the C: drive.

2. Right-click on the list of files, and select **New**. From the pop-up list that appears, select **Folder**.

3. A new folder will show up in the directory with a default name of "New Folder" with its name highlighted, probably in blue. Click in the little highlighted box and name the folder whatever you like, such as "Code."

4. Hit **Enter**, and the new folder is ready for you.

Creating the Script

Now you're ready to actually create the lines of Python code that will make up your script. To do this, go back to your IDLE window and select **New Window** from the File menu. You should see a new window pop up, as shown in Figure 3.3.

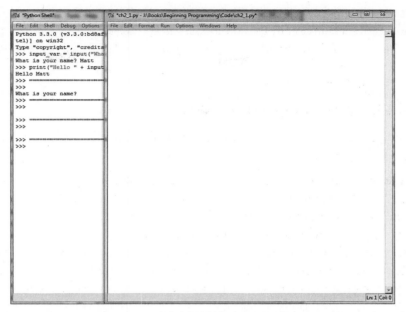

Figure 3.3: *A new editor window in IDLE.*

This window is used for code editing. You can create new scripts, edit existing scripts, and do many other things (such as syntax check code).

In this case, you're adding the script you learned earlier in the section to your new file. In the new window, type the following lines, remembering to press **Enter** after each line:

```
input_var = input("What is your name? ");
print("Hello " + input_var);
```

Save the file by selecting **Save** from the file menu; the IDLE editor will display the standard "Save As" dialog. Now put in the name you'd like to save the file under. In this case, I've chosen to save the file under the name "ch3_1" for Chapter 3, Example 1. I don't have to specify an extension for the file, since the editor will do that automatically. Finally, navigate to the directory you created (Code, in my case), and save the file.

ERROR MESSAGE

You can call the Python file anything you want, but it will make your life considerably easier if you do not have spaces in the file name. Finding a file with spaces in it in the operating system is difficult, and remembering whether you had them makes it even more so. Therefore, you should either condense the spaces (for example, Test1) or use an underscore in place of them (for example, Test_1).

Running the Script from the Command Prompt

Now that you have your script file created and saved to the proper location, it is time to actually run the script and see whether or not it works. To do this, you'll be using the command prompt you opened earlier in the process.

Go back to the command prompt window. The first thing you are going to need to do is change the current directory so it is where your script file is. In Microsoft Windows, as with most operating systems, programs operate on the "current directory" with respect to finding files, doing input and output, and the like. To change the current directory, you use the command *cd*, which is short for "change directory."

Let's suppose that you created a directory called *Code* on your C: drive and want to move to it from wherever you happen to be on your C: drive. To go from the current directory to the Code directory, you type in the following and then press **Enter**:

```
cd \Code
```

The command prompt is kind enough to tell you where you are in the prompt it displays, as shown in Figure 3.4.

Figure 3.4: *The command prompt showing the current directory.*

While these steps may seem incredibly strange at first, it will become second nature to you soon enough. The command prompt is actually much more efficient than working in the graphical user interface, once you get used to it.

You have created the script file, navigated to the directory where you saved it, and now can see the fruits of your labor. Finally, it is time to actually run the script! Type the following command at the command prompt and hit **Enter**:

```
python ch3_1.py
```

You should see the question "What is your name?" appear, and the blinking cursor indicating that the interpreter is waiting for your input. You will also notice you didn't see the interpreter prompt (the >>> sign), nor did you see the Python copyright or other information. This is intentional, so that none of that interferes with running your scripts.

Once you enter your name, the script should respond with Hello, followed by the name you entered, and then go back to the standard command prompt. It should look something like the screen shown in Figure 3.5.

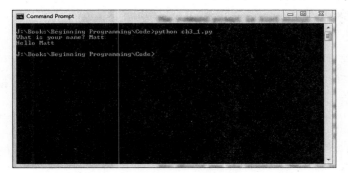

Figure 3.5: *The script runs!*

Congratulations, you have just written, loaded, and run your first Python script! Give yourself a nice pat on the back; most programmers take days to accomplish that much work.

When Bad Things Happen to Good Programmers

The good news is, your script ran perfectly and did what it was supposed to do. The bad news is, this is less common than you might imagine. Making mistakes is just a part of the programming process, and learning from those mistakes is what makes you a better programmer (and some say a better person, though I have my doubts). You should therefore learn how to deal with them in Python and all other computer programming languages.

To show you what might go wrong, I am going to introduce a deliberate error into the Python script I gave you. Now, you would never do this on purpose, but in this case, it helps to illustrate how you determine what is going wrong and fix it.

First, go back to the IDLE editor window you had open that contained your script file. Next, modify the script to add a single line to the bottom of it, so it reads like this:

```
input_var = input("What is your name? ")
print("Hello " + input_var)
something is not right with this line
```

PROGRAMMING TIP

If you closed the IDLE editor window with your script file, don't panic; it is easy enough to recover. Just go to the File menu and select **Open**. The standard file open dialog will be displayed. Navigate to the directory where you stored your script file, and select the file. A new window will appear showing you the code you entered last time.

Notice you've added a line that says, "something is not right with this line." This is a line that is not valid Python code, so the interpreter will have no idea what to do with it. Save the file (select **File** and **Save** from the menu), and then go back to your command prompt.

Once again, enter the following command and then press **Enter**:

```
python ch3_1.py
```

You will notice the process is very different from last time. Once again, the interpreter loads the script and starts to run it. But this time, the output looks much more like Figure 3.6.

Let's take a look at just what the interpreter is trying to tell you here. First, it spits out this wonderful piece of information:

```
J:\Books\Beginning Programming\Code>python ch3_1.py
  File "ch3_1.py", line 3
    something is not right with this line
                      ^
```

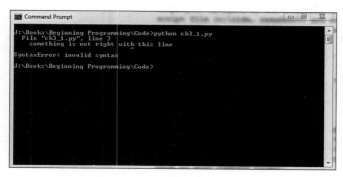

Figure 3.6: *Oh no! An error!*

There are two things to notice about this error message. First, you will notice that the interpreter tells you the exact file name and line number it is complaining about. In this case, you know it is the ch3_1.py file, which makes sense since that is the file you have been working on. Next, it tells you the error is on line 3 and displays the line in question. The little caret operator (^) shows you the place on the line that the interpreter is complaining about. In this case, it really has no idea what you are trying to do and is simply pointing at the first thing it did understand, which is the "with" keyword (I'll get into keywords in Chapters 4 and 5). Keywords are reserved in Python, meaning you can't use them for anything other than their intended purpose. "With" isn't used this way, so the interpreter complains.

The next thing you will see is the actual error that the interpreter found in the line it is pointing at. This is contained in the next bit of information displayed:

```
SyntaxError: invalid syntax
```

Python errors always have two parts to them at the very least. The first one is the kind of error that was encountered. In this case, the error is that the line found didn't match the proper syntax for the language. This is called a *syntax error.* You'll get quite used to syntax errors, unfortunately. The second part of the error message is supposed to be a more detailed description of what went wrong. In this case, Python simply has no idea what this line is supposed to do, so it displays the ever-helpful "invalid syntax."

Depending on what the problem is, fixing it can be either very simple or very complicated. In this case, it is the former, since all you have to do is remove the offending line from your script file. To do this, go back to the IDLE editor, highlight the third line using your mouse, and delete it by pressing either the **Delete** or **Backspace** key. Save the file and run it again in the command prompt, and you will see that it works like a charm. You have fixed your first bug!

The Least You Need to Know

- When writing a string, you can use single quotes (') or double quotes ("). However, do not enclose the information with one of each.

- Programming usually involves a whole bunch of code that needs to be processed at the same time to accomplish some task. You therefore have to create scripts or script files that contain all of the statements you want the interpreter to process.

- To move from the current directory to the directory where you've saved a script file, use the cd command.

- When there's an error in your script, Python gives you at least two pieces of information: the kind of error that was encountered and a more detailed description of what went wrong.

2

Learning Python

Python is not a complicated language, nor does it require a PhD to write and run scripts written in it. However, there are tricks and traps you need to understand before you can write your own programs. In this part, you learn about conditional constructs, such as the "if … then … else" condition. You also learn about looping constructs that allow you to perform an action many times.

Variables

Back in Chapter 3, I very briefly introduced the concept of a variable with input_var. In this chapter, I take you deeper into variables, including what they are, how to create them, and how to find their values and types.

In This Chapter

- Defining variables
- The concept of variable types
- How to create a variable
- The value of variables

Variables Defined

Put most simply, a variable is a little computer storage bin in your program that has a name. You can think of a variable as a folder in the filing cabinet that is your program. Each variable has its own folder, and the content of that folder is the value of the variable.

So variables have two essential characteristics: a name and a value. This isn't all that different from real life. For example, you might have two cars in your garage at home. Saying you have two cars is like saying you have two variables in your program. You need a way to indicate which one you are talking about, and you do that by name.

In your garage, say you have two Audi TT convertibles. (Well, at least you would be happy if you did.) How do you indicate which of the convertibles you are talking about? You might use the color of the car to talk about it: "Oh, yes, I am taking the red Audi TT convertible for a drive today." Red is the name of the car, at least for this example. You could even give it a variable name, like "RedAudi" as opposed to "BlueAudi," which might be the other car in the garage.

The value assigned to a variable is really up to you. Some languages restrict the kind of information you can store in different variables to specific types. Python, as you will see very shortly, has different types, but it doesn't restrict you to them. For the car example, let's say you have the two variables, RedAudi and BlueAudi, and you want to assign them value based on the amount of gas in the tank of each one. You might write code that looks like this:

```
RedAudi = "Half Empty"
BlueAudi = "Quarter Empty"
```

If you then printed out the values of the variables using IDLE, you would see something like the following:

```
>>> RedAudi = "Half Empty"
>>> BlueAudi = "Quarter Empty"
>>> print(RedAudi)
Half Empty
>>> print(BlueAudi)
Quarter Empty
```

Notice you send the name of the variable to the print() function (see Chapter 10 for more on functions), but it prints out the value of the variable. Computer programs don't care much about the names of variables, except to indicate which of the little folders to get information from.

(**PROGRAMMING TIP**)

It should be noted that it is perfectly valid to have a function called *print()*, as well as a variable called *print*. You add the parentheses to differentiate the two.

Variable Types

You just got through learning about what a variable was and how they contain values, but that isn't all you need to understand about the variable world. Probably the hardest thing for beginning programmers to really understand is the concept of variable types.

Variables are of certain types. Some of them are really quite self-evident. Consider the following list of information:

```
"Hello world"
123
123.456
[1, 2, 3, 4, 5]
```

As you learned in Chapter 3, the first item in the list is a string. Strings are just collections of alphanumeric data, letters and numbers, punctuation marks, and some strange characters like "{}|" and the like. You can really put just about anything you want between quotation marks and call it a string, so it is kind of like the catchall variable type.

The second item in the list, on the other hand, is a number. In the computer world, for mostly historical reasons, we differentiate between whole numbers (integers) and fractions (floating-point numbers). So 123 is an integer because it has no decimal point. However, the third item in the list, 123.456, is a floating-point number because it does have a decimal point.

(**PROGRAMMING TIP**)

Whole numbers and fractions are separated out due to the fact that computers handle them differently. There is even a separate part in your CPU to deal with fractions called a *floating-point unit*.

Computers really can't represent floating-point numbers like 123.456 completely accurately. If you remember significant figures from high school, you'll understand the problem, but realistically what happens is that computers drop digits out there somewhere to the right of the decimal point.

To a computer, the number 2.000000001 when added to the number 2.000000001 isn't always 4.000000002.

Whether it is or not is dependent on the way in which the floating-point math is handled on the computer. Again, this is not something you desperately need to know to be a programmer, but it is important when you do things like financial calculations. Odd side note: most financial work is done in whole numbers, with programmers representing dollars as the number of pennies in them. So, $1.00 is 100 pennies and used that way for math.

The fourth item in the list is the most interesting. Known as a *list* in Python and an *array* in other programs, it is just a convenient way to store a bunch of values in a single variable (see Chapter 7 for more about lists or arrays).

While you are not going to really get into a lot about the really complicated data types in Python, I think it is worth mentioning all the things available to you. I'll go into more detail on each one as it is used in the book.

Boolean Operators

Boolean is a really fancy way of saying true or false, which are the only two possible values you can get. The Boolean value is not really a type; any type in Python can be tested for a Boolean condition. In the programming world, false is normally a zero or zerolike value, such as zero, None, or an empty sequence. True, on the other hand, is set for anything that is nonzero and non-None.

Boolean values are represented in Python using the True and False keywords. You can assign a variable to one of the values, or test against one of the values:

```
>>> strNumber = True
>>> strNumber
True
>>> strNumber == True
True
>>> strNumber == False
False
```

PROGRAMMING TIP

In the preceding list, a single equals sign (=) means "assign a value to," while the double equals sign (==) means "is equal to." So the last two lines are asking "Does strNumber equal True?" and "Does strNumber equal False?" True means two things are equal, while False means they aren't.

The Complex Data Type

Unless you are a mathematician, as I have the misfortune (I mean, joy!) of being, you probably don't need to know much about complex numbers. Complex numbers have a real part and an imaginary part and use things like the letter i to represent the square root of -1. Yes, you were taught in school you can't take the square root of a negative number. They lied. Take it up with your teachers.

If you do ever have to work with complex numbers, know that they are used just like regular numbers, except they have two parts to them: real and imaginary. For example, if you want to write the complex number $3 + 2i$ (and if you are using complex numbers, you know what this means), you type in the following:

```
>>> cmplx = complex(3, 2)
```

You can then look at the real and imaginary components of the number by displaying the real and imag attributes:

```
>>> cmplx.real
3.0
>>> cmplx.imag
2.0
```

Decimals and Fractions

Decimal values are like floating-point number values, but much more accurate. The way in which financial applications get around the rounding and imprecision errors inherent in floating-point math is to use pennies instead of fractional dollars for their math. Decimal values are simply that concept implemented in Python directly.

The whole point to decimal numbers is they can be represented exactly on a computer. Decimals have a lot of applications, from financial to engineering, but they aren't really all that exciting to talk about. Here's how you work with a decimal number in Python:

```
>>> from decimal import *
>>> x = Decimal(1)
>>> y = Decimal(7)
>>> print(x/y)
0.1428571428571428571428571429
```

Compare this to the floating-point model:

```
>>> x = 1
>>> y = 7
>>> print(x / y)
0.14285714285714285
```

Note that the Decimal value is much more precise. If you need that kind of precision in your calculations, you use a Decimal object rather than a normal floating-point number.

Fractions, on the other hand, are exactly what you expect them to be. A Fraction object has a numerator and a denominator and can be added to either a whole number or another fraction.

Fractions are easy to use in Python:

```
>>> from fractions import Fraction
>>> x = Fraction(3, 4)
>>> y = Fraction(2, 4)
>>> print(x + y)
5/4
>>> print(x + 1)
7/4
```

As you can see, I added ¾ and ²⁄₄ and got ⁵⁄₄. In addition, I added the whole number 1 (⁴⁄₄ in the fractional world) to ¾ and got ⁷⁄₄. Both of these calculations are correct.

Python can also handle conversions to other bases:

```
>>> x = Fraction(2, 3)
>>> y = Fraction(3, 4)
>>> print(x + y)
17/12
```

In this one, Python converts ²⁄₃ and ¾ to ⁸⁄₁₂ and ⁹⁄₁₂ for you and gives you the answer of ¹⁷⁄₁₂. (Don't tell your small children about this one; they'll be using IDLE to do their math homework.)

Sequences

Python provides several classes for dealing with sequences. Sequences are just sets of values in a certain order that represent specific kinds of uses. The three main Python classes for sequences are list, tuple, and range.

A list is simply a list of values. The syntax is a little funky; you use the square brackets to indicate you want a list:

```
>>> myList = [1, 2, 3]
```

Once you have a list, you can print it out fully or print out pieces of it:

```
>>> myList
[1, 2, 3]
>>> myList[1]
```

Tuples are kind of cool. A tuple is a variable that holds multiple values. Unlike arrays, which also have multiple values, tuples are *immutable*—not changeable. Once you define a tuple, you can't add or remove from it or change any of the values already in it. Let's look at an example of a tuple:

```
>>> myTuple = (1, 2, 3)
>>> myTuple
(1, 2, 3)
```

 PROGRAMMING TIP

Tuples may not appear useful, but they are actually used in quite a number of places in Python programming, as they are the only way to return multiple values.

The range type represents, well, a range of numbers. Used mostly for looping constructs, the range generates a set of numbers. Here's a simple example of using the range type:

```
>>> x = range(1, 10)
>>> x
range(1, 10)
>>> x=range(43, 1, -1)
>>> x
range(43, 1, -1)
>>> print(x)
range(43, 1, -1)
```

The numbers represent the starting and stopping points of the range. So the first example has a range which represents the values 1 to 10, while the second represents a range that goes from 43 down to 1 (indicated by the -1). Ranges can go in either ascending or descending order.

All of the sequence functions have functionality to see if something is in them, called *in*. You use it as a separate word in a programming "sentence" like this:

```
>>> 2 in myList
True
>>> 8 in myList
False
```

If the value you are checking (the left part of the in statement) is in the sequence, the result is True. If the value is not in there, the result is False.

Sets

Sets are unique lists of values. Python provides pretty complete set functionality, which is built into the core of it.

PROGRAMMING TIP

Basically, you can think of a set as a collection of items, all of which are unique, kind of like a set of baseball cards or volumes of the encyclopedia. For example, if you have a large number of baseball cards and you put them all into a set, all of the duplicates will disappear and you will end up with a list of all the ones you have; this way, you can easily determine which ones you are missing.

To use sets, you use the curly bracket notation ({}) to indicate you want to create a set. You can either add items to the set initially or wait and add them later. For example, to create an empty set—that is, one with no items in it—you would write the following:

```
>>> mySet = {}
>>> mySet
{}
```

To create a set that had an initial content of the numbers 1 through 5, you could write this:

```
>>> mySet = {1, 2, 3, 4, 5}
>>> mySet
{1, 2, 3, 4, 5}
```

Note that in each case, IDLE shows you the contents of the set by typing in the name of the variable you used: mySet. The interesting thing is if you try to add a data element already in the set:

```
>>> mySet.add(5)
>>> mySet
{1, 2, 3, 4, 5}
```

You'll notice the set doesn't change. This is because there was already a value of 5 in the set. On the other hand, if you add a value that is not already in the set, like the following:

```
>>> mySet.add(6)
>>> mySet
{1, 2, 3, 4, 5, 6}
```

You can see that the unique value is, in fact, added to your set variable.

By the way, Python allows you to copy variables from one to another, so you could do something like this:

```
>>> myOtherSet = mySet
>>> myOtherSet
{1, 2, 3, 4, 5, 6}
```

However, a note about this. In the preceding case, myOtherSet is really just a "copy" of the original. This means if you change mySet by adding or removing elements, it will affect myOtherSet as well:

```
>>> mySet.remove(3)
>>> mySet
{1, 2, 4, 5, 6}
>>> myOtherSet
{1, 2, 4, 5, 6}
>>> mySet.add(7)
>>> mySet
{1, 2, 4, 5, 6, 7}
>>> myOtherSet
{1, 2, 4, 5, 6, 7}
```

This happens because when you assign a variable with a mutable value to another variable, you are really just pointing the new variable at the old one. If you want to create a brand-new set that isn't affected by the operations on the original, you can use the copy method:

```
>>> myOtherSet = mySet.copy()
>>> mySet
{1, 2, 4, 5, 6, 7}
>>> myOtherSet
{1, 2, 4, 5, 6, 7}
>>> myOtherSet.add(3)
>>> mySet
{1, 2, 4, 5, 6, 7}
>>> myOtherSet
{1, 2, 3, 4, 5, 6, 7}
```

As you can see, putting 3 in myOtherSet doesn't in turn put 3 in mySet; the sets stay separate.

Dictionaries

In the real world, dictionaries are big tomes in which you look up the meanings of words. In the computer world, the concept is similar; a dictionary is simply a mapping of a key (the word you are looking up) and a value (the meaning of that word).

You create empty dictionaries in Python using curly braces ({}). For example, you might have a dictionary that contains keys that represented the postal codes of individual states in the United States (like NY for New York), with values that are the actual names of the states:

```
>>> postalCodes = {}
>>> postalCodes['NY'] = 'New York'
>>> postalCodes['CO'] = 'Colorado'
```

As you can see, the square bracket notation ([]) is used to denote the key part of the dictionary, while the assignment statement (=) is used to put a value into that key. You can type in the following to look at the whole dictionary:

```
>>> postalCodes
{'NY': 'New York', 'CO': 'Colorado'}
```

Or you can look at a specific key in the dictionary by typing in the following:

```
>>> postalCodes['NY']
'New York'
```

Dictionary keys are most definitely case sensitive, so you have to match the key you put in there:

```
>>> postalCodes['ny']
Traceback (most recent call last):
  File "<pyshell#27>", line 1, in <module>
    postalCodes['ny']
KeyError: 'ny'
```

You notice in the preceding that you get an error if you supply a key that doesn't exist. You can get around that problem by using the in keyword in Python:

```
>>> 'ny' in postalCodes
False
>>> 'NY' in postalCodes
True
```

Classes

Python is an object-oriented language. Objects are computer representations of real-world things, like cars or books. They have attributes, which are simply things that describe them. A class is a template that indicates what kinds of attributes and functionality an object can have.

Classes are a major component of Python and most programming languages, because they allow you to encapsulate functionality in a single unit that can be reused—but not abused—by other programmers.

Creating a Variable

Creating a variable in most computer programming languages is a two-part process: declaration and implementation. Declaration is the process of telling a compiler (and some interpreters) the name of the variable and what type of variable it is. For example, in C++ language, also known as strongly typed language, you might declare a string called *foo* in the following way:

```
string foo;
```

The implementation phase of the process is simply using the variable. So for the variable foo, you would *assign* it the value "bar":

```
foo = "bar"
```

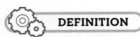 **DEFINITION**

Assignment simply means putting something on the right side of the equals sign.

Python does not have a separate declaration phase; variables only exist when you assign them a value. For example, if you try to use a variable you haven't assigned a value to, you'll get an error saying the variable name isn't defined:

```
>>> x = 1
>>> print(x)
1
>>> print(y)
Traceback (most recent call last):
  File "<pyshell#8>", line 1, in <module>
    print(y)
NameError: name 'y' is not defined
```

Finding and Looking at the Value of a Variable

The process for finding a value for a variable name, from the perspective of the Python interpreter, is pretty easy:

1. Look at the name of the variable.

2. Find a variable "folder" that matches that name in the list of variables for the program.

3. Return the value in the folder.

You can find the variable folder in one of two ways—using the print() function or typing in the name of the variable. For example, if you have a variable called *foo* and have assigned that variable the value "bar," the following show what you get if you use the print() function versus type in the variable name:

```
foo = "bar"
>>> print(foo)
bar
>>> foo
bar
```

Using the print() function is not really examining the variable value at all. IDLE doesn't know you are displaying the value; it simply knows you have called a function named *print,* and the single argument to that function is a parameter called *foo.* The side effect of calling the function is the value of the variable is displayed on the screen, but it could be sent anywhere.

The second method, typing in the variable name, is the preferred way to display a variable value. Typing the name of the variable will show you the value of it, as well as any other information about it. In the case of simple variable types, such as strings and numbers, all you will see will be the value. In the case of more complex types, such as classes or structures, you will see more information.

But what happens if there is no folder with the name of the variable you select? Well, let's take a look at that, using IDLE as our guide:

```
>>> print(GreenAudi)
Traceback (most recent call last):
  File "<pyshell#4>", line 1, in <module>
    print(GreenAudi)
NameError: name 'GreenAudi' is not defined
```

As you can see, there is no variable folder called GreenAudi in the program. The Python interpreter displays an error essentially saying it couldn't find GreenAudi anywhere. It is trying to be polite, but it is questioning your memory.

You can also run into trouble if you use improper capitalization for a variable. Variable names in Python are case sensitive; that is, if you name your variable BlueAudi, you have to keep calling it that. You can't then refer to blueaudi, Blueaudi, or blueAudi and expect to get back the same result. This can lead to some very strange results, especially if you happen to assign values to variables that look the same but aren't:

```
>>> blueaudi = "A very different car"
>>> print(BlueAudi)
Quarter Empty
>>> print(blueaudi)
A very different car
>>>
```

Computers, as I mentioned in previous chapters, are dumb. Unlike humans, who can recognize words no matter the case, computers do what you tell them to do, following the rules they were created to follow. Python was created to follow the rule that the case of all of the letters of a variable matters, so keep this in mind when naming and searching for variables.

Finding the Type of a Variable

Python knows what kind of data is stored in a variable, which defines the type of that variable. How can you find out that information? In Python, the combination of the type() function and the import keyword (see Chapter 14) can lead you to the variable type.

 PROGRAMMING TIP

Why is import used? Python is extensible; it is one of the pillars upon which the language was built. Extending Python is a matter of building modules, which can be reused by yourself or other developers. Using the import keyword allows you to access those modules.

The following code shows you how to use the import keyword and the type() function to determine what kind of value Python thinks is stored in a variable:

```
>>> x = 10

>>> type(x)
<class 'int'>
>>> x = "Hello world"
>>> type(x)
<class 'str'>
>>> x = 12.34
>>> type(x)
<class 'float'>
>>> x = 123424532432432432432324324
>>> type(x)
<class 'int'>
```

The type() function shows you both the values and the types that Python has assigned to the variable given to it. In this case, I've assigned various kinds of values to the variable x so you can see the different types that can be returned. For example, when the value of variable x is 10, you can see it says the type is an integer, or "int."

Changing the Value or Type of a Variable

Probably the most important thing to remember about variables stems from the fact that they're called *variables*. Something that is variable can change, and the values of variables can be changed at nearly any time. Remember from Chapter 3 when you wrote your input() function to get a name from the user?

```
input_var = input("What is your name? ")
```

The input() function returns a list of characters which represent the value of the text that the user types at the console. However, you could call this function numerous times and get numerous different results if the user types in different things. In each case, the value of the variable named input_var is changed to be the value that the user typed in.

Also, suppose you create a variable called *x* and assign it the value 10. Later on, you realize the value shouldn't be 10 at all; it should really be 20. That's perfectly fine with Python, as you can see using the IDLE editor:

```
>>> x = 10
>>> print(x)
10
>>> x = 20
>>> print(x)
20
```

You can change the type of a variable at any time, too:

```
>>> x = "hello world"
>>> print(x)
hello world
>>> x = 3
>>> print(x)
3
```

In the preceding code, not only has the value changed, it is now an integer (3) instead of a string (hello world). Clearly, a string is not the same as an integer, but Python is still able to recognize the value you've stored in the variable x.

You might also wonder how you could possibly know if a variable contains the kind of information you want it to. For example, suppose the user types in a string, and you want an integer. Strings and integers are not the same; you can't use one in place of another. And while you can do many of the same operations on strings and integers, the results are extremely different.

Python provides a number of conversion functions that can be used to convert one data type to another. Let's assume you have a string that contains a number. You want to convert that string into a real number you can use for math purposes—say a financial calculation.

The following is the number represented as a string:

```
strNumber = "123.45"
```

Now here's the number as a floating-point number:

```
floatNumber = float(strNumber)
```

Entering this into IDLE and looking at the results shows you the strNumber string has been properly converted into a floating-point number and stored in strNumber:

```
>>> strNumber = "123.45"
>>> floatNumber = float(strNumber)
>>> floatNumber
123.45
```

You might wonder how you know for sure it is a floating-point number. Well, you can multiply it by a value and see that real math is going on:

```
>>> floatNumber * 2
246.9
```

What would happen if you tried multiplying the string value by a value? One of the joys of programming is experimenting, so by all means, give it a shot:

```
>>> strNumber * 2
'123.45123.45'
```

Well, that was certainly unexpected, wasn't it? In fact, as you'll see a bit later, the multiply symbol (*) is used in strings to create additional copies of the value of the string. So what you really did was add an additional copy of the string to the end of the string.

By the way, you might wonder what happens if you convert a string and store the result in the original variable. Let's try that just to see what happens:

```
>>> strNumber = float(strNumber)
>>> strNumber
123.45
>>> strNumber * 2
246.9
```

As you probably had already guessed, Python does the conversion of the string to a floating-point number and then changes the type of the original variable to a floating point when it stores the value into it.

PROGRAMMING TIP

Notice how the variable is used twice in the same expression. That's perfectly okay; there is a very definite order to how things are evaluated. First, the stuff on the right side of the equals sign (the conversion, in this case) is done. The result of that expression is then stored in the variable to the left of the equals sign. That's why you don't get into some horrible loop trying to figure out what strNumber is at any given instant.

The Least You Need to Know

- A variable is like a folder in the filing cabinet that is your program. Each variable has its own folder, and the content of that folder is the value of the variable.
- Variables come in different types, such as strings, integers, floating-point numbers, lists or arrays, and so on.
- In most computer programming languages, creating a variable is a two-part process: declaration and implementation.
- You can find the variable folder in one of two ways—using the print() function or typing in the name of the variable.
- Python allows you to change the value or the type of a variable.

Conditional Programming

If writing computer programs were all about defining variables, assigning them values, and printing them out, what a terribly boring world it would be. Everything could only be done in a straight line one time. You couldn't change the program for any new kinds of input, nor could you make any kind of decision in your program to do things based on circumstances. That wouldn't be a lot of fun, would it? Of course not.

The programming world contains two concepts that I will discuss in this chapter—conditionals and branching—that make it possible to do all the fun things you see programs do in the real world.

In This Chapter

- What are conditions?
- Using the if statement
- Comparison operators for when things are not equal
- Applying else and elif statements
- Putting if statements inside of if statements with nesting
- If statements and lists

Conditions and the if Statement

Conditions allow you to make what-if kinds of decisions in your program. The most popular kind of conditional is the *if statement*. For example, imagine you want to only allow people to use your program if they are over the age of 18. You might ask them their age and base their access on the answer to that question.

You use a form called *pseudocode* to define the actions you want to take without getting into the details of the programming language. In pseudocode, which is really just plain English, your access granting process looks like this:

```
Ask the user how old they are
If the user is less than 18
    Exit the program
Otherwise continue
```

The basic syntax of a Python if statement is this:

```
if <some-condition> :
        Statements if the condition is true.
```

Both the if keyword and the colon (:) are required parts of the statement; you can't have an if statement without a colon at the end of it to tell the Python interpreter this is the condition to check. The important part of the "some-condition" part of the statement is that it must evaluate to a True or False condition. True is any nonzero value, or the Boolean value True. False, on the other hand, is any zero, None, or empty value, or the False Boolean value.

Let's take a look at an example. Imagine you have a password prompt, and you ask the user to enter their password. You are only going to have one password for every user in the system, though. (It isn't a very secure system, but what can you do?) You want to see whether or not the user entered the password, and, if not, exit the program. Here's how you might do this in Python:

```
import sys
password = input("Enter your password: ")
if password != "fred" :
   sys.exit()
print("You are good to go!")
```

PROGRAMMING TIP

You have a couple ways to do comparisons. To see if two variables (or a variable and a constant) contain the same value, you use the "==" comparator:

```
If x == y
```

On the other hand, if you want to see if they do not contain the same value, use the "!=" comparator:

```
If ( x != y )
```

If you run this in the command prompt (as you did in Chapter 3) with both a valid and invalid input, you'll see the following kind of output (save the file from IDLE as ch5_1.py):

```
C:\>python ch5_1.py
Enter your password: fred
You are good to go!

C:\>python ch5_1.py
Enter your password: derf
```

As you can see, a valid password gets past the if statement and prints the next line. An invalid password gets caught in the if statement and exits the program. The sys.exit() function simply terminates your current script and returns you to the operating system or command prompt, in this case.

Multiple Commands in an if Statement

To this point, every line of code you have written has been just that—a single line. However, with the introduction of if statements, I can now talk to you about blocks of code. In Python, code blocks are indicated by indentation—that is, you have something like the following:

```
if <some-condition> :
    Statement1
    Statement2
    Etc.
```

Let's look at an example based on the one in the previous section. Suppose you want to not only exit when you enter the wrong password, but you also want to print out a message telling you the program is ending abnormally. You could do something like Listing 5.1.

```
import sys
password = input("Enter your password: ")
if password != "fred" :
        print("You entered the wrong password!")
        sys.exit()
print("You are good to go!");
```

Listing 5.1

A simple password checker.

Now, when the program runs and the user enters an invalid password, the user will get some sort of useful feedback:

```
C:\>python ch5_1.py
Enter your password: derf
You entered the wrong password!
```

The important thing to take away from this is that the code in the block is executed when the interpreter enters the block. You define a code block in Python by indenting the code using the tab character. Every line that is at the same level of indentation and has the same number of tabs to begin the line is in the same code block.

PROGRAMMING TIP

Most other languages have a set of block characters or strings—such as "begin" and "end"—to denote the code blocks, but Python strives for simplicity.

For the example, what would have happened if you didn't indent the second line of the code block?

```
import sys
password = input("Enter your password: ")
if password != "fred":
        print("You entered the wrong password!")
sys.exit()
print("You are good to go!")
```

In this case, no matter what you enter, the program will exit after you enter a password. If you enter a wrong password, you will see the wrong password message, but you will never see the "good to go" line. Don't believe me? Try it.

But What If It Isn't Equal?

Up to this point, you have looked at equality as the sole comparison operator. Clearly, that's not it. Things can be equal or not equal, less than or greater than, and so on.

Python supports quite a number of comparison operators. Table 5.1 shows the operators and what they mean.

Table 5.1   Comparison Operators Supported by Python

Equal to (==)	The two values are equal in magnitude or value.
Not equal to (!=)	The two values are not equal in magnitude or value.
Greater than (>)	The first value is greater than the second value.
Less than (<)	The first value is less than the second value.
Greater than or equal to (>=)	The first value is greater than or equal to the second value.
Less than or equal to (<=)	The first value is less than or equal to the second value.

To see how this works, let's write a little program to input a value from the user and do some comparisons on it. Then you can look at the results and see what the actual meaning of each of the operators is.

This little program is going to take the balance of a checking account and figure out whether to charge a fee for the month, do nothing, or add interest to the account, all based on a set of simple rules. Here are the rules:

1. If the account is negative, apply a $10 fee.

2. If the account is zero, apply a $5 fee.

3. If the balance is up to $500, apply a $1 fee.

4. If the balance is $500, do nothing.

5. If the balance is over $500 but less than $1,000, the account gets 1 percent interest. (Yes, we are very generous here at the Python Savings and Loan.)

6. If the balance is at least $1,000 or more, the account gets a 2 percent interest.

Listing 5.2 shows the code you will be using.

```python
amount = int(input("Enter the current balance: "))

# If the amount is less than zero (negative) apply a $10 fee
if amount < 0:
    amount = amount - 10

# If the amount is zero, apply a $5 fee
if amount == 0:
    amount = amount - 5

# If the amount is up to $500, apply a $1 fee
if ( amount > 0 and amount < 500 ):
    amount = amount - 1

# If amount is greater than 500 but less than 1000, add 1%
if amount > 500 and amount < 1000:
    amount = amount + (amount / 100)

# And finally, everything over 1000, gets 2%
if amount >= 1000:
    amount = amount + (amount / 100) * 2

print("Your final balance is: ")
print(amount)
```

Listing 5.2

The checking account balance program.

There are some interesting things to note about this program, beside the basics of if statements and comparisons. First of all, notice the lines that begin with a pound sign (#). These are called *comments*. A comment is not read or understood by the Python interpreter. Instead, it is written in English (or whatever language you prefer) for other programmers to understand what you are trying to accomplish. In this case, you have written the comments to illustrate the rules by which the account balance is calculated.

Good programmers often use a technique called *code by comment*. This allows you to first think out the process of whatever you are trying to write code to do without getting tied up in the nitty-gritty of code syntax and such. It is a process you should seriously consider for your own coding, because the comments not only help you, they help the next programmer to come along to read your code. Unfortunately, since it can often be months or even years between when you write some code and then have to update it for another purpose, the next programmer may very well be you.

 **DEFINITION**

When you **code by comment**, you first write out a series of comments indicating what you plan to do, and then fill in the code between them as you implement it.

Beyond the comment issue, you have a line in Listing 5.2 that looks like this:

```
amount > 0 and amount < 500
```

The first and last parts of the line are fairly straightforward; they indicate comparing the value of the variable amount to the constants 0 and 500 and seeing whether the variable is within—but not touching—those bounds. Numbers like 1, 499, and 250 will all fit in this group, but numbers like 0, -1, 501, and 888 will not.

The middle of the line has the keyword *and*. The *and* keyword ties the two comparisons (greater than 0, less than 500) together. For *and* to be true, both sides of the equation have to be true, as you can see in Table 5.2.

Table 5.2   A Truth Table for the Keyword *and*

Value 1	Value 2	Result of *and*
True	True	True
True	False	False
False	True	False
False	False	False

As you can see, only the case of True for the first value and True for the second value results in a True when they are joined together using the keyword *and*.

Python also has the binary compare operator *or*. For *or* to be true, only one of them has to be true, as you can see in Table 5.3.

Table 5.3   A Truth Table for the Keyword *or*

Value 1	Value 2	Result of *or*
True	True	True
True	False	True
False	True	True
False	False	False

With the *or* keyword, only the case where both of the values are False results in a False when joined together. It is quite common for beginning programmers to mistake *and* and *or,* so referring back to these two tables may help you out.

The final thing to note in Listing 5.2 is one thing I haven't talked about:

```
amount = int(input("Enter the current balance: "))
```

You have used the input statement to get data from the user, but that data has always been in string form. You can't do math on a string, so you have to convert the input string into a number you can process. For this program, you use the int() function, which converts a string to a number. If you were using floating-point numbers, you'd use the float() function to convert a string to a floating-point number.

The rest of the code in Listing 5.2 should be pretty self-evident, as it is nothing I haven't covered before. However, before you move on, it is best to test the code and see if it does everything you expect. Let's look at some of the test cases you should consider when testing out this little program:

```
C:\>python ch5_2.py
Enter the current balance: -100
Your final balance is:
-110

C:\>python ch5_2.py
Enter the current balance: 0
Your final balance is:
-5

C:\>python ch5_2.py
Enter the current balance: 1
Your final balance is:
0

C:\>python ch5_2.py
Enter the current balance: 499
Your final balance is:
498

C:\>python ch5_2.py
Enter the current balance: 501
Your final balance is:
506.01

C:\>python ch5_2.py
Enter the current balance: 500
Your final balance is:
500
```

```
C:\>python ch5_2.py
Enter the current balance: 1000
Your final balance is:
1020.0

C:\>python ch5_2.py
Enter the current balance: 2000
Your final balance is:
2040.0
```

If you do the math, you will see that each and every case is correct, meaning your program has passed all of the tests.

ERROR MESSAGE

It is important to test your code. Otherwise, the only person that will ever see it break will be the users you wrote it for, and they won't be terribly happy.

The else Statement

When it comes to conditions, you may not always care about when something is true; sometimes, it may be a case of deciding what to do between two conditions. For example, if a stock is selling for $5 a share or less, I might want to buy 100 shares of it. If it costs more than that, on the other hand, I might only buy 50 shares of it. Python provides for this type of decision-making with the else statement. An else statement is always associated with an if statement; it can't exist on its own.

The pseudocode format of an else statement looks like this:

```
if <some-condition> :
    do something
else:
    do something else
```

The "do something" statement (or block, if you remember from earlier) will be executed if and only if the "some-condition" evaluates to True; in all other cases, the "do something else" statement or block will be executed. This is much easier to see with an example, so let's try one here.

Going back to the password example, say you want to print out a success message if you pick the right password and an error message if you pick anything else. You might write that like the following:

```
password = input("Enter your password: ")
if password != "fred":
    print("You entered the wrong password!")
else:
    print("You entered the right password, congrats!")
```

Notice the else statement, like the if that preceded it, is always followed by a colon. That is how you tell Python you are going to write a block or statement that should be executed when the else condition is met. Naturally, like the if condition, you can have multiple lines in the else condition, as you can see in Listing 5.3.

```
import sys
password = input("Enter your password: ")
if password != "fred":
    print("You entered the wrong password!")
    sys.exit()
else:
    print("You entered the right password, congrats!")
print("Logging you into the system.")
```

Listing 5.3

A multiline else condition block.

The elif Statement

Looking back at the account balance program, you will notice that you have a lot of if statements in a row. This isn't terribly unusual for the beginning programmer, but it is rather inefficient and hard to understand. For one thing, Python has to look at each if statement to determine whether or not it will ever be executed. Let's take a look at the code again to see what I mean:

```
amount = int(input("Enter the current balance: "))

# If the amount is less than zero (negative) apply a $10 fee
if amount < 0:
    amount = amount - 10
```

```
# If the amount is zero, apply a $5 fee
if amount == 0:
    amount = amount - 5

# If the amount is up to $500, apply a $1 fee
if ( amount > 0 and amount < 500 ):
    amount = amount - 1

# If amount is greater than 500 but less than 1000, add 1%
if amount > 500 and amount < 1000:
    amount = amount + (amount / 100)

# And finally, everything over 1000, gets 2%
if amount >= 1000:
    amount = amount + (amount / 100) * 2

print("Your final balance is: ")
print(amount)
```

If the amount is less than 0, you still have to execute each and every if statement after that, because they are separate blocks of code. Wouldn't it make more sense to simply execute the first one that fit the criteria and skip all the rest? After all, you always find something in the last place you look, right? Why? Because you stop looking after you find it. Programming is the same way; you should always stop when you have found the right point to execute your code.

To solve this problem, Python created the elif statement. Short for "else if," the elif statement is always found within an if block. Like the else statement, it can't live alone.

The general form of the elif statement is like the following:

```
if <some-condition> :
    do something
elif <some other condition 1> :
    do something if 1
elif <some other condition 2> :
    do something 2
else:
    default if nothing else was done.
```

 PROGRAMMING TIP

The elif statement seems like a bad typo, but it serves a lot of good purposes. Essentially, it is simply the equivalent of "else ... if <condition>," but allows for a default case (the else statement).

I'm sure that is all clear as mud, so perhaps an example will help. Let's rewrite the account balance program to use elif instead of multiple if statements:

```python
amount = int(input("Enter the current balance: "))

# If the amount is less than zero (negative) apply a $10 fee
if amount < 0:
    amount = amount - 10
# If the amount is zero, apply a $5 fee
elif amount == 0:
    amount = amount - 5
# If the amount is up to $500, apply a $1 fee
elif ( amount > 0 and amount < 500 ):
    amount = amount - 1
# If amount is greater than 500 but less than 1000, add 1%
elif amount > 500 and amount < 1000:
    amount = amount + (amount / 100)
# And finally, everything over 1000, gets 2%
elif amount >= 1000:
    amount = amount + (amount / 100) * 2
else:
    print("Amount out of range")

print("Your final balance is: ")
print(amount)
```

If you run the program now, you will find that each amount entered only goes up to the correct check and no further. You can put in print statements in each block if you want to verify this, which is slightly more efficient. But wait, running the program with one particular input gives you a strange result:

```
Enter the current balance: 500
Amount out of range
Your final balance is:
500
```

Why did you get an "amount out of range" error from the program? Looking at the list of if, elif, and else statements, you can see the amount exactly equal to 500 was never covered in the original program. This worked out fine, since that value had no changes for it. However, when you look at the coverage using a different method, it is no longer correct. This is easy to fix, of course; you just add a few new lines:

```
amount = int(input("Enter the current balance: "))

# If the amount is less than zero (negative) apply a $10 fee
if amount < 0 :
    amount = amount - 10
# If the amount is zero, add a $5 fee
elif amount == 0:
    amount = amount - 5
# If the amount is up to $500, apply a $1 fee
elif ( amount > 0 and amount < 500 ):
    amount = amount - 1
# Exactly 500, don't do anything
elif amount == 500:
    amount = amount
# If amount is greater than 500 but less than 1000, add 1%
elif amount > 500 and amount < 1000:
    amount = amount + (amount / 100)
# And finally, everything over 1000, gets 2%
elif amount >= 1000:
    amount = amount + (amount / 100) * 2
else:
    print("Amount out of range")

print("Your final balance is: ")
print(amount);
```

Now, if you run the program, you get the correct output:

```
Enter the current balance: 500
Your final balance is:
500
```

The problem with this particular way of doing things is that this line, while syntactically correct, is pretty dumb:

```
amount = amount
```

What you really want is a way to just skip that case, as you did originally. For this, Python provides the pass statement:

```
# Exactly 500, don't do anything
elif amount == 500:
    pass
```

The pass statement just tells the Python interpreter to skip past this line and do nothing. It isn't a very common thing to do in Python programming, but sometimes it makes code much more readable.

Nested if Statements

Like the old Russian nesting dolls, nested statements fit within each other and rely on their hierarchy for context.

While the if statement allows for conditional decisions and the elif statement allows you to condense multiple if statements into a single block, nested if statements serve quite another purpose. Imagine, for example, that you have to write a program that has the following rules for it:

1. For people making more than $100,000 per year, deductions are allowed for medical costs, but only if the medical costs account for more than 10 percent of their total income. Otherwise, they get only a flat $1,000 deduction.

2. For people making less than $100,000 per year, deductions are allowed for medical costs, but only if the medical costs are more than 2 percent of their total income. Otherwise, they get a flat $500 deduction.

Ah, if only these rules were true. That said, you would find the process of writing code to handle this very difficult using simple if or elif statements.

For this purpose, Python provides the nested if construct. Using pseudocode, you can try to write the algorithm that will be used for the preceding rules:

```
If income >= 100,000 then
    If medical costs > income/10 then
        Deduction = medical costs
    Else
        Deduction = 1000
Else
    If medical costs > income/50 then
        Deduction = medical costs
    Else
        Deduction = 500
End
```

As you can see, you have if statements inside of if statements, which is called *nesting.* Python allows the same construct in code, as you might expect. Let's take a look at the code that would be used for this little application:

```python
income = int(input("Enter your income: "))
medicalCosts = int(input("Enter your medical costs: "))

deduction = 0

if income >= 100000:
    if medicalCosts > income / 10:
        deduction = medicalCosts
    else:
        deduction = 1000
else:
    if medicalCosts > income / 50:
        deduction = medicalCosts
    else:
        deduction = 500

print("Based on your income, your deduction is: ")
print(deduction)
```

To verify your program is correct, try it with a variety of inputs. In this case, you want to make sure each branch of the if-else statements are hit. When you do this, you get the following output:

```
Enter your income: 110000
Enter your medical costs: 12000
Based on your income, your deduction is:
12000
>>>
Enter your income: 110000
Enter your medical costs: 2000
Based on your income, your deduction is:
1000
>>>
Enter your income: 50000
Enter your medical costs: 1100
Based on your income, your deduction is:
1100
>>>
Enter your income: 50000
Enter your medical costs: 1000
Based on your income, your deduction is:
500
```

If you run through all the scenarios, you will see that, in fact, your program is correct and produces the expected output in each case. This means your nested if statements are properly written.

Using if Statements with Lists

As you may remember from the last chapter, Python supports different kinds of lists, from simple lists of items to dictionaries and ranges. You might be wondering how one uses the if statement to work with such things, since the notion of equality or even less than or greater than makes little sense when talking about such a structure.

The answer lies in two Python keywords: *in* and *not in*. With *in*, you can verify whether an element exists within any sort of list; with *not in*, you can verify whether the element does not exist within that list. For example, suppose you create a list of commands that your user could enter into your program. You might implement that as a Python list like the following:

```
commands = ["open", "close", "exit", "undo"]
```

Now, let's imagine you want to write a program that reads some input from the user and compares it to your list. The thing is, though, you don't want to go through all the comparisons using if and elif if the command isn't valid in the first place. So the first thing you want to know is whether or not the command is okay. Let's use the "not in" construct to show how you can accomplish this. Listing 5.4 shows the code.

```
# This is our list of valid commands
commands = ["open", "close", "exit", "undo"]

# Get a command from the user
yourCommand = input("Enter a command: ")

if yourCommand not in commands:
    print("You must enter a valid command")
else:
    print("I'll be happy to do " + yourCommand+ " for you")
```

Listing 5.4

The command parser code.

Does it work? Let's find out. First, try a valid command:

```
Enter a command: open
I'll be happy to do open for you
```

Well, that worked okay. How about an invalid one?

```
Enter a command: blorg
You must enter a valid command
```

That one worked, too. As you can see, the in and not in constructs are powerful ways to work with lists easily.

A Slight Digression into IDLE

One thing you haven't looked at is actually running your little programs in the IDLE editor directly. If you open a new window in the IDLE editor (using the **File > New Window** menu or pressing the **Control** and **N** keys simultaneously), you will see the editor window. Figure 5.1 shows the editor window holding the sample program used in this chapter. You can get there yourself by doing a **File > Open** from the menu or pressing the **Control** and **O** keys simultaneously. In either case, notice the menu I've circled, which says "Run".

PROGRAMMING TIP

Most Python programmers will be testing their scripts or applications at the command line because that's how they will be run in the real world. However, when you are initially creating your application, it can make a lot of sense to always stay within the editor and just do your debugging and changing there.

Under this menu, you will see an option called *Run Module.* If you select this, Python will run the existing code in this window back in the original shell window (the main window that opens when Python starts). You can also do the same thing by hitting the **F5** key while in this window.

Most programmers prefer the keyboard to the mouse, so nearly all important commands in programming tools have keyboard shortcuts. Because you spend most of your time typing, it is easier to stick with the keyboard than to move your hands around to the mouse regularly.

To see this in action, first go to the editor window and hit **F5**. You will see the shell window come to the front and your program begin running, as shown in Figure 5.2.

Figure 5.1: *The code editing window in IDLE.*

Figure 5.2: *The run command in action.*

The Least You Need to Know

- Conditions allow you to make what-if decisions in your program, the most popular of which is the if statement.
- Python supports a number of comparison operators, such as equal to, not equal to, greater than, less than, greater than or equal to, and less than or equal to.
- For else statements, the "do something" statement will be executed if and only if the "some-condition" evaluates to True; in all other cases, the "do something else" statement or block will be executed.
- The elif statement allows you execute the first piece of information that fits the criteria and skip all the rest.
- Nested if statements helps you write code that would require a lot of if or elif statements.
- The *in* keyword helps you verify whether an element exists within any sort of list, while the *not in* keyword helps you verify whether the element does not exist within that list.

Loops

One of the things computers do best is repetitive task completion. Computers can do the same thing over and over all day and never get bored, never get tired, and never make a mistake. So it makes sense that there would be some sort of a way to have a computer repeat a command or series of commands in a programming language. That repetitive way of doing things is called *looping*.

In this chapter, I talk about different types of loops, as well as how you can use and combine them with some of the other things you've learned in the book so far.

In This Chapter

- Learning how loops work
- Using loops to calculate values
- Avoiding errors with the break and continue statements
- Infinite and nested loops
- Changing the direction of a loop
- How to print out lists of commands

Introducing Loops

A loop, much like it sounds, is something that begins and ends at the same point. In programming parlance, a loop is a repetitive construct that may or may not terminate. Python supports two kinds of loops: the for loop and the while loop. When you think about doing something over and over, think about loops as an answer to your problems.

How do loops work? Well, a loop has three basic parts:

1. **The entrance to the loop:** A loop always begins with some sort of initialization and entry point. This is the point the loop returns to each time it finishes an *iteration*.

2. **The body of the loop:** Whatever you are trying to accomplish in the loop—whether it be making calculations, printing out data, or simply passing the time of day—it goes in the body of the loop. Like an if statement, the body is the part between the colon following the entrance and the end. It can be a single statement or a block of statements.

3. **The termination clause of the loop:** This is actually optional, since some loops never terminate. However, most loops have a termination clause, which is a condition whereby they stop looping.

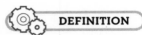 **DEFINITION**

In programming, an **iteration** is the repetition of a block of statements within a program. Multiple iterations mean multiple times through the loop.

The while Loop

The easiest way to understand the looping constructs in Python or any other language is to look at a simple example. Before you get into the syntax of the code, however, let's look at it in pseudocode so you can get a better idea of what is going on. For this example, let's assume you have a program that has to do the following:

• Input a string from the user.

• Check to see if the string is an exit command.

• If not, convert the string to a number and add it to the total.

• If it is the exit command, exit the program.

• Repeat until the exit command is found.

In pseudocode, this looks like the following:

```
Repeat
Get Data from User
If Exit command, exit loop
Convert string to number
Add to total.
Until Exit command found
```

Python does not have a "repeat until" loop, but it does have a while loop. Let's use the while loop to implement the pseudocode requirements and create the program. The code to do the task is shown in Listing 6.1.

```
done = False
total = 0
while not done:
    inputVar = input("Enter a value or 'exit' to exit the program: ")
    if inputVar == 'exit':
        done = True
    else:
        total += int(inputVar)
print("You entered a total of ")
print(total)
```

Listing 6.1

A simple while loop in Python.

The output from this program looks something like this, depending on your inputs:

```
Enter a value or 'exit' to exit the program: 10
Enter a value or 'exit' to exit the program: 20
Enter a value or 'exit' to exit the program: 30
Enter a value or 'exit' to exit the program: exit
You entered a total of
60
```

Let's go over the pieces of this program to see how it works. The first couple of lines in Listing 6.1 just initialize some variables, including the signal variable *done.* This variable will be used to terminate the loop, which happens when the user has entered the correct command. Next, you have the loop itself, which begins with the following line:

```
while not done:
```

Since done is a Boolean variable that has been assigned the value *False,* the loop will continue.

ERROR MESSAGE

While loops only execute while the terminating condition is not true. If you initialize the terminating condition to be true, the loop will never start at all. Likewise, if you don't set the terminating condition to be true at all, the loop will never finish. This is known in programming parlance as an *infinite loop*, because, well, it will run for infinity.

For example, if you changed the value of *done* to *True* at the top of the program, you'd see that the loop is never executed at all. In fact, you'd get the following output when you run the program:

```
You entered a total of
0
```

The code for the loop itself is the block after the colon of the while loop. As I've mentioned before, Python works by indentation for blocks, so all statements that are indented after the start of a block are run when the statement is executed, which in this case is the while loop.

Unlike an if statement, however, the while loop continues back up at the top when it finishes the block it is executing. The process is something like this:

1. Check the signal value.

2. If it is false, run the block.

3. Go back to step 1.

The loop block in Listing 6.1 is pretty simple—you retrieve a value from the user. Notice that you are doing no conversion on the value at the time of input, so it remains a string. This is because in this case, you don't know at the start whether the input string is a number or the exit command, so you leave it a string.

Following the input, you check the input for the exit command and, if it is found, you set the terminating condition to *True*. This will force the loop to exit the next time it reaches the top. As this is inside of an if-else statement block, there is nothing more to be done, and it drops to the bottom of the block. That loops around to the top, and the done value is checked again.

ERROR MESSAGE

If the input was not the exit command, you may assume the input is a number. As you'll see later on in the book, though, this may not be a good assumption and could in fact cause some serious problems. For now, however, you can simply make sure you either enter **exit** or a valid number. The number will be converted and then added to the total value.

Looping for Math

Nothing says that a while loop has to be done simply to wait for some kind of exit condition. In fact, a while loop is often used to calculate a value.

Suppose, for example, you wanted to add numbers 1 through 10 and report the result to the user. You could write some code like what's in Listing 6.2.

```
count = 1
total = 0
while count <= 10:
    total += count
    count += 1
print("The total = ", total)
```

Listing 6.2

An additive loop in Python.

Running this program, not surprisingly, gives you the total:

```
The total = 55
```

As you can see in Listing 6.2, Python allows for some shorthand commands where math is concerned called *augmented assignment operators*. In this case, you used the operator "+=," which can be read as the following:

```
total = total + int(inputVar)
```

There are several such augmented assignment operators in Python, which you can find in Table 6.1 along with what they mean. There are a few more than this, but since I haven't discussed the other operators in general yet, I'll stick to the ones you know.

Table 6.1   Augmented Assignment Operators in Python

+=	Add a value to the current variable.
-=	Subtract a value from the current variable.
*=	Multiply the current variable by a value.
/=	Divide the current variable by a value.

PROGRAMMING TIP

Up to this point, you have printed out a single value, whether it be a string or a number. If you take a look at the print() function in Listing 6.2, however, I've elected to show you how to print the whole thing on one line. The print statement can have as many arguments as you want, each one separated by a comma, and it will print out each of the arguments on a single line with a space in between them.

The break and continue Statements

Sometimes when you are in a while loop, you just need to get out of it. An error occurs, something finishes—whatever the case, you need to finish the loop right then and there. For this reason, most programming languages provide a method for doing so. In Python, this method is the *break statement*. The break statement tells the interpreter to drop past the bottom of the current loop. This means only the current loop is affected when you use the break statement.

For example, say you want to input commands from the user and echo them back until they enter a terminating command—in this case, let's use *quit* as the terminator. Until the user enters quit, the program will just continue to loop. Listing 6.3 shows what the program looks like.

```
while True:
    command = input("Enter a command: ")
    if ( command == 'quit' ):
        break
    print(command)
print("All done")
```

Listing 6.3

The break statement.

If you run the preceding little program and enter some commands or strings, you'll see something like the output shown here:

```
Enter a command: fred
fred
Enter a command: george
george
Enter a command: harold
harold
Enter a command: quit
All done
```

As you can see, the break statement immediately drops you out of the loop. This can be effective when you are looking for a specific value in a loop or when a problem occurs.

Similar to the break statement is the *continue statement*. The continue statement drops to the bottom of the loop but does not exit it. Continue statements are usually used when you either do not need to process a bit of information or when a problem occurs if you do process the information.

Consider the case where you want to divide a given number by a series of other numbers. You might loop, asking the user for a value with which to divide. If they enter a value of zero, which can't be used in division, you want a way to print out an error message and skip that value. To do this, you should have a program that looks something like Listing 6.4.

```
value = 123456
while value > 1:
    div = int(input("Enter something to divide the value by: "))
    if div == 0:
        print("You cannot divide by 0!")
        continue
    value /= div
    print("The value is now ", value)
print("Done with the loop")
```

Listing 6.4

The continue statement.

As you can see, you loop until the value of the value variable (say that three times fast) becomes less than 1.

> **PROGRAMMING TIP**
>
> You might wonder how that can be when *value* is clearly a whole number. In fact, Python will "cast" a variable to a different type when an operation requires it. Because dividing by a number will likely result in a fractional result, Python casts the variable *value* to be a floating-point number. Floating-point numbers will eventually become less than 1.0 when you successively divide them by larger values.

Let's see how this works:

```
Enter something to divide the value by: 345
The value is now  357.8434782608696
Enter something to divide the value by: 34
The value is now  10.524808184143223
Enter something to divide the value by: 0
You cannot divide by 0!
Enter something to divide the value by: 456
The value is now  0.023080719702068472
Done with the loop
```

As you can see, when you entered the value zero, the program did not do the division, nor did it print out the new value of the variable. At the same time, however, it did not exit the loop either, indicating that the continue statement was merely moving you past all of the code to the bottom of the loop.

While you can accomplish the same thing using a complicated set of if and else statements in most cases, the continue and break statements allow you to write the information in a simpler and more readable way. And that's what Python is all about.

Infinite Loops

One of the most interesting things about programming is that certain classes of problems occur over and over, and even though you are fully aware of them, you continue to make them happen. One of the most insidious of the known programming bug classes is the infinite loop.

As I mentioned earlier in this chapter, looping constructs have to have a terminating condition in order for them to exit. If you don't provide a terminating condition, or that condition is never met, you will continue to go up and down the loop forever. This clearly isn't what you—or your program's users—want. Therefore, you need to understand what causes an infinite loop and how to avoid one if you want to be a successful programmer in the long run.

Listing 6.5 shows a particularly nasty form of the infinite loop that's pretty much specific to the Python programming language.

```
i = 0
while i < 10 :
    print("I = ", i)
i += 1
print("Done")
```

Listing 6.5

An infinite loop.

Because Python relies on indentation to indicate where a block begins and ends, the following line is actually outside of the loop, even though the programmer clearly meant for it to be inside:

```
i += 1
```

Because the variable *i* is never incremented, the terminating condition of i >= 10 is never met, and the loop never exits. If you run this program, you will see the same statement over and over, telling you the variable is equal to zero. You can then exit the program by pressing **Ctrl + C** while the focus is on the Python window. You should see something like this:

```
I =  0
I =  0
I =  0
I =  0
I =  0
I =  0
I =  0
I = Traceback (most recent call last):
  File "F:/Books/Beginning Programming/Chapter 6/ch6_5.py", line 3, in
  <module>
    print("I = ", i)
  File "C:\Python33\lib\idlelib\PyShell.py", line 1318, in write
    return self.shell.write(s, self.tags)
KeyboardInterrupt
```

Looping Backward

Up to this point, every loop you have looked at has counted forward—that is, from 1 to some higher number. There is no particular reason that loops have to go in rising order; in fact, they can just as easily count downward. The point of a loop is simply to do an iteration of something; the interpreter doesn't care what you consider an iteration.

For example, suppose you want to print out a string backward. You might write code like that shown in Listing 6.6 using the while loop.

```
myStr = input("Enter a string: ")
i = len(myStr) - 1
myReverseString = ""
while i >= 0:
    myReverseString += myStr[i]
    i -= 1
print("Reversed, the string is: ", myReverseString);
```

Listing 6.6

A string reversal program.

As you can see, the loop runs very happily backward. There are a bunch of other interesting things I've introduced in this little program using the backward loop, so let's take a look at them.

In the preceding code, the len() function is used to determine the length of a string. If you recall, a string is just a sequence of characters. For historical reasons, the string characters are numbered from zero to the length of the string minus 1. For example, for the string "Hello," the characters are labeled like the following:

```
Hello
01234
```

The len() function simply counts the number of characters in a string, including punctuation marks, spaces, and all the rest. For the string "Hello," the length of the string would be 5.

Next, another string operation, the "+=" operator, appends something to the end of a string. So you could append a full string:

```
>>> s = "Hello"
>>> s += " world"
>>> s
'Hello world'
```

Likewise, you could append a single character:

```
>>> s = "Hello"
>>> s += 's'
>>> s
'Hellos'
```

You can't append a number directly to a string:

```
>>> s = "Hello"
>>> d = 123
>>> s += d
Traceback (most recent call last):
  File "<pyshell#13>", line 1, in <module>
    s += d
TypeError: Can't convert 'int' object to str implicitly
```

The reason for this has to do with type safety and the fact that the addition operator means different things for a string and a number. You can accomplish this task by converting the number to a string, though:

```
>>> s += str(d)
>>> s
'Hello123'
```

Finally, as I think I've mentioned in the past, the "-=" operator subtracts a value from the current variable. So, writing the following simply subtracts 1 from the variable *i*:

```
i -= 1
```

PROGRAMMING TIP

Addition and subtraction are the most common operations in programming. For this reason, most languages provide methods for adding and subtracting values from the current variable. In the case of Python, those methods are "+=" and "-=".

Nested while Loops

Like you were able to do for if statements in Chapter 5, Python allows you to nest loops. A nested loop is simply a loop that resides inside of another loop. There are lots of good reasons to use nested loops, from processing matrices to dealing with inputs that require multiple processing runs. Here, I'll show you how to make a nested while loop (nested for loops are discussed later in this chapter).

Suppose you are given the task of implementing a program that accepts a number from a user and then determines whether it is a prime number. The program also has to continue to accept values from the user until the user enters a zero.

As I'm sure you remember from math class, to determine if a number is prime, you divide it by the values beginning at 2 and ending at the number. If none of those values results in a number without a remainder, the value is prime; if any one of the values does result in a number without a remainder, the number is not prime.

But how do you put that information in a program? In pseudocode, the process of finding a prime number looks like this:

```
Set divisor = 2
Loop
    Divide number by divisor
    If remainder is 0 then number is prime. Stop
    Add one to divisor
Until divisor > number
```

You can implement the prime number check using the following code, which includes a loop, an if statement, and a break statement. I also include the modulus (%) operator, which divides one number by another and returns the remainder:

```
divisor = 2
number = 13
isPrime = True
while divisor < number:
    # Stop as soon as you find a prime number
    if number % divisor == 0:
        isPrime = False
        break
    divisor += 1

if isPrime == True:
    print("The value ", number, " is prime")
else:
    print("The value ", number, " is NOT prime")
```

You can change the value of *number* in the preceding code to check various values. For example, for the values 13 (which is prime) and 14 (which is not prime), you get the following outputs:

```
The value  14  is NOT prime
The value  13  is prime
```

This is what you would expect. However, the original requirements state the user wants more than that—he wants to be able to enter a value repeatedly until he enters a zero. How could you do this? The answer is to encase the preceding code, without assigning the number directly (that should come from the user, not the program), in a loop itself, as you can see in Listing 6.7.

```
while True:
    number = int(input("Enter a value: "))
    if number == 0:
        break
    divisor = 2
    isPrime = True
    while divisor < number:
        # Stop as soon as you find a prime number
        if number % divisor == 0:
            isPrime = False
            break
        divisor += 1

    if isPrime == True:
        print("The value ", number, " is prime")
    else:
        print("The value ", number, " is NOT prime")

print("Done")
```

Listing 6.7

The prime number program in Python.

PROGRAMMING TIP

If you take the original code and add the new lines shown in Listing 6.6, make sure you use the Tab key on the keyboard to indent the existing code; otherwise, Python will complain about improper indentations. If you are using IDLE, it already knows how to do this. If you are using a different text editor than Python, though, this might require consulting the documentation on how to insert a tab character.

Remember, you need to have a terminating condition for your loops—in other words, when the done variable is set to *True,* or the break statement is encountered. In this case, the break statement is hit as soon as the user enters the signal value zero.

By the way, you might note that you terminate the loop using the break statement when the zero is encountered. Why do you do this instead of first processing the value? The answer is that the value zero is neither prime nor not prime, and the algorithm makes no sense for it. In this case, you would see that it reports zero as a prime number if you remove the break statement.

Nested loops like you see here with the while loop can be a very powerful and very elegant solution to a number of problems in computer programming. However, they can also be very expensive in terms of processing time. This is because each item in the outer loop causes the inner loop to execute. So if you have a large number of items in the outer loop, the process could take quite a while!

So, for example, if you were to run the prime program for a really big number, you might have to go out and get some coffee or maybe some dinner before it finished running. So much for computers being fast, right? However, using nested while loops for this kind of process is much faster than if you did the same process by hand, which might require you to turn it over to your grandchildren to finish.

The for Loop

If the while loop is a general-purpose tool, the for loop is more of a targeted one. One type of information for loops work with is ranges.

A range is what it sounds like—a set of values from one end to another. For example, the values from 1 to 10 form a range and can be expressed using the range() function in Python:

```
range(1,10)
```

The range() function can provide you either a list of inclusive integers—in this case, 1 to 10—or a list from zero to whatever you choose:

```
range(6)
```

Finally, the range statement can be provided with an increment value (in this case, 2):

```
range(1, 10, 2)
```

Because you told the range statement to increment each value by 2 and to stop when it reached 10, the range will be 1, 3, 5, 7, 9.

The for loop syntax for ranges looks like this:

```
for somevariablename in somerange:
    do something.
```

The "somevariablename" and "somerange" are things you can select. The "do something" is either a single statement or a block of statements following the colon that you want executed for every value in the range.

The end of the range is not included in what's printed. For example, if you use a range of 0 to 10, the for loop would be executed 10 times, meaning you'd get back 0 through 9. Let's take a look at the world's simplest for loop so you see what I mean:

```
>>> for i in range(0, 10):
    print(i)
```

The output from this little Python snippet is the following:

```
0
1
2
3
4
5
6
7
8
9
```

As you can see, the variable *i* is assigned a new value for each iteration of the loop. This is called *enumerating* a loop. The keyword *in* is used here to denote that you only care about the values which are in the range() function returned values.

You don't have to use a range with for loops—any sort of enumerable value will do. That includes lists, sets, dictionaries, and even arrays.

For example, if you want to print out each character in a string:

```
>>> myStr = "Hello world"
>>> for s in myStr:
    print(s)
```

The program produces the following output:

```
H
e
l
l
o

w
o
r
l
d
```

Yes, it seems a little odd, but when you think about it, it makes perfect sense. Enumerating is simply stepping through a list of things. In this case, the "things" are characters in a string.

You can do the same thing with tuples:

```
>>> mySet = ("hello", "goodbye", "greetings", "aloha")
>>> for s in mySet :
   print(s)
```

The code produces this output:

```
hello
goodbye
greetings
aloha
```

ERROR MESSAGE

You can't change strings and arrays while you are enumerating them. This is considered a bad thing and is to be avoided at all costs. The reason for this is how things are implemented behind the scenes: Python assumes the block that represents the string or set is fixed and won't go back to refigure how where it is in the string if you change it. This very rarely comes up in the real world but is important to consider up front.

The nice thing about for loops is that you don't have to know how many values you are going to process. Because the length of each element is built into itself, Python simply asks the element (set, list, or string) how big it is and then uses that many iterations of the for loop to process it.

Descending Loops

A for loop can operate in either direction, incrementing upward or decrementing downward. The range() function, however, only works downward unless you tell it otherwise. You might think that if you wanted to count down from 10 to 1, you could write the following:

```
>>> for i in range(10, 1):
   print(i)
```

In fact, if you run this in the Python IDLE interpreter, you see it produces no output at all. That is because the range generated is empty, since the beginning plus the default increment value of one is greater than the end. You can accomplish the task of counting down by including an increment value like this:

```
>>> for i in range(10, 1, -1):
    print(i)
```

The output from this bit of code is the following:

```
10
9
8
7
6
5
4
3
2
```

PROGRAMMING TIP

Remember, the end of the range is not included in the output. Therefore, if you want to count down to 1, you have to have a range from 10 to 0 and an increment of -1.

Nested for Loops

Like while loops, for loops can be nested inside each other. You can nest them to a more or less infinite degree (although I can't really think of a good reason to do so). As a simple example, imagine you want to print out a calendar. A calendar, of course, has two parts to it: a line showing what day you are looking at and a series of lines showing the dates within that month (see Chapter 11 for more on calendars).

Listing 6.8 shows a very simple calendar-like display. It does not worry about starting dates for the month, always beginning on the first day, but it would be pretty easy to change the code to accommodate that need as well.

```
# First, print out the days
days = ["S", "M", "T", "W", "T", "F", "S"]
for d in days:
    print("{0:4s}".format(d.rjust(4)), end="")
print("")

# Next, we'll set the number of days in the month, for now
# just assume 31
daysInMonth = 31

# Calculate the number of weeks we need
numberOfWeeks = int(daysInMonth / 7)

# Outer loop handles the weeks
currentDay = 1

for w in range(numberOfWeeks):
    # Inner loop handles the current week
    for cw in range(0, 7):
        print('{0:4d}'.format(currentDay), end="")
        currentDay += 1

    # Print a new line
    print("")

# Now, print out any remaining days
for d in range(currentDay, daysInMonth + 1):
        print('{0:4d}'.format(d), end="")
print("")
```

Listing 6.8

Printing a calendar.

This program using nested for loops has some interesting pieces you should get to know. First, you have the line that looks like this:

```
print("{0:4s}".format(d.rjust(4)), end="")
```

Up to this point, you've only looked at the very basic print statement—that is, dumping out variable values to the console. The print statement is capable of a considerable amount more than just that. The part of the line that reads "{0:4s}" is what is called a *formatting requirement*.

This part says to create a four-space-wide field to print out whatever is attached to the string. In this case, the something to print out is the ".format()" stuff.

The format() function, applied to the formatting string, indicates what variable to print. You want to print out the current value of the day of the week string, so you pass that in. The rjust() function does a right justification (that is, the string is aligned to the right side of the area in which to print it). The rjust() function takes a single argument—the width of the area in which to justify.

 PROGRAMMING TIP

> If none of this information about formatting makes a lot of sense, play with it a bit and know you are going to learn about formatting to a greater degree in Chapters 8 and 9.

The end= part of the line indicates what the print() function should do when it has reached the end of the values to print. Normally, as you've seen, the print() function moves the cursor to a new line when it is done, much like you hitting the Enter or Return key in a word processor. You can change this, though, using the end attribute. In this case, you don't want the cursor to move, so each string for the day of the week remains on the same line.

Rather than bore you with a lot of technical jargon, let's first look at the output of this little code fragment:

```
 S   M   T   W   T   F   S
 1   2   3   4   5   6   7
 8   9  10  11  12  13  14
15  16  17  18  19  20  21
22  23  24  25  26  27  28
29  30  31
```

As you can see, it does resemble a calendar quite closely!

The else Clause

When it comes to loops in general, one of the strangest Python constructs is the else clause. You can use the else clause after a for or while loop, and it has the same effect. Once the loop has terminated, the else clause will be invoked. Why would you do this? In a while loop, you can use the else clause to handle searching through a list or set and not finding something.

Consider the following example, as shown in Listing 6.9. This asks the user for a command and looks for that input in a given list of commands. If it finds it, it exits; otherwise, it prompts again.

```
commands = {"open", "close", "save", "exit" }


while True:
    cmdStr = input("Enter a valid command: ")
    for c in commands:
        if ( cmdStr == c ):
            break
    else:
        print("You didn't enter a valid command")
```

Listing 6.9

A very simple command processor.

Because the code is far from clear as to how it will end up working, let's take a look at the output when you run it:

```
Enter a valid command: badcommand
You didn't enter a valid command
Enter a valid command: close
```

As you can see, when you enter a valid command—in this case, *close*—the program exits the loop due to the break statement in the body of the "if" shown in bold.

On the other hand, if you do not enter a valid command, the loop will go through all of the elements in the commands set and won't find anything to match. In this case, the while loop exits without setting the done variable and without breaking out of the loop. Here, the else clause is invoked and the invalid command is printed out.

So the rules for the else clause are simple:

1. If the loop goes to completion, the else clause will be called.

2. If the loop does not go to completion due to a break statement, the else clause will not be called.

Hopefully, you can see where this might be useful in the real world. In the code sample, you don't have to worry about them not entering a valid command because it will always be dealt with. It also shows that the break statement works the same way with for loops that it does with while loops. Naturally, the continue statement works the same way, too.

Printing List Indexes with Items

The last topic you are going to examine when talking about loops is that of printing out more information for lists. Because this is such a common practice in the programming world, it is useful to be able to print out a "menu" of items with an index representing the item value. For example, you might display a menu like this:

```
1. Open a new project
2. Close the current project
3. Exit the program
Enter a value (1-3):
```

In many cases, it is a lot easier for the user to enter a number representing the option than to type in a command. In a graphical user interface, of course, you rarely do this, but it is also nice to be able to offer keyboard shortcuts to commands, which can be numbered.

Suppose you have a list of commands like the preceding. You want to print them out, along with the index of the command, so the user can enter a value to instruct the program as to what he wants to do. Listing 6.10 shows you how to do just that.

```
# The list of menu commands
commands = ['Open', 'Close', 'Exit' ]

# List the commands with their index
for index, value in enumerate(commands, start=1):
        print(index, value)
```

Listing 6.10

Displaying a menu with indexes.

The commands list, of course, shows us the list of commands. The start parameter to the enumerate() function indicates where to start in that list.

The enumerate() function returns a tuple—that is, multiple results from a single function call. This is something fairly unique to Python and very powerful. In the case of this particular function, it returns the index of the command within the list, as well as the string at that index, or position, within the list. You can think of a list as being like this:

```
1 - Open
2 - Close
3 - Exit
```

When you ask for an indexed value, such as commands[1], Python scans the indexes, or values on the left, and then returns the string on the right. All the enumerate() function is doing is returning both of them at the same time.

The Least You Need to Know

- Loops are one of the key structures in any programming language.
- You can use loops to iterate over a list or to skip through a list without changing anything.
- Loops can be embedded in other constructs, such as if statements or other loops.
- Loops should always have a terminating condition.
- Enumerate can be used to create a list that a loop iterates over.

Arrays

To this point, I have discussed several methods for storing more than one value in a variable. Lists, sets, and dictionaries all allow a Python programmer to create data structures that contain multiple data elements. Sometimes, however, you don't need all the overhead of using one of these constructs and instead prefer to just have something simple that contains a bunch of elements.

Nearly every programming language in existence supports the concept of an array, which is simply a block of fixed-size chunks that contains the same kind of variable in each chunk. In this chapter, I teach you about arrays and what you can do with them in programming.

In This Chapter

- Crafting an array in Python
- Printing out individual array elements
- Changing arrays to lists and reversing lists
- Removing items from an array
- Copying and slicing arrays
- Creating multidimensional arrays

What Are Arrays?

You can think of an array as a kind of expandable file folder, with each folder holding the same kind of data.

In most Python examples, when programmers refer to an array, they are really talking about a list object. Lists look like this in Python:

```
myArrayWhichisReallyAList = [1, 2, 3, 4]
```

You can use the list elements individually, like so:

```
print(myArrayWhichisReallyAList[1]);
```

Or you can use "slices" of the list, as shown here:

```
print(myArrayWhichisReallyAList[0:2]);
```

A slice is just a selection of the elements in the list. In this case, you are looking at three elements, starting at the beginning of the list (0) and going up to—but not including—element 2.

Arrays can be used in much the same way as lists; however, they are stored much more efficiently. Also, unlike lists, an array type is only available for numeric values and is *homogenous,* meaning you can only store the same kinds of numeric data in a single array.

 **DEFINITION**

Data that is all of the same type is **homogenous**. Data that is of different types is referred to as *heterogeneous.*

Creating an Array in Python

To create an efficient array in Python, you need to first import from the array module and then use the array syntax, as shown in the following:

```
import array
array.array(type, values);
```

For example, to create an array of whole numbers, you would use the following code, as shown in Listing 7.1.

```
import array
a = array.array('i',[1, 2, 3, 4, 5])
for i in a:
    print(i)
```

Listing 7.1

Creating an array of whole numbers in Python.

Notice the first character in the array function call: i. This letter represents the type of data you want to store in the array. Table 7.1 shows all of the data types the array type supports.

Table 7.1   The Array Data Types Supported in Python

Letter	Meaning
b	A single byte with a *signed* value
B	A single byte without a signed value
u	A unicode character
i	A single signed integer
I	A single *unsigned* integer
l	A signed long integer
L	An unsigned long integer
f	A floating-point number
d	A double-length floating-point number

 **DEFINITION**

Python, like most languages, supports both signed and unsigned value types. A **signed** value type allows for both positive and negative values (for example, -1 or 1), while an **unsigned** value allows only for positive values. Attempts to set an unsigned value to a negative value results in an OverflowError error message.

As you can see from the table, Python allows for both small values and really big values. The integer, or whole number, type supports values from 0 to a value represented by 2 raised to the power of 31 − 1. The long value is system dependent, but you can find it using the sys module in IDLE:

```
>>> import sys
>>> sys.maxsize
9223372036854775807
```

That's a pretty big number!

Unicode characters are for working with foreign languages, which is outside the scope of this book. You rarely run into a problem with arrays of unicode characters, but it's helpful to know it just in case.

Floating-point numbers represent decimal values, such as money ($1.23) or percentages (15.5 percent). Floating-point numbers aren't represented exactly on a computer, so you should never use them for extreme precision applications. This is because you can't really make a decimal value out of zeroes and ones!

Working with Individual Array Elements

You can get at any individual element in an array by using the indexing operator ([]) and specifying the number, or index, of the element you want. However, there is a slight trick to working with arrays and lists of all types in Python. Arrays always start from position zero and run until the number of elements in the array minus one. For example, for an array that contains the elements 1, 2, 3, 4, and 5, the first element is at index 0, and the last element is at 4. You can print out the elements individually using their index as well as the len() function to tell you how many elements an array contains, as shown in Listing 7.2.

```
import array
a = array.array('i',[1, 2, 3, 4, 5])
l = len(a)
for i in range(0, l):
    print("Element ", i, " is ", a[i])
```

Listing 7.2

Array indexing.

When you run this little program, the output shows you just what you should expect:

```
Element  0  is  1
Element  1  is  2
Element  2  is  3
Element  3  is  4
Element  4  is  5
```

PROGRAMMING TIP

If you want more information on the array object and all the available methods for it, you can use the help() method and specify "array" as the argument to it: help(array). If you do this in IDLE, you will see a display that gives you a rundown of what an array is and the methods you can use with it.

Arrays as Stacks

A stack is a data structure that allows you to push things on and pop things off. It is most analogous to a dish holder in a cafeteria or a gun ammunition magazine—you push in things at the top, and they come out in the opposite order. This is also known as a *Last In, First Out (LIFO)* structure. The array object in Python lends itself extremely well to a stack, using the built-in methods of the object itself.

Suppose, for example, you want to reverse the values in a list. You have a list with the numbers 1 through 10 in order, like this:

```
originalList = [1, 2, 3, 4, 5, 6, 7, 8, 9, 10]
```

What you want when you are finished is an array that contains the numbers 1 through 10 in reverse order. How could you accomplish this?

If you look at the layout of the list, it looks like this:

1	2	3	4	5	6	7	8	9	10

You want to move the first element so it would be here:

									1

And the next element would go here:

								2	1

What is it you are doing here? It would appear you are adding elements to the end of an array. Certainly, you could do that by just moving element 0 to element 9, 1 to 8, and so forth. But there is an easier way, and that involves using a stack.

The method you care about in the array is called *insert()*, which accepts two arguments:

1. The position in the array at which you want to insert the value

2. The value you want to insert at that position

If you insert at the beginning of the array, at position zero, you push everything in the array back one element. So insert(0, 1) would do this to an empty array:

1	<empty>

If you then insert another value, like 2, using insert(0, 2), you would get the following:

2	1	<empty>

Hopefully, you can see how this moves along. Now, let's write a little Python to take the original list and convert it to an array in reverse order. Listing 7.3 shows the code you will be implementing.

```
import array

# This is your original list
originalList = [1, 2, 3, 4, 5, 6, 7, 8, 9, 10]
print(originalList)

# This is the array you will put the list into
newArray = array.array('i', [])

# Reverse the list
for o in originalList:
    newArray.insert(0, o)

print(newArray)
```

Listing 7.3

Reversing a list with an array structure.

Here is the output from this little program:

```
[1, 2, 3, 4, 5, 6, 7, 8, 9, 10]
array('i', [10, 9, 8, 7, 6, 5, 4, 3, 2, 1])
```

As you can see, the result is what you expect—the array contains the list's elements in reverse order.

PROGRAMMING TIP

There is a slightly easier way to do this, since reversing the order of elements in any kind of sequence is a pretty standard computer programming problem. You could simply have written the following:

```
>>> originalList = [1, 2, 3, 4, 5, 6, 7, 8, 9, 10]
>>> originalList
[1, 2, 3, 4, 5, 6, 7, 8, 9, 10]
>>> originalList.reverse()
>>> originalList
[10, 9, 8, 7, 6, 5, 4, 3, 2, 1]
```

The reverse() function does exactly what you want with less code. However, it applies only to lists, not arrays.

Converting an Array to a List

Arrays are extremely useful programming constructs in Python, but they do have a fair amount of overhead involved in them. Sometimes, it is easier just to use a list primitive (a built-in type in Python, rather than a constructed one) instead of using an array. To do this, the array class provides a method called *tolist()*, which converts your array into a simple list. You use it like this:

```
>>> import array
>>> myArray = array.array('i', [1, 2, 3, 4, 5])
>>> myList = myArray.tolist()
>>> myList
[1, 2, 3, 4, 5]
```

As you can see, it is simple enough to do. But why would you want to do this? If you recall, I said that arrays were homogenous. That means if you create an array of integers, you can't do something like this:

```
>>> myArray.append("hello world")
```

If you try to add letters, the Python interpreter will tell you that you've made a mistake:

```
Traceback (most recent call last):
  File "<pyshell#15>", line 1, in <module>
    myArray.append("hello world")
TypeError: an integer is required
```

Lists, on the other hand, allow you to put any kind of data you want into them:

```
>>> myList.append('hello world')
>>> myList
[1, 2, 3, 4, 5, 'hello world']
```

As you can see, a list is a better choice if you don't care what goes into your sequence of data. However, if you want to make sure the only data that goes into your sequence is of the right type, stick with an array.

Removing Data from an Array

Sometimes, you want to get rid of data in an array. For example, you might have added a value that no longer makes sense. The array class provides the remove() function to do just that. The remove() function takes a single argument—the value of the element you want to remove. Suppose you have an array with the values from 1 to 10:

```
myArray = array('i', [1, 2, 3, 4, 5, 6, 7, 8, 9, 10])
```

Suddenly, your manager comes along and tells you the number 6 has been stricken from the corporate lexicon. (No, really, they do things like this in the corporate world.) To remove the value 6 from your array, you write:

```
myArray.remove(6);
```

Enter the whole thing into the IDLE interpreter and see what happens:

```
>>> import array
>>> myArray = array.array('i', [1, 2, 3, 4, 5, 6, 7, 8, 9, 10])
>>> myArray
array('i', [1, 2, 3, 4, 5, 6, 7, 8, 9, 10])
>>> myArray.remove(6)
>>> myArray
array('i', [1, 2, 3, 4, 5, 7, 8, 9, 10])
```

Poof! The value of 6 is no longer in the array, and management is happy.

But what would happen if you tried to remove a value that didn't exist in the array in the first place? Say you try to remove 12 from your array of 1 through 10:

```
>>> myArray.remove(12)
Traceback (most recent call last):
  File "<pyshell#25>", line 1, in <module>
    myArray.remove(12)
ValueError: array.remove(x): x not in list
```

Python is smart enough to realize the value you have selected doesn't exist in the array, and tells you about it. The error message is called an *exception,* since it is an exceptional event outside of the expected results (see Chapter 12 for more on exceptions).

Determining the Number of Elements in an Array

Although you can easily iterate through an array and print out or work with the elements, it is sometimes nice just to know how many things are in the array. This is kind of like having a bucket of nails and wanting to know if you have enough nails to finish a project. The len() function works on all sequence types in Python and can be used to show you how many elements are filled up in an array:

```
>>> myArray
array('i', [1, 2, 3, 4, 5, 7, 8, 9, 10])
>>> len(myArray)
9
```

As you can see, the len() function returns the number of slots used.

ERROR MESSAGE

The len() function tells you how many elements there are in an array; however, it does not tell you how many *unique* elements there are. For example, if you have two entries with a value of 7, it would tell you that there are two elements, not one 7. This shows how important it is to distinguish between the value of the elements and the number of them.

Finding an Array Element

There are two ways you can find an element with a specific value in an array. One way is the brute force method, searching through the array until you find the first element that has the right value and returning the index of that particular element. Because this is the way it used to be done all the time, let's take a quick look at how that might be done.

If you have the array you've been working with that has the elements 1 through 10 and you want to find which one has the value of 6, you could write what's shown in Listing 7.4.

```python
import array
myArray = array.array('i', [1, 2, 3, 4, 5, 6, 7, 8, 9, 10])
pos = 0
for i in myArray:
    if i == 6:
        print("Found the value six at position: ", pos)
        break
    pos += 1

if pos == len(myArray):
    print("Didn't find value of six")
```

Listing 7.4

Finding an array element by brute force.

If you run the program, not surprisingly, it finds the element in the array:

```
Found the value six at position:  5
```

So element 5 has a value of 6.

On the other hand, you could use the built-in index() function—the second way to find an element with a specific value—to accomplish the same thing:

```
>>> import array
>>> myArray = array.array('i', [1, 2, 3, 4, 5, 6, 7, 8, 9, 10])
>>> myArray.index(6)
5
```

As you can see, this way is much simpler and works fine. In your little code snippet, you print out a message if the value was not found. What happens with index()? Let's try putting in a value that doesn't exist in the array:

```
>>> myArray.index(12)
Traceback (most recent call last):
  File "<pyshell#33>", line 1, in <module>
    myArray.index(12)
ValueError: array.index(x): x not in list
```

You get back an exception indicating the value was not found, which is the same thing that would happen if you entered a nonexistent value using the brute force method code.

So which is easier for you to deal with? The way you choose to accomplish this is entirely up to you.

Adding and Extending Arrays

If you have two arrays and want to combine them into a single array with all the values in it, what do you do? You could loop through each of the values in the first array and append them to a new array, and then do the same for the second array. However, there's an easier way to manipulate arrays to add or extend them, as you can see in Listing 7.5.

```
import array
aa = array.array('i', [1, 2, 3])
bb = array.array('i', [2, 3, 4])

# Add two arrays
cc = aa + bb
print(cc)

# Create two copies of one array
dd = aa * 2
print(dd)
```

Listing 7.5

Array manipulation in Python.

It may not be intuitive, or for that matter very clear, but the lines marked with the comments "Add two arrays" and "Create two copies of one array" are actually doing an enormous amount of work. If you look at the output from this snippet, you can see what happens:

```
array('i', [1, 2, 3, 2, 3, 4])
array('i', [1, 2, 3, 1, 2, 3])
```

In the first case, you are appending the entire contents of the second array (bb) to the first array (aa) and storing the result in a new array called "cc." If you print out the original arrays, you'll see they haven't been changed:

```
>>> aa
array('i', [1, 2, 3])
>>> bb
array('i', [2, 3, 4])
```

When you add two arrays in Python, the result is an array that is the *concatenation* of the two. However, it is important to note that because arrays are homogenous, the two arrays have to be of the same type. You can't, for example, add an array of floating-point numbers to one of whole numbers.

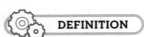 **DEFINITION**

A **concatenation** is a sequential link of two or more pieces of information.

In the second case, you can see that when you multiply an array by a numeric constant in Python, you get a new array that is created by appending copies of the original array. The number of copies is specified by the constant. By multiplying the first array (aa) by the constant 2, you get a new array that has six elements—two copies of the three original elements in the original array. You can either assign this new array to a new variable or use the original variable and overwrite the existing data in the array.

Adding New Elements to an Array

You may have noticed that when you create an array, you specify the data that goes into it. Say you use the array class as follows:

```
a = array.array('i', [1, 2, 3])
```

Once you have done this, you have created three elements in the array. So trying to use the fourth element will result in an error.

If you want more elements in your array, you can use the append() method to add new elements so they can be used in your program. For example, you can create an empty array like this:

```
>>> import array
>>> a = array.array('i', [])
>>> a
array('i')
```

As you can see, there is nothing in the array. Now, let's append things to the array, using *a* to stand in for the name:

```
>>> for i in range(10):
    a.append(i)
>>> a
array('i', [0, 1, 2, 3, 4, 5, 6, 7, 8, 9])
```

Your array, a, now has 10 elements, and you can assign values to any of them.

Python also provides a shorthand version for doing this, known as the list generator. The code for that is as follows:

```
>>> b = array.array('i', [0 for j in range(10)])
>>> b
array('i', [0, 0, 0, 0, 0, 0, 0, 0, 0, 0])
```

The little bit of code within the statement "0 for j in range(10)" is called *list comprehension*. It creates a list of 10 elements, all assigned the value zero, and then puts that into the array called *b*. As you can see from the display, array b correctly has those 10 elements.

Slicing Arrays and Other Sequences

Python supports an operation called *slicing*, which allows you to get at selected parts of an array, list, or other sequence variable. For example, suppose you have an array of 10 elements, from 1 to 10. For some purpose, you might only want some of them. Perhaps you are doing a scheduling program or something where you can only look at four elements at a time. The slicing operator allows you to get only the ones you want at the time you want them.

The slicing operator looks like this:

```
variable[start:end]
```

For example, if you have an array like the following:

```
>>> mya = array.array('i', [1, 2, 3, 4, 5])
```

And you want the second and third elements of it, you might write this:

```
>>> mya[1:3]
```

And IDLE would respond with the following:

```
array('i', [2, 3])
```

Note that the first element is zero based—that is, if you want the very first thing in an array, you use the value zero. The second element is where you want it to end, not including that value, so the value "3" really means go to element two.

You can omit the second value and get all elements from the starting value on to the end of the array:

```
>>> mya[2:]
array('i', [3, 4, 5])
```

Or, you can omit the first value, and get everything from the start of the array up to the point you want:

```
>>> mya[:3]
array('i', [1, 2, 3])
```

Slicing is a very powerful technique in Python, so please review it and play with it a bit until you really understand it.

Multidimensional Lists

In arrays, dimensions are the number of rows and columns. For example, if you have a "normal" array with six elements in it, you really have one row of six columns:

1	2	3	4	5	6

On the other hand, you might want to have something more like a spreadsheet and have several rows with multiple columns each. Let's say your spreadsheet represents a number of weeks. It has seven columns, with each representing the amount you might sell for a given day, and a row for each week. Your spreadsheet might look like this:

1, 1	1, 2	1, 3	1, 4	1, 5	1, 6	1, 7
2, 1	2, 2	2, 3	2, 4	2, 5	2, 6	2, 7
3, 1	3, 2	3, 3	3, 4	3, 5	3, 6	3, 7
4, 1	4, 2	4, 3	4, 4	4, 5	4, 6	4, 7

In this case, I've labeled the individual cells (that is, the intersections of rows and columns) with the cell number. The cell numbers all look like "row, column," so, for example, the value "1, 5" represents the fifth column in row one, while the value "4, 3" represents the third column in row four.

The spreadsheet motif is very common in computer programming due to mathematical entities called *matrices*. If you don't know what a matrix is outside of the movies by the same name, don't worry about it. They are pretty complex things, and well outside the scope of this book. However, the concept of a matrix is that of a multidimensional array, which is what I am talking about here.

Sadly, there is no way to create an array of arrays. However, Python does have the list construct, which is perfectly capable of doing lists of lists (and even lists of lists of lists and so forth). The creation of a list looks like this:

```
my1DList = [1, 2]
```

This creates a one-dimensional list with two elements in it—in other words, it has one row and two columns.

To create a two-dimensional list, you simply write the following:

```
my2DList = [[1, 2], [2, 3]]
```

This statement creates a list that contains two lists with one row each, making it a two-row, two-column list. Remember, the numbers you are looking at are values, not indexes. So the breakdown is as follows:

```
>>> my2DList
[[1, 2], [2, 3]]
>>> my2DList[0][0]
1
>>> my2DList[0][1]
2
>>> my2DList[1][1]
3
```

Of course, it isn't really useful to have such a construct, unless you can work with it. So, how do you refer to the elements in a two-dimensional list? The answer is exactly what I've been talking about all along: rows and columns.

Because my2DList is just two lists smushed together, you can think of it this way: my2DList[0] is the first list, while my2DList[1] is the second list. These are the rows in the multidimensional list construct my2DList.

Within the rows, you have the columns. To represent the first row and the first column of the first list, you'd write as follows:

```
my2DList[0][0]
```

This represents the first row (remember, list indexes start at zero) and the first column of that row. In this case, that would be the value 1.

Likewise, the end of the multidimensional list is the second column of the second list, which is as follows:

```
my2DList[1][1]
```

Or the value 3.

To see what it all looks like, just enter it into IDLE and allow the interpreter to show it to you:

```
>>> my2DList[0][0]
1
>>> my2DList[1][1]
3
```

Of course, because lists are mutable (that is, changeable) in Python, you can change the values of the list elements. For example, you could change the last element to have a value of 5 like so:

```
>>> my2DList[1][1] = 5
>>> my2DList
[[1, 2], [2, 5]]
```

However, you can't assign a value to an element that doesn't exist. So, if you tried to set the third column of the first row in my2DList to a value, you'd get the following error:

```
>>> my2DList[1][2] = 3
Traceback (most recent call last):
  File "<pyshell#6>", line 1, in <module>
    my2DList[1][2] = 3
IndexError: list assignment index out of range
```

PROGRAMMING TIP

While I've talked about matrices or multidimensional lists as being "square"—having the same number of rows and columns—they don't have to be that way. You can create a matrix with two rows and five columns, five rows and two columns, and so on anytime you want.

The Least You Need to Know

- Arrays are constructs that store data in memory.
- Lists are mutable constructs that store data in memory.
- Arrays can be converted to lists.
- You can "slice" arrays and lists to form subsets of them.
- You can create multidimensional lists in Python for matrices.

String Basics

Strings really are the backbone of programming languages. Outside of mathematical programming, nearly every program is heavily involved in string processing, whether inputting, outputting, manipulating, or saving the strings. Python provides a wealth of string functionality, some of which you've looked at before, and some of which you haven't. In this chapter, I give you a more in-depth look at Python strings, showing you how to work with them and what kinds of formatting you can do with them.

In This Chapter

- Working with string literals
- Using escape sequences
- Setting up formatted output
- How to convert bases

String Literals

Usually, when I think about strings and programming, I think in terms of string literals. A string literal is simply the name for a string value typed in Python code, such as "Hello."

In Python, you define string literals using one of three ways. The first two you've already looked at extensively: single and double quotes. As you know, Python really doesn't care which set of quotes you use, so you can have string literals that look like either one of the following:

```
'Hello world!'
"Hello again world!"
```

The third string literal is one I haven't really talked about yet: triple quotes (""""). The triple quotes way is used for strings that go over multiple lines. Here's a good example of what you can do with triple-quoted strings:

```
>>> longstring = """This is a test
of the emergency broadcast system.
I can use single quotes in my test, 'like this'
or I can use double quotes in my test,
"sort of like this"
but nothing changes until I end it with my
triple quote!
"""
>>> longstring
'This is a test\nof the emergency broadcast system.\nI can use single quotes
    in my test, \'like this\'\nor I can use double quotes in my test,\n"sort of
    like this"\nbut nothing changes until I end it with my\ntriple quote!\n'
```

Notice it doesn't matter if you wrap over two or more lines or put single, double, or both kinds of quotes in a triple-quoted string.

Triple quotes are usually used for blocks of text you want to display on a web page, a help page, or something like that. You don't normally use the triple quote for something like a help prompt; it makes the code harder to read and keep up to date, since you need to find matching quotes.

Naturally, because Python doesn't care whether you use a single quote or a double quote, you can do a triple-quoted string using double quotes, like shown previously, or single quotes:

```
>>> longsinglestring = '''This is a test, This is
only a test. If this had been a "REAL" emergency, you
would have been given warning.
'''
```

```
>>> longsinglestring
'This is a test. This is\nonly a test. If this had been a "REAL" emergency,
   you\nwould have been given warning.\n'
```

Escape Sequences

In the example of a triple-quoted string, you may notice that when you print out the value of the string in IDLE, you see some weird characters in the string, like "\n" and "\" characters. These strange things are called *escape sequences* (which are not to be confused with escape hatches, escape from the planet of the Python programmers, or anything like that). An escape sequence is made up of two parts. First, you have a backslash character (\). The second part (which you must always have) is another backslash, a letter, or quote marks. Take a look at Table 8.1, which shows you all of the available ones that Python recognizes. I'll then show you how you use them and what they mean.

Table 8.1   Escape Sequences in Python

Character	Meaning
\\	Insert a backslash in a string.
\'	Insert a single quote character.
\"	Insert a double quote character.
\b	Insert a backspace character.
\n	Insert a newline character.
\r	Insert a carriage return character.
\t	Insert a tab character.
\oOO	Insert a character with octal value OO.
\xHH	Insert a character with hexadecimal value HH.

Some of these characters are very important, even at this stage of your programming development. For example, the ability to insert a single or double quote into a string makes readability much easier. Likewise, the newline character (\n) is used quite a bit when outputting data to the screen. Tab characters (\t) are used quite often to line up columns for reports. The remainder of the escape sequences aren't likely to show up in your early programming experiences, but it is nice to know what they are when reading other people's code.

Octal characters are expressed in base 8 (I'll discuss what this means later in the chapter). For some special characters stored in files or transmitted over the internet, these are important. You will likely never use them unless you do system-level programming. Likewise, hexadecimal is base 16 and allows you to output numbers like 10 as "A." Once again, I doubt you will use these unless you work at the lowest level of programming. A carriage return, which is a holdover term from typewriter days, simply advances a line and goes to column zero.

PROGRAMMING TIP

The only real way to get better at programming is to write programs.

For strings, write yourself a little program that outputs a given string in different formats. For example, you might write out each character in a string in hexadecimal format:

```
var c = hex( ord( c ) )
```

The ord() function simply converts the character to its integer representation and the hex character converts that to a hexadecimal output.

Formatted Output

One the greatest uses of strings in Python is in formatted output. Python, like most modern programming languages, provides excellent control over what your output looks like, how things line up, and the like. You've looked at output briefly using the print() function in the past chapters. Mostly, it has been things like this:

```
a = 1234
print(a)
```

This works, but all it does is "dump" the value of the variable a to the console window (or IDLE). Sometimes, you want a bit more elegant answers.

Suppose, for example, you want to output data that is in a nice set of columns, so it can easily be read by a user. If you have three variables, such as this:

```
>>> col1 = "Fred"
>>> col2 = "Jones"
>>> col3 = "1313 Mockingbird Lane"
```

You could try to write these variables out using the simple print statement you know and love:

```
>>> print(col1, col2, col3)
Fred Jones 1313 Mockingbird Lane
```

The output is readable, certainly, but it isn't really clear where one column ends and another begins. That is fine if you are trying to run words together so the user sees them as a single statement, but it isn't so good when you are trying to make a pretty report.

Using the Tab Character

Looking back at the list of escape sequence characters, you can see there is a tab (\t) character. The tab concept dates way back to typewriters, where you could set *tab stops*. For computers, the concept is similar. Tabs move the output a given number of positions. Normally, for computers, the tab is the equivalent of eight spaces. (Why, I have no idea. I'm old, but I'm not that old.)

DEFINITION

Tab stops are the points to which you can advance the printing of letters. These are often used to align text.

The important thing about tabbed output for code is that it moves the output out to a position that is an even multiple of eight spaces. Therefore, the first tab moves to position 8 (assuming you are currently between positions 1 and 7), the second moves you to position 16, and so on.

To give you an idea of what tab positions look like, consider the following:

```
12345678911111111112
         01234567890
```

If you read the preceding numbers vertically, you can see they amount to the numbers from 1 to 20. Now, look at this:

```
12345678911111111112
         01234567890
       !         !
```

The exclamation points below the list show you where the tab stops will be for that line. So when you encounter the first tab character in the format string, you automatically move to the first tab position (8, in the previous diagram). Well, kind of, but that's not entirely true. You see, the tab moves to the next available tab stop given the current position on the line. So if you have already output 8 characters, it will actually move to position 16. Just think of it as moving to the next available eight spot on the line and you will do fine.

This may still be about as clear as mud, but once you see it in code, it makes more sense. Take a look at the following sample code:

```
>>> print("%s\t%s\t%s" % (col1, col2, col3))
Fred   Jones  1313 Mockingbird Lane
```

For the moment, ignore the weird stuff inside the print() function call and just look at the output. You can see columns are no longer running into each other; instead, there is now some spacing between them.

You can better see how this looks when printing out a bunch of data. First, however, you need to create some data to work with. In this case, you'll have three lists with the first and last names of your users and another with the name of the street they live on:

```
>>> FirstNames = ["Mark", "Joel", "Adam", "Irving"]
>>> LastNames = ["Smith", "Jones", "Telles", "Glockenspiel"]
>>> Streets = ["Elm", "Mott", "Lee", "Maple"]
```

Now, you print them out in a loop, with the tab character separating the three lists:

```
>>> for i in range(4):
    print("%s\t%s\t%s\t" %(FirstNames[i], LastNames[i], Streets[i]))
Mark   Smith  Elm
Joel   Jones  Mott
Adam   Telles Lee
Irving Glockenspiel  Maple
```

Well, that's certainly interesting, isn't it? It places the information in three columns, though the last line isn't in alignment with the other lines. Before you learn how to fix the alignment issue, though, you need to understand a little bit about those other funky characters inside the print() function call. Let's break those down a little bit.

Other Python Characters Used for Formatting

Within the print() function call, the first thing you see is a string value with all kinds of weird characters in it:

```
"%s\t%s\t%s\t"
```

Naturally, all of those funky characters mean something.

In Python, as well as numerous other programming languages, formatting is done by a series of formatting characters that tell the interpreter what kind of data you want to format and how you want that data to appear.

The character that triggers all the formatting in Python code is the percent sign (%). When you see a percent sign followed by anything other than a space in a string, you know you are looking at some kind of formatting information.

What follows the percent sign determines what kind of formatting will be performed. For example, the "s" following the percent sign in the preceding string means the formatting is done as a string. There are other formatting characters you can use in place of that "s," as you can see in Table 8.2 (I'll go over what the bases mean in the next section).

Table 8.2   The Formatting Characters for Python

Character	Meaning
c	Outputs the data as a single character format.
d	Outputs the data in decimal (numeric) format.
o	Outputs the data in octal (numeric) format, or base 8.
x	Outputs the data in hexadecimal (numeric) format, base 16, with lowercase letters for numbers 10 to 16.
X	Outputs the data in hexadecimal (numeric) format, base 16, with uppercase letters for numbers 10 to 16.

There are other characters, I might add, that are used for mathematical output, things like exponential output and fixed floating-point numbers. I'm not really going to get into those in this book, but it is good to know they exist.

The Formatted Data

It is all very well and good to say you are formatting something as a string and making it align to tab stops and all that other good stuff, but the real question is, how does it apply to what you are formatting and printing?

Let's go back to the original print() function call:

```
print("%s\t%s\t%s\t" %(FirstNames[i], LastNames[i], Streets[i]))
```

As you can see, your print() function call breaks down into four "pieces." First, you have the function name itself, the word "print." Next, you have the formatting string I've talked about a bit already. The next thing is the infamous percent sign. Python has removed the percent sign in their new-style formatting (see Chapter 9), but the old way I'm showing here is still perfectly valid and quite often used. Therefore, I want to make sure you understand it.

ERROR MESSAGE

With programming languages, old constructs rarely die. You have to get used to seeing things being done a dozen different ways, because while the methods have evolved over time, that doesn't mean everyone's going to use the most up-to-date ones. At the very least, you should of all of the possible ways to do things, since you may run into other people's code that uses a method you aren't accustomed to.

With the old-style formatting, the format string (the part that has %s and \t) is separated from the data to format by the percent sign. So you can read this as follows:

```
Formatted-string % formatted-data
```

Each of the elements in the formatted string that begins with a percent sign is "mapped to" an element in the formatted data section of the print() function call. So for your code, the first %s goes to FirstNames[i], the second to LastNames[i], and the last one to Streets[i].

You can think of it this way:

1. The interpreter finds a %s (or any other formatting character) in the format string.

2. The interpreter looks at the formatted data section to be sure there is an element matching the format string.

3. The interpreter formats the data element in the way specified by the programmer in the formatting string and outputs it.

What happens if you don't have enough pieces of data in the formatted data section to match the number of formatting strings? You'll get an error, of course. For example, if you accidentally added another column to your name and street code, you'd get the following error:

```
for i in range(4):
   print("%s\t%s\t%s\t%s" % (FirstNames[i], LastNames[i], Streets[i]))


Traceback (most recent call last):
  File "<pyshell#39>", line 2, in <module>
    print("%s\t%s\t%s\t%s" % (FirstNames[i], LastNames[i], Streets[i]))
TypeError: not enough arguments for format string
```

Converting Bases

If you recall, Table 8.2 listed a number of "base" output formats. What are bases?

When you count, you normally do so in what is called *base 10*. This is because most of us have 10 fingers and 10 toes, so our math system is based on counting on them. (I don't know about you, but I still do that some of the time.) You probably remember back in grade school when the teacher talked about the ones place, the tens place, the hundreds place, and so forth. In base 10, each of those "places" is a power of 10.

For other bases, such as eight, the "places" are powers of that base. So in base eight, you have 1 through 8, 9 through 16, and so forth. In binary, also known as base two, you only have two numbers to work with: zero and one.

Suppose you want to find out what numbers look like in other bases. You could write a little Python program, like the one shown in Listing 8.1, to do just that. Let's take a look at the code, and then I can explain how it works.

```
# Get a number from the user. We'll use 0 as the signal to stop
done = False

while not done:
    num = int(input("Enter a number to convert: "))
    if num == 0:
        done = True
    else:
        print("Num (decimal): %d" % num )
        print("Num (octal)   : %o" % num )
        print("Num (hexadecimal) : %x" % num )
        print("Num (binary) : %s" % bin(num))
```

Listing 8.1

A base conversion program in Python.

If you run this little program, you can enter numbers to your heart's content and see what they look like in other bases. When you are finished, just enter a zero and the program will end, as shown here:

```
Enter a number to convert: 5
Num (decimal): 5
Num (octal)   : 5
Num (hexadecimal) : 5
Num (binary) : 0b101
Enter a number to convert: 10
Num (decimal): 10
```

```
Num (octal)   : 12
Num (hexadecimal) : a
Num (binary) : 0b1010
Enter a number to convert: 20
Num (decimal): 20
Num (octal)   : 24
Num (hexadecimal) : 14
Num (binary) : 0b10100
Enter a number to convert: 0
```

> **PROGRAMMING TIP**
>
> You might wonder why you call the bin() function to print things in binary, rather than using a formatting string. The answer is pretty simple—the designers of Python chose not to include a binary print format when they released Python 3.3. The reason for this is that the bin() function already does this and, really, how often do you want to see something in binary?

As you can see from the listing, the number outputs are all different, even though the number you are printing is always the same. For example, the number 20 is 2 × 10 in decimal (the normal 1 through 10 you know), which is displayed as 20, while it is 2 × 8 + 4 in base 8, which is displayed as 24. The number 10 is clearly 10 in decimal, while it is 8 + 2 or 12 in octal (1, 2, 3, 4, 5, 6, 7, 10, 11, 12). But in hexadecimal or base 16, the number 10 is shown as "a," because hexadecimal uses the letters a through f to replace the numbers 10 through 16 (1, 2, 3, 4, 5, 6, 7, 8, 9, a, b, c, d, e, f).

Because computers work in bits and bytes, knowing how numbers are represented is important. It isn't really all that essential you understand how to read binary, octal, or hexadecimal because, as you can see, it is trivial to convert one to the other. It is important to know what is available to you, though. The more you know, the better off you are.

The Least You Need to Know

- Strings are one of the most powerful data types in any programming language.
- Strings can be formatted or unformatted.
- Computers work in bits and bytes, so it's important to know how numbers are represented.

The New Way of Strings

One of the most important things in the programming world for nonprogrammers is formatting. Whether it be on screen fields, reports, or just information presented to them, users expect data to be formatted correctly. This means strings need to be justified, money needs to be displayed properly, and dates need to be in the correct format for the user. In this chapter, you learn about formatting information in the new-style Python way.

In This Chapter

- Positional arguments
- The importance of precision
- Dynamically formatting strings
- Filling, padding, and slicing strings

New-Style Formatting

As I mentioned in the previous chapter, Python is moving away from the old-style print() format specification to a newer style. The new-style formatting revolves around the format() string method. Rather than embedding the string formats in a print() function call or using the odd formats required, the new format() method allows you to specify what you want printed where and how, if you choose to. Let's look at an example first:

```
>>> x = [123, "Hello world", 12.345]
>>> print(x)
[123, 'Hello world', 12.345]
>>> print("Values. Number = {0}, String = {0}, Floating Point={2}".
    format(x[0], x[1], x[2]))
```

The output from this, before you run off to type it into your IDLE environment, looks like this:

```
Values. Number = 123, String = 123, Floating Point = 12.345
>>> print("Values: {0}".format(x))
Values: [123, 'Hello world', 12.345]
```

So how does it all work?

Arguments and Positioning

A function consists of two parts—the name of the function and the arguments to the function (you'll learn more about functions in the next chapter). It looks something like this:

```
func( arg1, arg2, …)
```

The number of arguments can vary by the function and can be called anything; I've simply chosen the names arg1 and arg2 to indicate they are arguments. The ellipsis (…) indicates there could be more arguments to follow; you don't type that when you call the function.

For the print() function, the number of data elements to print is variable. That is, you can print out one string, two whole numbers, three squawking geese, or whatever makes you happy. So let's take a look at how you are printing things using the print() function.

```
print("Values: {0}".format(x))
```

First of all, the single string value being passed to print() is the string returned from the format() method. The format() method is being called on the string "Values: {0}." The format() method inserts values into strings in one of three ways: the default order, the specified position, or the name of the argument. Whatever the case, the number represents the position in the variable list passed to format().

Default and Positional Ordering

To understand the positional argument a little better, let's try printing something out with multiple arguments. You will print out a string that contains a name, an age, and a score of some sort, which will look like this in IDLE:

```
>>> name = "Matt"
>>> age = 51
>>> score= 99.99
>>> print("Values: {0}, {1}, {2}".format(name, age, score))
Values: Matt, 51, 99.99
```

As you can see, the output is what you would expect. However, the numbers in the curly brackets mean something. For example, if you change the line to read like this:

```
>>> print("Values: {2}, {0}, {1}".format(name, age, score))
```

You get an output that looks like this:

```
Values: 99.99, Matt, 51
```

As you can see, the number in the curly brackets represents the position of the argument that you want to print out. Arguments, like everything else, are numbered from zero upward, so, for example, if you want the second argument, you use a one.

What if you don't want to worry about the numbering of the arguments and just want to print things in order, like you have been doing in the past? For that, Python offers what is called *default ordering*. Default ordering just uses placeholders—that is, curly brackets with no number inside them—to indicate where you want a value printed. It then reads the values in order from the format() function and prints them out in that default order, which is shown in the following:

```
>>> print("Values: {}, {}, {}".format(name, age, score))
Values: Matt, 51, 99.99
```

As you can see, I didn't specify any numeric ordering here; therefore, I got the name, age, and score variables in the order they were entered into the format() function.

As a simple exercise, change the print string so it prints out the information in the order of age, name, and score. If you came up with this, you did great:

```
>>> print("Values: {1}, {0}, {2}".format(name, age, score))
Values: 51, Matt, 99.99
```

You also have the option of using default ordering and just changing the ordering of the arguments in the format() function:

```
>>> print("Values: {}, {}, {}".format(age, name, score))
```

As long as your methodology works for you and doesn't break the system, it is fine to do it any way you want.

Ordering by Name

As I mentioned previously, there is a third way to display arguments in Python that is known as the named argument method. This one is by far the most confusing to use, and often the least useful, but it is valuable to know what you are looking at if you run into it in someone else's code.

For named arguments, rather than a number in the curly brackets, you use the name of the argument you want displayed in that position. In the format() function, you specify the name as part of the argument by placing a "name=value" in there, as you can see in this example:

```
>>> print("Values: {nm}, {a}, {s}".format(nm=name, a=age, s=score))
Values: Matt, 51, 99.99
```

In this case, I've given the three output slots the names "nm," "a," and "s."

PROGRAMMING TIP

I could have called the three outputs anything, including "name," "age," and "score"; while those are clearer, it could be confusing to the reader to read:

```
print("Values: {name}, {age}, {score}".format(name=name, age=age,
   score=score))
```

Still, if you type that line into IDLE, you'll get the exact same output. That's because Python can do the work of figuring out which "name" you really meant by the place it finds the string in the print() function call.

Why choose names over positions or vice versa? There is no single good answer for that except personal preference. There may be times when you want to make it very clear what you are printing, which leads you to use the named argument approach. Most of the time, though, you will just use the default argument method, with no numbers or names at all. Still, knowing about the other choices makes it easier to understand other people's code.

Formatting Output

Now that you understand arguments, positions, and all that jazz, let's get into more of the art of formatting data in Python.

Python provides a wealth of options when it comes to formatting output. Chances are you won't use the vast majority of them, but it is good to know what they are there when you need them. Let's take a look at a few choices using the print() function that will allow you to accomplish common programming tasks.

Setting the Width

First, let's reconsider printing issue you had with the name and state report. If you recall, when you tried printing things out with tabs, you ended up with some problems, mostly when the string exceeded the length of a tab stop (eight characters). If you want to avoid that issue, you can define exactly how long you want the string to be in the formatting part of the print() function.

When you want to use codes to manipulate the output width, justification, or anything else in the format string, you use a colon (:). This indicates to Python you are trying to change something about the way the data is output. In the case of creating columns, what you want to do is create a fixed width for each column so it looks like a real table. In other words, you want to print the first column in some number of characters, the second column in some other number, and so forth. It looks something like this:

```
←-    First Column →|← Second column →|Third column
```

You may or may not care about the length of the third column, since it is the end of the line. In this example, though, let's set the widths of each one of the columns, just as if it were a real report.

Listing 9.1 shows the code that prints the report, along with the data that it uses.

```
FirstNames = ["Mark", "Joel", "Adam", "Irving"]
LastNames = ["Smith", "Jones", "Telles", "Glockenspiel"]
Streets = ["Elm", "Mott", "Lee", "Maple"]


for i in range(len(FirstNames)):
    print("{:20s} {:20s} {:30s}".format(FirstNames[i], LastNames[i],
  Streets[i]))
```

Listing 9.1

Printing a report in Python.

Checking the output, you see that it looks like this when run in the interpreter:

```
Mark                 Smith                Elm
Joel                 Jones                Mott
Adam                 Telles               Lee
Irving               Glockenspiel         Maple
```

As you can see, the report looks pretty good!

Now how did you accomplish this? Looking at the formatting section of the print() function call, you can see it is pretty similar to what you've been doing so far in this and the previous chapter. There are three arguments to the format() function with no positional values, so the arguments will simply be taken in the order they are presented. The strange part is the stuff after the colon, such as ":20s." In Python, you can put the format in form ":xx," where xx is the minimum width of the entry you want displayed. If you could count the characters, you'd see the columns are as wide as indicated in the code. The "s" part of the format indicates the argument is to be treated as a string.

Being Precise

There may be times when you don't have enough room on the page for the widths you have selected. Suppose your boss does not like the big spaces between the columns. You therefore decide to make the width of the first column smaller, since nobody has really long first names anyway, right? Listing 9.2 shows the width change to the first column.

```
FirstNames = ["Mark", "Joel", "Adam", "Irving"]
LastNames = ["Smith", "Jones", "Telles", "Glockenspiel"]
Streets = ["Elm", "Mott", "Lee", "Maple"]


for i in range(len(FirstNames)):
    print("{:10s} {:20s} {:30s}".format(FirstNames[i], LastNames[i],
  Streets[i]))
```

Listing 9.2

The amended report program.

Notice the section in bold? It is the new width of the FirstNames column. What happens when you run the thing? Well, as expected, you get something like this:

```
Mark        Smith           Elm
Joel        Jones           Mott
Adam        Telles          Lee
Irving      Glockenspiel     Maple
```

Great, you think, *I've made it just the way the boss wanted it.* Of course, as with all great plans, something comes along to ruin it. You get a new person with a long name for your report, so the data now looks like this:

```
FirstNames = ["ReallyLongFirstNameOfPerson", "Mark", "Joel", "Adam",
  "Irving"]
LastNames = ["ReallyLongLastNameofPerson", "Smith", "Jones", "Telles",
  "Glockenspiel"]
Streets = ["AStreetNameThatIsLong", "Elm", "Mott", "Lee", "Maple"]
```

What happens when you run the program now?

PROGRAMMING TIP

Notice, by the way, that you always run the for loop over the number of elements in the FirstNames list, so no matter how much data you add, it will always display it all.

```
ReallyLongFirstNameofPerson ReallyLongLastNameofPerson AStreetNameThatIsLong
Mark      Smith              Elm
Joel      Jones              Mott
Adam      Telles             Lee
Irving    Glockenspiel       Maple
```

Uh oh, that doesn't look good. That first line is completely out of whack with the rest of them. How can you fix this problem so the boss doesn't rip her hair out and yell at you? In Python, you can put the format in form ":xx.yy," where xx is of course the width, while yy is the precision. The answer lies in the "precision" part of the format.

While the width part of the format tells Python that you want the field to be at least that wide, the precision part lets you inform the interpreter that you don't want it to be any wider than a certain amount. So if you want the first field to be 10 characters wide and only 10 characters wide, you would write it as "{:10.10s}."

If you update the code to print out the fields in widths of 10, 20, and 30 for the three fields, you'd get something that looks like Listing 9.3.

```
FirstNames = ["ReallyLongFirstNameOfPerson", "Mark", "Joel", "Adam",
  "Irving"]
LastNames = ["ReallyLongLastNameofPerson", "Smith", "Jones", "Telles",
  "Glockenspiel"]
Streets = ["AStreetNameThatIsLong", "Elm", "Mott", "Lee", "Maple"]


for i in range(len(FirstNames)):
    print("{:10.10s} {:20.20s} {:30.30s}".format(FirstNames[i], LastNames[i],
  Streets[i]))
```

Listing 9.3

The updated report program.

PROGRAMMING TIP

Remember, the part before the colon would be the position or name of the variable you want printed; in the examples in this section, however, I am just having you use the default, meaning the interpreter will take the fields as you give them to it.

Now, running the thing gives you an output that looks like this:

```
ReallyLong ReallyLongLastNameof AStreetNameThatIsLong
Mark       Smith               Elm
Joel       Jones               Mott
Adam       Telles              Lee
Irving     Glockenspiel        Maple
```

As you can see, the really long names have been truncated to fit in the space you asked for, making the report look much prettier and your boss much happier.

Justifying Your Existence

One thing you might notice when looking at your report output is that all of the printed data shows up nicely aligned along the left side of its intended column. The process of moving text so it lines up along a given axis is called *justification*.

There are three sorts of textual justification: right, left, and center. Right-justified text aligns with the right side of the column, left-justified text aligns with the left side of the column, and center-justified text is centered in the entire width of the column.

To give you an idea of each type, here's what they look like in print:

This is left justified

                                                        This is right justified

                            This is centered

Modern word processors can do this at the click of a button, and process in Python is pretty simple as well.

One of the ways you can justify text in Python is with formatting characters. Not surprisingly, there are three characters that represent left, right, and center justification, which you can see in Table 9.1.

Table 9.1　Justification Formatting Characters in Python

Left justification	<
Right justification	>
Center justification	^

How do you use them? The following shows you how they're placed in code:

```
>>> "{:>25}".format("This is a string")
'            This is a string'
>>> "{:<25}".format("This is a string")
'This is a string         '
>>> "{:^25}".format("This is a string")
'     This is a string    '
```

As you can see, the formatting character goes after the colon—since that marks the end of the position part of the argument—and before the width of the string. You can use it with precision arguments as well to make sure the string is truncated if it is too long, but obviously that will negate any justification (since it would take up the entire width no matter how it was justified).

Because Python is trying to move away from the embedded characters that have weird meanings and more into a function-based object-oriented programming language, newer versions of Python (3.x and above, mostly) have functions in place of the justification characters. The three justification functions are shown in Table 9.2, along with their character equivalents (in case you have gotten attached to them in the last few moments).

Table 9.2   The String Justification Functions in Python

Left Justification	ljust()	<
Right Justification	rjust()	>
Centered	center()	^

Rewriting the justification character examples with function calls yields code that looks like this:

```
>>> "{}".format("This is a string".rjust(25))
'            This is a string'
>>> "{}".format("This is a string".ljust(25))
'This is a string         '
>>> "{}".format("This is a string".center(25))
'     This is a string    '
```

 PROGRAMMING TIP

Whether the characters or the functions are more readable is really a matter of opinion. The formatting characters will likely be around for quite a while, so if it makes you happier to use them, by all means. For myself, I prefer the clearer look of the function calls.

The functions for these in Python can actually return a value. That is, you can write the following:

```
s = "{}".format("This is a string".center(25));
```

The variable s will then have the centered string "This is a string" stored in it. Try it out in IDLE and you will see what I mean. The nice part about this is that you can hold onto the value of the string and use it again and again without having to format it each time. Calling a function (or printing with the formatting character) does take time and processing power, so it's a nice way to get around doing that over and over.

Numeric Formatting for Floating-Point Numbers

Like strings, numbers allow you to define the width you are printing out into, as well as the precision of the number you want to print. In the case of floating-point numbers, however, precision doesn't mean the absolute width. Precision for floating-point numbers means the number of places to the right of the decimal point.

Python provides formatting strings that allow for most of the numeric types. You looked at the ones for strings and simple (whole) numbers in Listing 8.2 in Chapter 8, so Table 9.3 shows the formatting options for only floating-point numbers.

Table 9.3   Python Floating-Point Formatting Characters

Character	Meaning
e	Lowercase the exponential output.
E	Uppercase the exponential output.
f	Lowercase the floating-point output, if necessary.
F	Uppercase the floating-point output, if necessary.
g	Lowercase either the floating-point or exponential output, depending on the value.
G	Uppercase either the floating-point or exponential output, depending on the value.

To see some examples of how this works, you can write a small program that outputs the same numbers using different formatting characters. Along the way, you will see just how powerful an interpreted language can be in terms of flexibility and control. Listing 9.4 shows a little program; study it first and see if you can figure out what it does.

```
formatOptions = ["{:f}", "{:F}", "{:e}", "{:E}", "{:g}", "{:G}"]
value = 1234.567789
for f in formatOptions :
    print(f, f.format(value))
```

Listing 9.4

A formatting program in Python.

Running the program will result in the following output. Let's take a look at that first, and then I'll explain how it all works:

```
{:f} 1234.567789
{:F} 1234.567789
{:e} 1.234568e+03
{:E} 1.234568E+03
{:g} 1234.57
{:G} 1234.57
```

Okay, so what is going on here? First, you declare a list of strings, which look suspiciously like formatting strings. In fact, that's exactly what they are. Python doesn't care if your string is *hard coded*; when it gets down to the actual formatting process, the interpreter just looks at the value of the string and takes whatever action is appropriate.

 **DEFINITION**

Something is **hard coded** when it is written directly into a program, potentially in multiple places, where it can't be easily modified.

So you have a list of strings, and you walk through them one at a time using a for loop (see Chapter 6). Nothing magical here; you've done this a dozen times already to this point in the book. The magic comes in with this line:

```
print(f, f.format(value))
```

As I mentioned, the format function works on any string, based on the content of the string variable. So what is really happening here is the print() function grabs the format string and gets whatever happens to be in it. For the first string, it reads "{:f}," because that is the first value in your list. Looking at the format string, the interpreter then decides it needs to grab a floating-point value out of the argument list (from the format() function). The value of the "value" variable is then formatted and the result is displayed for the user. That's a lot going on in a simple statement!

Dynamic Formatting

One of the things the example in Listing 9.4 shows off to the maximum is the ability of Python to do things dynamically. Dynamic formatting means you can change the output format at runtime rather than using a hard-coded string for the format.

In the early days of programming, everything had to be stated statically and absolutely to the interpreter or compiler. You couldn't change the format or value of an output on the fly; you had to go in and make code changes when someone wanted something different.

Today, though, you can create a format string by saving the output into a list, as you've seen, or you can actually create one from scratch while the program is running. Let's write a little bigger program this time, one in which you actually reformat things based on user input.

First, study the code in Listing 9.5 and the output that follows.

```
done = False
while not done:
    num = float(input("Enter a floating-point number: "))
    if num == 0.0:
        done = True
        break
    print("How do you want the number formatted?")
    print("[1] As an integer (whole number)")
    print("[2] As a floating-point number")
    print("[3] As an exponential number")
    choice = int(input("Enter your choice from 1 to 3: "))
    if choice == 1:
        print("Number: {:d}".format(int(num)))
    elif choice == 2:
        decpts = int(input("How many decimal places do you want?"))
        fmt = "{:." + str(decpts) + "f}"
        print("Number: " + fmt.format(num))
    elif choice == 3:
        print("Number: {:e}".format(num))
    else:
        print("Please enter a valid choice!")
```

Listing 9.5

Dynamic formatting in Python.

Some sample output from running this program might look something like this:

```
Enter a floating-point number: 123456.456
How do you want the number formatted?
[1] As an integer (whole number)
[2] As a floating-point number
[3] As an exponential number
Enter your choice from 1 to 3: 1
Number: 123456
Enter a floating-point number: 12345.35676
How do you want the number formatted?
[1] As an integer (whole number)
[2] As a floating-point number
[3] As an exponential number
Enter your choice from 1 to 3: 2
How many decimal places do you want?3
Number: 12345.357
Enter a floating-point number: 1234512312.123123
How do you want the number formatted?
[1] As an integer (whole number)
[2] As a floating-point number
[3] As an exponential number
Enter your choice from 1 to 3: 3
Number: 1.234512e+09
Enter a floating-point number: 0
```

Most of what you see here—the input statement, as well as conversions to float and integer (see Chapters 3 and 4)—I have already discussed quite a bit. The menu structure is also familiar to anyone who has worked in a command-line-oriented system; it isn't a pretty graphical user interface (GUI), but then that's not what I am going for here. What is interesting is the building of the dynamic formatting string in this line:

```
fmt = "{:." + str(decpts) + "f}"
```

As you can see, there is nothing special about Python formatting; it is just a string that is in a certain format. This example shows that as a programmer, you can create strings in any format or layout you wish.

You build the format string by concatenating pieces of the string together. This part simply takes the start of a formatting string for Python and adds to it the string version of the number of decimal points the user requested in their input:

```
"{:," + str(decpts)
```

You then add the floating-point format to that, along with the terminating curly brace that makes it a complete format string:

```
+ "f}"
```

The plus operator (+) takes two strings and combines them by putting the second one at the end of the first one, returning the result.

Play with this little program a bit. You can add as many strings as you want; the result will be a single string with all the pieces combined into it.

Miscellaneous String Formatting Options

I've covered most of the biggies with respect to string formatting in Python and programming in general. However, there are a few other things that will likely come up when you are writing programs you should know about.

Padding and Filling

Programmers often get requests to write strings or other data to files that are in a *fixed format*. As you've seen, you can do this with the precision and width arguments, as well as the justification functions; the default is to fill in all empty space with spaces.

Once in a great while, though, that's not what you need. Suppose you are writing a Hangman-like game and want to print out the characters the user guessed, along with the underscore for those the user hasn't guessed. This is where padding and filling come in.

> **DEFINITION**
>
> A **fixed format** means each line in the file has data that appears at a specific position.

Filling means that you want all of the spaces in a string filled in with the character of your choice. Once upon a time, this meant writing some code that looked something like the one shown in Listing 9.6.

```
s = "      dog       "
o = ""      # The output string
for i in range(0, len(s)):
    if s[i] == ' ': # A space
        o = o + "@"
    else:
        o = o + s[i]

print(o)
```

Listing 9.6

Filling a string with a character.

Looking at the code listing, you see it works its way through the length of a string. Each character is examined using the indexing operator ([]). If the character is not a string, it is appended to the output string. If the character is a space, the signal character—in this case, the at (@) sign—is appended instead. Running the program shows it works, though it's a bit clunky:

@@@@@dog@@@@

Fortunately, the new functionality of the Python format() function allows you to bypass a lot of this clunkiness. You can write the same code shown in Listing 9.6 in one line:

```
'{s:{replacechar}^{width}}'.format(s='dog',width=12,replacechar='@')
```

The output from this, if you type it into IDLE, is as follows:

@@@@dog@@@@@

As you can see, the format() function is pretty powerful! The {replacechar} argument to the formatting string tells Python to fill the string with the character indicated by the replacechar variable in the format() function. The width is simply the entire width of the output string you want. The up arrow character (^) indicates you want the string you are passing in (dog) to be centered.

Now, if you don't happen to like the arcane sequence of characters used in the format string, you can do this another way. The justification functions in Python (rjust(), ljust(), and center()) all accept an optional second parameter that indicates the character to fill out the string with. By default, this justification character is the space, but you can override that as follows:

```
>>> "dog".center(12,'@')
'@@@@dog@@@@@'
```

That certainly seems easier to me and much more readable, but Python allows you to use your preference.

PROGRAMMING TIP

By the way, if you have questions about how to use a function, IDLE has a very cool feature to help you. If you type the name of the function and the open parenthesis that starts the argument list and wait, IDLE will display a little "tool tip" window that shows you the options for that function. This can be extremely useful when you can't remember exactly how a function is called or what the optional parameters that you rarely use are.

Another method for filling and padding is the zfill() method. This function allows you to prepend zeroes to a string. You can do this in a number of other ways, but the zfill() method is particularly useful when you are writing out fixed-length strings to a file or other output device.

One of the most common problems in programming is communicating between different systems. One program expects data in one format, while another program wants the data in a completely different format. Fixed-format files are a common interchange method between two programs. In this case, you write out the data you want input into the second program in a single line, with each character on the line meaning something.

Let's say, for example, you have to write a 20-character string to program <x>. This program expects four numbers to be sent to it:

```
Date of Birth
Age
ID Number
Salary
```

Date of birth is a pretty well-understood string; it will be in the format "MMDDYYYY," where MM is the month from 1 to 12, DD is the day from 1 to 31, and YYYY is the four-digit year (for example, 2014).

The age is expected to be three digits, from 0 to 999. However, if the age is less than three digits, the remaining digits should be filled in with zeroes.

The ID number is just some string; in this case, let's make it five characters long.

The salary field is in thousands of dollars and allows for four digits (0 to 9999), which also need to be padded with zeroes.

To do this, you use the zfill() method. This method, which applies to strings, takes a single argument: the total width of the output string. Let's take a look at how you might accomplish the program <x> task you have been given. Listing 9.7 shows the code.

```
DateOfBirth="09301967"
Age=47
IDNumber ="12345"
Salary=20

# Our output string must be:
# DateOfBirth
# Age zero filled to 3 characters
# IDNumber
# Salary zero filled to 4 numbers.

line = DateOfBirth + str(Age).zfill(3) + IDNumber + str(Salary).zfill(4)
print(line)
```

Listing 9.7

The zfill() method in action.

Does it work? Running the little program in IDLE reveals that, yes, it does! The output looks like this:

```
>>>
09301967047123450020
```

Now, that might not mean anything to you or I, but it does to program <x>, and that's really all you should care about. Sometimes, your job as a programmer is just to do things, whether they have meaning to you or not.

Slicing

Slicing is the Python way of getting pieces of a string, or any other list or array, to use individually. In its simplest form, a string slice is simply a range of characters that make up a string. The basic syntax for slicing is "str[start:end]."

For example, if you have a string with the value "Hello world." and you want the first five characters ("Hello"), you would write the following:

```
>>> s = "Hello world"
>>> s[0:5]
'Hello'
```

You don't have to use the first argument, if you don't want to; it defaults to the beginning of the string. So you can also write this and get the same result:

```
s[:5]
```

Likewise, you can omit the second argument if you want everything through the end of the string and get everything after "Hello" in the string:

```
s[5:]
```

You can also use slicing to remove a character from a string. For example, say you want to remove the space in "Hello world." You could take the first five characters and everything after the sixth character and combine them as follows:

```
>>> s = s[0:5] + s[6:]
>>> s
'Helloworld'
```

As you can see, slicing is a pretty powerful feature in Python. But wait, there's more! String slicing also allows for negative numbers, which count backward from the right side of the string. So, for example, if you want the last five characters of the string, you could write:

```
>>> s = "Hello world"
>>> s[-5:]
'world'
```

There is a method for strings called *find()* that will give you back the position of a given string within your string. It can be used in conjunction with string slicing to give you back a substring as well.

```
>>> s[0:s.find("world")-1]
'Hello'
```

This works by finding the position of the string "world" within the string "Hello world". If you count the characters, you'll see this should be position 6. That will be the start of the string (the "w"), so subtracting one from that gives us the position right before the space. You then slice that part of the string and get back "Hello."

The Least You Need to Know

- Strings provide for justification, padding, and truncating of output, which allows you to make well-formed reports.
- With dynamic formatting, you can change the output format at runtime rather than using a hard-coded string for the format.
- Slicing is the process of taking a smaller part of a string from a larger string.

Basic Programming Concepts

Python, one of many programming languages, is a building-block language. The original designers of the language provided the very basic tools—conditionals, loops, functions, and classes—that permit you to build more-complicated constructs. In this part, you learn to put those constructs into bigger things, like building a house from bricks and wires.

## CHAPTER 10

Functions

Functions are the building blocks for the programming world. Like most programming foundation work I've discussed in this book, functions are not in any way unique to Python, so they're something you need to understand to move forward in your programming life.

In this chapter, I talk about what functions are; how you define them; how you work with them; and, of course, how they are implemented in Python. By the end of this chapter, you'll not only know how to implement functions—which are a major part of programming—but also have more of an insight into how programmers really work.

In This Chapter

- Setting up a function
- Putting comments in code
- Creating a function
- Using function arguments
- Learning about scope

What Is a Function?

Programming defines a *function* as "a set of statements grouped together to perform a specific purpose." So a function is simply a set of programming statements that perform a common action.

Functions are to programming languages what routines are to people's lives. You get up, get your coffee, go to work, and come home—these are all steps in the process you call your workday. Likewise, functions consist of steps that make up a process that a program utilizes. These sets of programming statements can be reused in other parts of a program or even in other programs.

So what exactly does that all mean? Let's talk about a simple process—say, determining if a number is odd or even. The actual functionality of this is simple enough; you just check to see whether the number is divisible by 2, and if it is, it must be even. Well, no, not quite. After all, zero is neither odd nor even and is divisible by 2; therefore, you have one special case. Also, are negative numbers odd or even? There's a fair amount of debate about that one, so maybe you have to make a decision. Either way, the same thing will happen—you'll end up with the same code littered all about your program, doing the same thing.

What happens when your boss decides you have to handle negative numbers differently than what you've written in the code? You'll have to go through all of the code and change it so the checks for even numbers are correct. That is very unproductive and frustrating. Enter the function to save the day!

> **PROGRAMMING TIP**
>
> Functions are used to collect the same code into a single place, where you can maintain and use it. Functions save time and energy when changes have to be made.

Reusing Code

One of the things functions do is collect code into a single place to be reused.

When programming first began, the idea was simply to write code that solved a problem. The code would then be modified to do new things, or it would be thrown away and new code written to solve new problems. This works, of course, but it is terribly inefficient. For one thing, it means reinventing the wheel every time you have a problem to solve. There aren't really all that many new problems in the world—most of them are simply variants on something old.

Because most problems are not new, it makes sense to use the code you've written in the past to fix problems that come up today, or in the future. This process is called *software reuse.* If you have the same code all over your program and need to change it, it is a long process; however, if you have the code in one place and somehow use it from all over your program, changes to the one place are pretty easy.

 ERROR MESSAGE

Reusing software does have some issues associated with it. For one thing, of course, when you reuse old software components, you inherit all the problems that were in that software in your new software. That's sometimes a pain in the neck when you are creating new functionality.

Encapsulation

Functions also allow you to hide the implementation of an algorithm, also known as *encapsulation.* The programming world defines encapsulation as an information-hiding mechanism that prevents access to the internals of an object. That's a really complex way of saying that encapsulation allows you to treat parts of your program as a black box. A function performs one or more actions, possibly based on some kind of input you give to it, and then either gives you back other data or just finishes.

That may be a bit hard to grasp at first, but there are plenty of real-world situations for which this applies. For example, your car contains an internal combustion engine, a transmission, a steering column, and miscellaneous other components. You don't really need to know how the engine works to drive it, but you could if you wanted to. The engine is a function of the car—it provides certain uses without you needing to understand how those uses are generated. The engine might be gasoline powered, it might be electric powered, or it might be a hybrid of the two. The fact is, you don't know, and you don't care. All you care about is that the car moves when you step on the accelerator. Similarly, functions hide all of the behind-the-scenes processes that users don't necessarily want or care to know about a program.

Similarly, when someone calls a function, they don't—and shouldn't—need to think about how that function was implemented, what code went into it, how the comments were written, or what the variable names inside the function are. All the programmer should care about is what the function does and what information they need to provide to the function, as well as what information is returned from the function.

Encapsulation is a very important part of object-oriented programming. Instead of thinking about how someone did something, the idea is to think about what is already out there that does the job for you. That's something to always keep in mind with functions.

Determining a Function

Creating reusable code is one of the hallmarks of a great software developer. Anyone can write code to accomplish a task, given a halfway decent algorithm to implement. Where the greatness emerges is in recognizing pieces that other developers would also need to create and pulling them out into smaller, reusable, and functional units.

Defining a Function

So how do you go about creating a function? You first define the function, which is a three-step process:

1. Determine the common functionality in your application.

2. Create a single point that contains all of that common functionality.

3. Test the common functionality with a variety of inputs to verify that it does what it is supposed to.

> **PROGRAMMING TIP**
>
> I talk about the last step in greater detail in Chapter 18, but it is still an important consideration now. When you are creating something that can potentially be used by many other programmers, you need to make sure that it works. By "works," I mean that the function does what it is supposed to do and doesn't do what it isn't supposed to do. That's an important piece many programmers never understand.

The most important thing to remember about creating functions is they are meant to do one thing, to do it very well, and to not create problems. If you try to do more than one thing, you will likely end up doing several things badly. If you don't do something very well, nobody is going to use your function to do anything. If your function creates problems (as I'll show you in a bit), it won't be used by anyone, including yourself. Stick to doing one thing well, and you'll do just fine.

Designing a Function

Designing a function is a multistep process. First, you need to determine just what the function is going to do. In many cases, functions are very simple things—perhaps adding two numbers or verifying some input data from the user. Once you've decided what the function is to do, the next step is to outline the process of what the code in the function will do.

For example, let's say you are writing a function to input some data from the user that will be used in a square root formula. The steps involved in the function look like this:

- Get some input from the user.
- Verify the input.
- Return the input to the calling code.

The "calling code" is whatever called your function. As a function writer, you can't really be sure when or how your function will be called, and it really shouldn't matter to you. It is kind of like answering the phone. You don't know who is out there calling you—you just answer and say hello. Don't make assumptions about the state of the system—always make sure you verify anything you assume.

You can now write some pseudocode that shows how your function will be implemented. If you recall, pseudocode is important because it abstracts the nitty-gritty details from you while allowing you to see the big picture of what you are trying to accomplish.

Your pseudocode for the input function you are writing might look like this:

```
while we don't have data :
   get data from user
   verify the data for type and length
   convert the data to the program's needs if necessary
   if the data is valid, return data to calling code
   go back to the beginning of this loop
```

 ERROR MESSAGE

One of the most important things to remember as a programmer is that you need to think through what you are going to do before you do it. Writing code on the fly can get the job done in the short run, but it tends to cause a lot of problems in the long run. Think through what your code needs to do and how it needs to do it, as well as any things you can think of that might go wrong. That way, when you settle down to write the code, you'll know exactly what to do.

What Do You Know? What Don't You Know?

Up to this point, the programming problems you have looked at have been extremely simple. They were straight-line programs that did a number of things in a row without concern for what might go wrong or what other things might be going on. That really isn't very normal in a programming environment. You need to consider all of the variables (pun unintended, I assure you) before you start writing code.

One of the biggest variables in writing software is knowing the things you know to go into a function, as well as the things you don't know. If something is new to you, there is time required to investigate how to do it, and what the potential pitfalls are in doing that task. Let's take a look at the tasks you've outlined in the pseudocode and see what you already know how to do, what you don't know how to do, and what might be a problem in writing the code for a function:

Step 1: While we don't have data. Clearly, this is a looping construct of some sort, and you know how to do this.

Step 2: Get data from user. Again, this is something you've done numerous times before—inputting data from the user. There probably aren't any serious pitfalls here.

Step 3: Verify the data for type and length. Ah, now you begin to get into things that aren't quite so clear. What does "verify" mean in this context? What are the proper types and lengths of data? This is something you will need to either have spelled out or discover on your own by working with your users.

Step 4: Convert the data to the program's needs if necessary. Again, what are the program's needs? This isn't quite clear, although you've done a fair amount of conversion in the past. This is probably something that is a "low-priority" issue.

Step 5: If the data is valid, return data to calling code. You can assume that figuring out how to determine if the data is valid will answer the first part of this step, but what does "return data" mean to your function? This is again something you'll need to investigate.

In your case, the only user you have is me, so I'll be happy to answer the questions. (Nice of me, isn't it?) The first question, which comes from step 3, is how to verify the input. Clearly, the input has to be numeric, since taking the square root of a string is problematic. In addition, the square root function accepts only positive numbers, so the value has to be greater than zero. For simplicity, I will also presume that the maximum value allowed is 1,000. There's no particular reason for this, but then many *requirements* are arbitrary, so you should get used to it.

The next requirement question centered around the data type the program needs. In this case, you will presume the program works only with floating-point numbers.

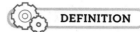

DEFINITION

The elements of what a program needs to do are called **requirements**. The process of determining whether you know how to implement code to satisfy those requirements is called *requirements gathering*. Most requirements are specified by the user of the program, and working with users is a major part of the programming process for developers.

Finally, you have the requirement to return the data to the calling code. What does this mean? In your case, if the data is valid, you will return the square root of the number entered by the user. If the number is not valid according to the rules specified previously, it will return -1, indicating an error.

Coding by Comment

Before you actually start writing a function, I'd like to take a minute to tell you about a developer methodology called *code by comment*. While some might sneer at the idea of comments (and this is a big foofaraw in the development community), they do serve a useful purpose. Comments tell you what the developer meant the code to do, not necessarily what it does. For example, you might see a comment that looks like this:

```
# Now double the value to account for slop
value = value + 2
```

Clearly, the comment is wrong. Or is it the code? Some developers will tell you that comments are useless, since the code is the ultimate source of documentation. I disagree, since the code can only tell you what the program does, not what it was intended to do. In the preceding case, the developer said quite distinctly that he was going to double the value, yet the code adds two to it. I would guess that the code is incorrect here.

Code by comment is a way of outlining your code to make it clearer not for the reader or maintainer of the code, but rather for yourself as you are writing it.

To implement code by comment, you simply write out a list of comments indicating what each block of code is going to do. For example, in your little square root function code, you might start out by saying the following:

```
# Input data from user
# Validate that the data is proper for floating-point numbers
# Validate that the data is within the proper bounds
# Compute the square root of the input
# Return the valid value to the calling code
```

From the comments, you see exactly what you need to do. In fact, you can even write snippets of code under each comment to determine exactly how your program is going to work well before you convert it to a function. In the programming world, this is known as *exploratory programming,* because it explores what you need to do.

So you want to write the code that corresponds to the processes. Each of the comments tells you exactly what that little piece of code needs to do without worrying about the other pieces. The code that implements your first cut at the exploratory phase of the program is shown in Listing 10.1.

```python
import math, sys

# Input data from user
strNum = input("Enter a number to take the square root of: ")

# Validate that the data is proper for floating point numbers.
# To be a valid floating point number, each character of the string
# needs to be a digit, and there can be only one decimal point
hasDecimal = False
sError = ""
for c in strNum:
    if not (c.isdigit() and c != '.'):
        sError = "Invalid number - bad character!"
    elif c == '.':
        if hasDecimal == False:
            hasDecimal = True
        else:
            sError = "Invalid number, too many decimal points!"
if sError != "":
    print("Error converting: " + sError )
    sys.exit()

# Validate that the data is within the proper bounds
fVal = float(strNum)
if fVal <= 0 or fVal > 1000 :
    print("Error: value out of range 0-1000")
    sys.exit()
# Compute the square root of the input
fSquare = math.sqrt(fVal)

# Return the valid value to the calling code
print("Square root of {} is {}".format(fVal, fSquare))
```

Listing 10.1

Your first stab at a square root function.

The only really new things here are using the math library (math.sqrt[])and using a function in the string library (isdigit[]). The math library is imported via the import statement, which is how you get access to all of the goodies that other people have written in Python.

PROGRAMMING TIP

Rather than writing your own functions to do everything, always verify there is not already something out there to do the job for you. You can gain access to any module in Python by using the "import" statement. Once you have the module imported, you can get access to any of the functions inside of it by using the syntax "module.function," where "module" is the name of the module in the import statement and "function" is the name of the function you want to call.

The isdigit() method simply checks to see if a given character is a number or not. Floating-point numbers clearly have to have all digits and can only have one decimal point, which is what you are checking in your validation piece. The isdigit() method will also return False if called on the blank string.

Finally, you verify the number is in the range specified by the requirements (0 to 100) and then take the square root of it.

Turning It into a Function

Once you have explored the basic functionality needed to implement the code for a function, it is time to actually turn it into a function. Let's do that here, and skim over the important lines of code added. Listing 10.2 shows you the function I created from the code I just talked about. You'll notice there are very few big changes; the lines that differ are shown in bold.

```
import math, sys

def compute_square_root():
    "Inputs a string from the user and returns the square root or -1 for
    error"

    # Input data from user
    strNum = input("Enter a number to take the square root of: ")

    # Validate that the data is proper for floating point numbers.
    # To be a valid floating point number, each character of the string
    # needs to be a digit, and there can be only one decimal point
    hasDecimal = False
    sError = ""
    for c in strNum:
```

```
    if not (c.isdigit() and c != '.'):
        sError = "Invalid number - bad character!"
    elif c == '.':
        if hasDecimal == False:
            hasDecimal = True
        else:
            sError = "Invalid number, too many decimal points!"
if sError != "":
    print("Error converting: " + sError)
    sys.exit()


# Validate that the data is within the proper bounds
fVal = float(str)
if fVal <= 0 or fVal > 1000:
    print("Error: value out of range 0-1000")
    sys.exit()

# Compute the square root of the input
fSquare = math.sqrt(fVal)

# Return the valid value to the calling code
return fSquare
```

Listing 10.2

The square root function.

As you can see, there isn't much to making something into a function in Python or, really, any other programming language.

Functions have a definition line, which tells you the name of the function and a list of any arguments it takes. Because your function doesn't take any arguments, the list between the parentheses is empty.

The next line, which appears to be a string literally in the middle of nowhere, is a Python-specific thing. This line allows you to document your function so the help system understands what to tell the programmer using the function about it. This line is optional, but it is a good idea to always document your functions.

PROGRAMMING TIP

The best forms of documentation for any kind of code are those that are attached to it. Documents like help files or text documents that tell you how to use functions or programs are nice, but they can become separated from the original code and be easily out of date. It is worth writing a few extra lines of documentation and embedding it in your code through whatever system your programming language supports.

The only other changes to your code are the return statements where your comments to do something used to live. Seems pretty simple to create a function, doesn't it? In fact, it is, because the creators of programming languages wanted the language to be extended, and the function concept is one that helps that end goal. By adding new functionality via functions, you extend the ability of the language to do new things.

Using the Function

If you enter the function code in Listing 10.2 into the IDLE editor and there are no syntax errors, you will be able to run the code. Select "run module" from the run menu. When you do this, you might be a little surprised to see that absolutely nothing happens! Why is that?

Well, a function isn't really executable code. It is more of a template for executable code, the way that a variable is a holder for data rather than the data itself. In order to see the function in action, you have to execute it. Enter the following command into the IDLE shell and you should see the output you expect:

```
>>> compute_square_root()
Enter a number to take the square root of: 16
4.0
```

As you can see, when you run your function, the interpreter calls the code you've written and returns the value. The "4.0" beneath the call shows the return value from the function, not a print statement's output. If you don't believe this, simply assign the return value from the function to a variable:

```
>>> x = compute_square_root()
Enter a number to take the square root of: 16
>>> x
4.0
```

As you can see, the function itself doesn't print anything out, unless there is an error. This is good programming practice, although there are even better ways to handle errors (as you'll see in Chapter 12). Your function should do what it is supposed to and not interfere in the remainder of the program in which it is embedded.

Congratulations! You have written your first function. Of course, programming is a never-ending battle, so there will be changes, right?

Yes, It's a Function, but Is It a Good Function?

One of the cornerstones of programming is change. Sometimes change is good, and sometimes it is bad. When the change comes from the development side and not the business side, it's called *refactoring*. This means you are updating the code for the sake of making it better, cleaner, or less buggy.

 ERROR MESSAGE

Refactoring is an important part of programming. You refactor to make things better, more efficient, or both. The danger in refactoring is never finishing. One of the hardest things to learn as a programmer is when you are really done.

Always look over your code for inefficiencies, or places where it could be made easier to reuse by others. These are excellent locations for refactoring. Do not refactor your code just because you want to refactor your code. Always have a reason in mind.

In this case, there is certainly room for improvement to the function that's been written. When you are looking to refactor your code, ask yourself a single question: What is the purpose of this function, block, class, or whatever it is you are looking at? Write out a single-line description of what it should do, and then examine the code. Is it necessary to have pieces in there? Do they fit under the umbrella of "What is this code supposed to do?"

The purpose of your function, according to the name of it, is to compute a square root. The question is, what parts of the code are really necessary, and what parts should be moved to some other function or section of code?

Clearly, the actual process of computing the square root is necessary. In addition, the validation checks are necessary, because they are a part of the business logic for this function. The standard square root function doesn't do the checking you need it to, which is why the function was written in the first place. So those two segments of code need to stay. But what about the input from the user? Does that really need to stay in this function?

The answer is probably no. Input is something that is normally tied directly to your program, rather than reusable functions that are used in multiple programs. So how can you fix your function to remove the input of the data? The answer to that question lies in function arguments.

Redesigning the Function

In order to remove the input from your function, you need to redesign it a bit. First, obviously, you need to remove the input from the function itself. That's easy enough to do. But then how do you get the information from the user?

Instead of simply requesting information from the user directly, let's allow the calling code to provide it for you. That is, you'll move the input() function into the larger program that calls your function, rather than leaving it inside the routine that computes the square root. When you do this, your function will look like the one shown in Listing 10.3.

```
import math, sys

def compute_square_root():
    # Validate that the data is proper for floating point numbers.
    # To be a valid floating point number, each character of the string
    # needs to be a digit, and there can be only one decimal point
    hasDecimal = False
    sError = ""
    for c in strNum:
        if not (c.isdigit() and c != '.'):
            sError = "Invalid number - bad character!"
        elif c == '.':
            if hasDecimal == False:
                hasDecimal = True
            else:
                sError = "Invalid number, too many decimal points!"
    if sError != "":
        print("Error converting: " + sError)
        return -1.0


    # Validate that the data is within the proper bounds
    fVal = float(str)
    if fVal <= 0 or fVal > 1000:
        print("Error: value out of range 0-1000")
        return -1.0

    # Compute the square root of the input
    fSquare = math.sqrt(fVal)

    # Return the valid value to the calling code
    return fSquare
```

Listing 10.3

The square root function without input.

Of course, there is a rather major snag to this function, as you will see if you try to call it in IDLE:

```
>>> compute_square_root()
Traceback (most recent call last):
  File "<pyshell#0>", line 1, in <module>
    compute_square_root()
  File "F:\Books\Beginning Programming\Chapter 10\ch10_2.py", line 9, in
  compute_square_root
    for c in strNum :
NameError: global name 'strNum' is not defined
```

Oh, well, that's clear, right? Actually, what Python is complaining about is that the variable "strNum" is no longer defined. That's true, since you removed it. So how do you get the value into the function so it can be validated and the square root calculated? The answer is as a "function argument," which is simply data that is passed to a function. You've been using function arguments all along, even if you were unaware of it. For example, when you write a statement like the following:

```
print(x)
```

This statement, as you know, outputs the value of "x" to the console. In this case, "x" is the function argument that the print() function expects to print out.

In your case, you need only make one very minor modification to your code to add an argument:

```
def compute_square_root(strNum):
```

Notice that the compute_square_root() function now takes one argument—the string which you want to convert and compute the square root of. Now try calling the function the way you have been:

```
>>> compute_square_root()
Traceback (most recent call last):
  File "<pyshell#2>", line 1, in <module>
    compute_square_root()
TypeError: compute_square_root() missing 1 required positional argument:
 'strNum'
```

As you can see, the interpreter knows the function takes one argument and complains that you haven't supplied it. On the other hand, if you supply the argument:

```
>>> compute_square_root("16")
4.0
```

You can see your function works as you expect it to. Function arguments are a major component to programming in any programming language, so it is something you really need to understand.

PROGRAMMING TIP

You can have zero, one, or multiple arguments to a function—it is completely up to you. Function arguments make it possible for you to change the behavior of your functions based on outside influences. This is kind of like changing your function based on user input, but more from the programming side. Allowing arguments to your functions makes them much more extensible and usable in the long run, so always think about allowing the passing in of an argument rather than hard coding it or requesting it directly from the user.

Named Function Arguments

You can call a function with arguments in either positional order or using names. What do you have to do to make this work with your functions? The answer, thankfully, is nothing—Python will do all that work for you.

For example, suppose you have a function that simply prints out the arguments it receives in order:

```
>>> def func1(arg1, arg2, arg3 ):
    print("Variables: {}, {}, {}".format(arg1, arg2, arg3))
```

You could call this function with arguments in positional order:

```
>>> func1(1,2,3)
Variables: 1, 2, 3
```

Alternatively, you could call the function with arguments in named order. The name of the argument is simply the name that appears in the function definition line. In your case, the three named arguments are "arg1," "arg2," and "arg3."

```
>>> func1(arg1=1, arg3=2, arg2=3)
Variables: 1, 3, 2
```

A Word About Scope

Scope is something that is extremely important when writing functions. Up to this point, I have talked about two kinds of variables—those that you define and those that are arguments to functions. It is important to understand when those variable names mean something and when they don't. The life of a variable is called its *scope*. All programming languages have scope in one form or another, although some vary in which they define. Let's take a look at the kinds of variable scopes, and look at some examples of each.

Scope is the area in which a variable or function exists and can be called. You can think of it as "line of sight." If you can see the variable, you can use it; if you can't see it, it doesn't exist as far as your program is concerned. Things that prevent you from "seeing" a variable include function definitions, blocks within loops, and blocks within if statements.

Functions exist within the file they are defined and can be imported into other areas of the code via the module concept (see Chapter 16).

The idea of scope is complicated, so don't be too upset if you don't get it at first. Worse, there are all sorts of little gotchas with scope, as you'll see shortly. Rather than try to explain it with words, I want you take a look at a simple example of scoping and see what is involved. Listing 10.4 shows you the code you will be looking at.

```python
# This variable is program level in scope
gA = 10

# Variables defined in the function are local to the function.
# Functions can use program level variables

def myfunc1():
    lA = 5
    print("Local value of a in myfunc1 = {}".format(lA))
    print("Program level value of a = {}".format(gA))

def myfunc2():
    lA = 10
    print("Local value of a in myfunc2 = {}".format(la))
    print("Program level value of a = {}".format(gA))

def myfunc3():
    gA = 20   # Line 1
    print("In myfunc3, gA = {}".format(gA)) # Line 2

# This line is ok
print("Program level variables are ok here: {}".format(gA))

# And they don't change in local functions
```

```
myfunc1()

# But program level variables can be changed anywhere.
# or can they?
myfunc3()
print("Program level variable is now: {}".format(gA)) # Line 3
# This line will produce an error
#print("Local variables are not: {}".format(lA))
```

Listing 10.4

Scoping as illustrated in Python.

 PROGRAMMING TIP

What is very important to understand is that nothing you are examining with respect to scope is different in any other language. While you have done a lot of work looking at the specifics of how Python implements certain functionality, scope applies across the board.

Where a Variable Starts and Stops Being Valid

Scope is defined by where a variable starts and stops being valid. For example, if you run the program shown in Listing 10.4, you will see the following output:

```
Program level variables are ok here: 10
Local value of a in myfunc1 = 5
Program level value of a = 10
In myfunc3, gA = 20
Program level variable is now: 10
```

Let's take a look and see exactly what is going on here.

The first few entries in the output are hardly surprising. You set a variable at the program level, print it out at the program level, and it is the same. By "program level," I mean the main program, not one of the functions. For a function, a variable declared within the function has the value you expect it to. Likewise, a variable that is declared outside of the function has the value it was given outside the function. No surprise there either.

The interesting bits occur in the function myfunc3. As you can see by the lines marked "Line 1" and "Line 2" in the comments of Listing 10.4, you set the "global" program variable gA to 20 and then print it out. Not surprisingly, the value of the variable is, in fact, 20 when it is printed. What is more surprising is the value of the variable when you get out of the function, on the line marked with the comment "Line 3."

You would think, since the variable appears to be in the full program scope, that the value of the variable "gA" would be 20, since that's the last thing you set it to in the function myfunc3. When you look at the output, however, that is not the case. The value of the variable "qA" is still 10, as you see from the program output. How can this be?

This is an interesting issue in Python and many other programming languages. Using a local version of a "global" (available everywhere) variable creates a "shadow version" of that variable that is only available in the scope in which it is defined. When you wrote the function myfunc3:

```
def myfunc3():
    gA = 20  # Line 1
    print("In myfunc3, gA = {}".format(gA)) # Line 2
```

It is really as if you wrote it like this:

```
def myfunc3():
    localqA = globalaQ
    localqA = 20  # Line 1
    print("In myfunc3, gA = {}".format(localgA)) # Line 2
```

PROGRAMMING TIP

There are three kinds of variables in programming. First, you have local variables that are defined within a local scope like a function or block of code. Next, you have program-level variables that can be used anywhere in the code after they are defined but can't be modified outside of the scope in which they were defined. Finally, you have "global" variables, which are available anywhere and can be modified anywhere.

This can be hard to understand, but really, anytime you use a variable inside of a function, you either have to specifically tell the interpreter you want the global version, or you will get a local "copy" of that variable. The local copy inherits the value of the outside variable (gA) but changes to it do not apply to the outside variable, only to the copy.

So, essentially, here are the rules:

- Variables are valid within the scope they are defined.

- Scope is always a block-level operation. A block is usually a function but could be a class as well.

Variables used outside the block do not have the same value as those inside the block. You can see an example of this in Listing 10.5.

```
def add_to_var(x):
    x = x + 1
    print("in add to var, x = {}".format(x))

x = 1
for i in range(0,10):
    add_to_var(x)
print(x)
```

Listing 10.5

An illustration of scope.

You might think that x, in the main program, would go from 1 to 10, since the add_to_var() function adds 1 to its value. But the x in the function definition is not the same as the one outside the function. So instead, you get the following:

```
in add to var, x = 2
… <repeated several times>
in add to var, x = 2
1
```

"Okay," you say, "I can see that." After all, you called the variable to the function x, but that's an argument, not a global variable. No problem; let's remove it and use the "program-level" variable called *x,* as you can see in Listing 10.6.

```
def add_to_var():
    x = x + 1
    print("in add to var, x = {}".format(x))

x = 1
for i in range(10):
    add_to_var()
print(x)
```

Listing 10.6

Modification to use the global variable x.

The output from this little code snippet might surprise you. IDLE gives you this:

```
Traceback (most recent call last):
  File "Q:/Books/Beginning Programming/Chapter 10/ch10_6.py", line 7, in
  <module>
```

```
    add_to_var()
  File "Q:/Books/Beginning Programming/Chapter 10/ch10_6.py", line 2, in add_
  to_var
    x = x + 1
UnboundLocalError: local variable 'x' referenced before assignment
```

What is going on here? If you recall from Listing 10.4, the "program variable" was defined before you defined the function that used it. Python, like most languages, uses variables in the order in which they are defined. So it was available to the functions but can't be changed there. In Listing 10.6, however, the variable is defined after the function, and therefore isn't available to it. Think in terms of "top down"—things defined before the current position in the code are available to you as the programmer, while things defined after the current point in the code are not.

PROGRAMMING TIP

Think of using a variable with a function as a metaphor for time. You can use things that were created before you were born, since they exist. But you can't use things that were created after you died, since you don't exist.

Global Variables

But what if you want to change a variable that is outside the scope of your function? For this, Python and most other languages use the concept of global variables.

Let's go back to the code in Listing 10.6 and make one minor modification, which you can see in Listing 10.7.

```
def add_to_var():
    global x
    x = x + 1
    print("in add to var, x = {}".format(x))

x = 1
for i in range(10):
    add_to_var()
print(x)
```

Listing 10.7

The updated global variable routine.

Notice the line marked in bold. The global statement is Python specific, but similar functionality exists in virtually every other programming language. What you are telling the interpreter is that the variable x should be treated as global in scope, available to the function and outside the function. When you run this snippet, you now get the following correct output:

```
in add to var, x = 2
in add to var, x = 3
in add to var, x = 4
in add to var, x = 5
in add to var, x = 6
in add to var, x = 7
in add to var, x = 8
in add to var, x = 9
in add to var, x = 10
in add to var, x = 11
11
```

As you can see, the variable is changed inside the function as well as outside of the function. This is what you wanted, and what you expected, so it is good!

There is more, of course, to working with functions, but this chapter should give you a decent basis for them.

The Least You Need to Know

- Functions are bits of code that perform a single action.
- Functions help to extend the usage of a language by making it easier to do things.
- Functions can be global or local.

Does Anybody Really Know What Time It Is?

Of all of the concepts in the programming world, the one that is the most familiar and the most confusing at the same time is that of dates and times. We all have to track the numbers on a calendar and the hours in the day, and computers are no different. Computers have things like schedules that run certain processes at certain times. They also have deadlines and expirations, such as when to remind you to change your email password (*again*) at work.

In this chapter, I show you how to set up these types of programs and more in Python.

Understanding How Computers Measure Time

The first step to working with date and time functions in Python—or any other programming language—is to realize that computers don't think in terms of hours, minutes, and seconds. They don't really know anything about dates, either. Rather, computers measure time by counting what are called *ticks*. A tick is one iteration of the system CPU clock, which runs at the speed of the processor. Once upon a time, ticks were somewhat random, in that they changed when the speed of the processor in the machine changed. Today, however, ticks are standardized.

Thankfully, you don't need to use ticks to measure time; instead, you use seconds—in particular, seconds since the "beginning of computer time," or *epoch*.

To determine the amount of time that has gone by since the epoch, Python provides the time module and a function within it called *time*. (If that isn't redundant enough, I don't know what is.) To see the number of seconds since the beginning of the Unix epoch, use the following code in IDLE:

```
>>> import time
>>> seconds_since_epoch = time.time()
>>> seconds_since_epoch
1379515288.967928
```

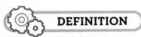 **DEFINITION**

An **epoch** is a memorable event or date, or an event that marks a new period of development. For computer time, the Unix epoch is usually January 1, 1970.

If you'd like to know the epoch on your computer, you can figure it out in Python easily. Use the following code to print out the beginning of the epoch for your machine:

```
>>> import time
>>> t = time.gmtime(0)
>>> print("The EPOCH began on {0}/{1}/{2}".format(t.tm_mon, t.tm_mday, t.tm_
    year))
The EPOCH began on 1/1/1970
```

And so you see the Unix epoch began, at least for Python, on January 1 (the first day of the first month), 1970, which is pretty much the standard.

The Time Structure

Looking at the little snippet of code that printed the epoch date, you can see that you used a function called *gmtime()*. This function returns the time based on Greenwich Mean Time (GMT), which is the base standard for all time across the world. Every time zone is simply an offset (positive or negative) from GMT, so you can figure out what time it is anywhere you want to call or visit in the world.

The gmtime() function actually produces a *structure*, which you can look at by displaying it in IDLE. In this case, instead of simply calling the gmtime() function, you have to specify time.gmtime() so Python knows it needs to grab the gmtime() function from the time module. Let's type this in and then discuss what it is you are looking at:

```
>>> import time
>>> t = time.gmtime(0)
>>> t
time.struct_time(tm_year=1970, tm_mon=1, tm_mday=1, tm_hour=0, tm_min=0, tm_
    sec=0, tm_wday=3, tm_yday=1, tm_isdst=0)
```

The display of the *t* variable shows you that *t* is of type "time.struct_time." The "time." part of the name means the struct_time thing is found in the time module, while the "struct_time" part is a description of what the object you are looking at is (in this case, a structure).

 **DEFINITION**

A **structure** is simply an assemblage of data elements grouped under a single name. A structure contains other objects that can be simple (such as numbers, strings, and so on) or complex (such as other structure objects).

The object returned from the gmtime() function in the time module contains "pieces" you can look at for various bits of information. Table 11.1 shows you the list of items in the structure and what they mean to you.

Table 11.1   The Time Structure Returned by gmtime()

Field	Meaning
tm_year	The four-digit year.
tm_mon	The month of the year, from 1 (January) through 12 (December).
tm_mday	The day of the month, from 1 to the number of days in the month (maximum of 31; minimum of 28).
tm_hour	The hour of the day, from 0 to 23.
tm_min	The minute of the current hour, from 0 to 59.
tm_sec	The second of the current hour, from 0 to 59.
tm_wday	The day of the week, represented as a number from 0 (Monday) to 6 (Sunday).
tm_yday	The day of the year, from 1 to 366. This is same as the Julian calendar day and includes leap days.
tm_isdst	Indicates whether this time uses Daylight Savings Time. A -1 indicates the library determines this, a 0 says no, and a 1 says yes.

Printing a Calendar

One of the most common uses for time and date functions in any programming language is showing users a calendar they can either simply view or select new dates from. Whether it's to make an appointment or simply to look at how far out a due date of a project is, calendars are a basic component of the business world.

I talked about calendar printing briefly back in Chapter 6, but really just from the perspective of looping through the days of a hard-coded month. Here, I want to show you how to print out a calendar month in Python, which couldn't possibly be easier.

```
import calendar
month = int(input("Enter the month number from 1 to 12: "))
if month > 1 and month < 12 :
    year = int(input("Enter the year (four digits) to print the month for:
 "))
    cal = calendar.month(year, month)
    print(cal)
else :
    print("You entered an invalid month number!")
```

Listing 11.1

A monthly calendar printer in Python.

As you can see in Listing 11.1, you simply need to enter the month number and four-digit year. The following is the output from this small program if you use the code to create a calendar for September 2014:

```
Enter the month number from 1 to 12: 9
Enter the year (four digits) to print the month for: 2014
    September 2014
Mo Tu We Th Fr Sa Su
 1  2  3  4  5  6  7
 8  9 10 11 12 13 14
15 16 17 18 19 20 21
22 23 24 25 26 27 28
29 30
```

PROGRAMMING TIP

Most languages contain the basic functionality to print a calendar, allowing you to retrieve all the pieces you need to display it; Python is no different. The only thing that is really easier in Python than most other so-called "higher-level" languages is that the print() function automatically displays the calendar in the correct format for the location. This is a nicety, but you can easily implement this functionality yourself if you work in another language.

Converting Base Time to Local Time

One important thing to be aware of with respect to dates and times on computers, particularly involving programming languages, is that the date and time are rarely stored or produced in "local time." As you learned earlier, time is based on GMT; each locality has a time offset (often called a *time zone*) which is used to convert the base time to the local time.

When working with most time functions in almost all languages, you will find that the time is actually returned to you in the base (GMT) values. There are conversion functions—some of which the date routines use automatically—that will use time zones to figure out what the local time is.

To understand time zones, you can use the system settings on your computer to check out the information on your time zone. In Windows, you do this by going to Control Panel (**Start > Control Panel**) and selecting the **Date and Time** option, as shown in Figure 11.1.

Figure 11.1: *Control Panel showing Date and Time options.*

From there, you will be taken to the Date and Time options panel, which shows you a number of items about the settings for your current computer. This panel is shown in Figure 11.2, with the current time zone circled for simplicity.

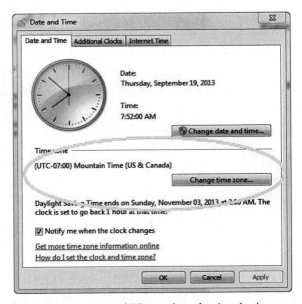

Figure 11.2: *Date and Time options showing the time zone.*

Notice that the time zone is shown as an offset (in my case, -7 for Mountain Time) from GMT. This number is what you add or subtract from GMT in order to convert it to the local hour. The computer automatically handles things like Daylight Savings Time, so you don't have to worry about that.

In Python, as with many programming languages, the designers of the language have made it a bit easier to convert from GMT to the local time. Rather than going through all the work of determining your time zone offset and converting the time yourself, you can use the Python function called, not surprisingly, *localtime()*. Open up IDLE and type the following into it, one line at a time, and you'll see what I mean:

```
>>> import time
>>> time.gmtime()
time.struct_time(tm_year=2014, tm_mon=9, tm_mday=19, tm_hour=13, tm_min=57,
  tm_sec=16, tm_wday=3, tm_yday=262, tm_isdst=0)
>>> time.localtime()
time.struct_time(tm_year=2013, tm_mon=9, tm_mday=19, tm_hour=7, tm_min=57,
  tm_sec=22, tm_wday=3, tm_yday=262, tm_isdst=1)
```

As you can see, the year, month, day of the month, day of the week, and day of the year are the same. The hour, however, is changed from the GMT of 13 to my local time of 7. I wrote this code during Daylight Savings Time, so rather than the -7 you saw in the options panel, the actual offset is -6. The good news is that you don't have to keep track of all that; you can simply use the localtime() version of the clock to get the number you really want to show or use.

Formatting Dates

The time module is actually quite large and contains all sorts of functions that provide you with the ability to not only display and inquire about the current time, but also to format the time information into a user-friendly display. One of these functions is called *strftime()*.

The strftime() function formats (the "f" part of the name) a time value (the "time" part of the function name) and returns it to you as a string (yes, you guessed it, the "str" part of the name).

While this description tells you that the function allows you to format strings, it doesn't really tell you *how*. (This is an unfortunate thing about programmers; they do tend to assume you know what they are thinking.)

The strftime() function accepts two arguments: the format string and the "tuple" that represents the time. You can get the latter from any of the time retrieval functions, such as gmtime() or localtime(). Let's look at a simple example of how to do this:

```
>>> l = time.localtime()
>>> time.strftime("%B %d %Y", l)
'September 19 2013'
```

This seems simple enough—you get the local time and format it as the current month, day of the month, and full year with century. Okay, but where did all of those magic numbers come from? The answer lies in the formatting string, the first argument to the function.

 ERROR MESSAGE

Sadly, the preceding code is a common way that programmers choose to format strings. Rather than create something that just said, "use the month, use the day, use the year," they choose arcane format codes that mean nothing to anyone else. When you write your own code, make it as simple to use and as easy to understand as you possibly can. Perhaps we can change the programming world just a little.

Table 11.2 shows the formatting options available for dates in Python using the strftime() function.

Table 11.2   Format Characters for the strftime() Function

Characters	Meaning
%a	Abbreviated weekday name
%A	Full weekday name
%b	Abbreviated month name
%B	Full month name
%c	Century number
%d	Day of the month (01 to 31)
%e	Day of the month (1 to 31)
%u	Weekday as a number (1 to 7)
%U	Week number of the current year (1 to 53)
%w	Day of the week as a number; Sunday is 0
%y	Century as a two-digit year (for example, 2014 is 14).
%z	Time zone

You could begin with something as simple as the following to format the date:

```
>>> time.strftime("%a/%d/%y")
'Fri/20/13'
```

The strftime() function just takes the formatting arguments you pass to it and returns a string that represents the data in that format. If you don't specify a date, the function will use the current date and time. (It returned this information for me because I wrote it on Friday, September 20, 2013.) It doesn't care whether they format makes any sense or whether it is in a "standard" format—all the function cares about is whether the formatting characters are correct or not.

If the characters are not correct, you will get an error like this:

```
>>> time.strftime("%q")
Traceback (most recent call last):
  File "<pyshell#5>", line 1, in <module>
    time.strftime("%q")
ValueError: Invalid format string
```

Since "%q" is not one of the valid formatting characters, the function doesn't know what to do with it and simply displays an error. This isn't the best choice of how to handle such things, as you'll see when you start writing your own modules and classes, but it is the most common way (see Chapters 14 and 16).

Now, that is not to say you can't put your own information into the formatting string—you certainly can. You just can't use any of the "percent character" formats that don't exist. So, for example, if you want to use strftime() to format something that indicates what you're displaying, you could do so:

```
>>> time.strftime("This is the two digit year: %y")
'This is the two digit year: 13'
```

Using Your Own Dates

The most common date usages work with the current date, because that's just what most programs need to display. That doesn't mean, however, you can't create your own date values and format them. The notion of "creating a date" is available in most programming languages. While the date does have to be valid (you can't create February 31, for example), it doesn't have to be one that has already occurred. You could create a date for next Tuesday, if you wanted to.

To work with the date functions, you need to import the datetime module. This is slightly different from the time module, but the overall functionality is similar. For example, suppose you want to create a date based on someone's birthday:

```
>>> import datetime
>>> abirthday = datetime.date(1967, 9, 30)
>>> abirthday
datetime.date(1967, 9, 30)
```

The date function of datetime works with the year, month, and day of the date, so this represents a date of September 30, 1967, a good date in history.

You can also use the formatting functionality on this date, just as you could with the current date and time, like this:

```
>>> abirthday.strftime("%d-%b-%Y")
'30-Sep-1967'
```

Notice that you use the function strftime() directly on the actual abirthday object. This is called an *object method*, something I will talk about at length in Chapter 14.

PROGRAMMING TIP

When you are writing functions and code, it is best to think long term. Make the functions as generic as possible in order to be reused by others. If you make your code as simple as possible, people will not be afraid to reuse it.

Dates and Math

With math, you are quite accustomed to normal addition and subtraction. You can add one and one, subtract one from six, and so forth and so on. But what does it mean to work with math using dates?

Like many programming languages, this problem has come up so often in Python that the developers of the language have built in functionality for working with date math. In Python, the specific functionality is found in the timedelta() function. This function allows you to create a "delta," or change in some unit of time or date, and then apply that to an existing date.

For example, suppose you create a date for January 1, 2015:

```
>>> import datetime
>>> d1 = datetime.date(2015,1,1)
```

You then decide you want to add two days to this date, so it's the third day of the year:

```
>>> d1 = d1 + datetime.timedelta(days=2)
>>> d1
datetime.date(2015, 1, 3)
```

Why would you want to do this? There are really many reasons. For one thing, you might get paid every two weeks. If you know, for example, that you got paid on September 13 and would like to know when your next two pay dates are, you could use a very simple Python script to determine it, as shown in Listing 11.2.

```
import datetime
pd = datetime.date(2014,9,13)
for i in range(0,4) :
    pd = pd + datetime.timedelta(weeks=2)
    print("You get paid on: {}".format(pd))
```

Listing 11.2

Calculating biweekly pay dates.

The output from this little script would be the following:

```
You get paid on: 2014-09-27
You get paid on: 2014-10-11
You get paid on: 2014-10-25
You get paid on: 2014-11-08
```

Pretty cool, isn't it? As an exercise, try writing your own little script that calculates getting paid on other schedules, such as weekly, every 15 days, or whatever your heart desires.

To change the period you get paid, you simply change the argument to the timedelta() function. Instead of, say, "weeks=2," you would say "days=15" and the function would do the rest. (That is a great function for reuse, wouldn't you say?)

You can also use date math to do things like determine what day of the week a given date fell on for multiple years. Suppose, for example, you were born on June 10. You can determine the day of the week on which you'll have your birthday by doing this—in this case, I'm using the year 2013:

```
import datetime
d = datetime.date(2013, 6, 10)
print(d.strftime("Day %w of the week (a %A)."))
```

As you can see, you're using the format characters %w and %A to find the day of the week as a number and the full weekday name respectively. The output would show you the following:

```
Day 1 of the week (a Monday).
```

So if your birthday is June 10, your birthday was on a Monday in 2013—not ideal, but a pretty decent way to start the week.

Now, you would think if you wanted to count backward through the years, you could do something like the following:

```
import datetime

d = datetime.date(2013, 6, 10)
for i in range(0,10):
    print(d.strftime("Day %w of the week (a %A)."))
    d = d - datetime.timedelta(years=1)
```

After all, in the preceding code, you are simply subtracting one year and printing out what day of the week it is, right? Surprise, it doesn't work. The timedelta() method doesn't allow for years:

```
Traceback (most recent call last):
  File "F:/Books/Beginning Programming/Chapter 11/ch11_3.py", line 6, in
  <module>
    d = d - datetime.timedelta(years=1)
TypeError: 'years' is an invalid keyword argument for this function
```

So how would you manage this? Well, you can simply re-create the date object with a new year, as shown in Listing 11.3.

```
import datetime

d = datetime.date(2013, 6, 10)
year = 2013
for i in range(0,10) :
    print(d.strftime("Day %w of the week (a %A)."))
    year = year - 1
    d = datetime.date(year, 6, 10)
```

Listing 11.3

Calculating the day of the week backward for years.

Now, when you run this little program snippet, you can see that it works properly:

```
Day 1 of the week (a Monday).
Day 0 of the week (a Sunday).
Day 5 of the week (a Friday).
Day 4 of the week (a Thursday).
Day 3 of the week (a Wednesday).
Day 2 of the week (a Tuesday).
Day 0 of the week (a Sunday).
Day 6 of the week (a Saturday).
Day 5 of the week (a Friday).
Day 4 of the week (a Thursday).
```

ERROR MESSAGE

Date math is important in programming, and understanding how it works will get you far when you are writing your own programs. As you can see in the timedelta() examples, however, sometimes it isn't quite as straightforward as you might want it to be. It's okay to be frustrated when code doesn't work the way you want it to—after all, you are often working with other people's code. When facing such moments of frustration, take a deep breath and try to look at the problem from a different viewpoint. Often, you will find that the programmer that wrote the original code wasn't as dumb as you thought they were, and was simply looking at the issue in a different manner. Understanding how code was meant to be used will often lead you down the right path. Plus, thinking things through and realizing that you can do things other ways is an important attribute for a programmer.

Another thing you can do with date math is calculate the difference between two dates very easily using the datetime() functions. If you have two dates, such as the following:

```
>>> import datetime
>>> d1 = datetime.date(1961, 10, 5)
>>> d2 = datetime.date(1967, 9, 30)
```

You can subtract one from the other, and get the number of days between them:

```
>>> d2 - d1
datetime.timedelta(2186)
```

The preceding code shows there are 2,186 days between 10/5/1961 and 9/30/1967. Okay, perhaps not the best of examples, but you can see why this might be important.

Calculating the aging of invoices, for example, requires you know the difference in days between them. If you had sent out an invoice on July 1 and it is now August 10, clearly more than 30 days has gone by. How many sets of 30 days have gone by, though? Is it just 30, or has it moved to 60 or 90? These are important issues in accounting that can be answered with a program.

You can calculate this easily enough, as you can see in the code in Listing 11.4.

```
import datetime
original_invoice_date = datetime.date(2013, 7, 1)
current_invoice_date = datetime.date(2013,9,10)
# Calculate the number of days
days  = current_invoice_date - original_invoice_date
print("days = {}".format(days))
print("Number of 30-day cycles: {}".format(int(days.days / 30)))
```

Listing 11.4

Calculating invoice cycles.

As the listing shows, the first step is to calculate the actual number of days between the two dates. This is done with straightforward date math, as shown in the line which reads "Calculate the number of days." If you run the preceding program, the first output line is the following:

```
days = 71 days, 0:00:00
```

This may seem a bit strange—you are just calculating the number of days between the two dates, right? The days variable is actually a timedelta() object, which stores the number of days, as well as the time offset between the two dates. So the days portion of the timedelta() represents, as expected, the number of days.

PROGRAMMING TIP

If you just wanted to see the whole number of days between the two dates, you could write the following:

```
print("days = {}".format(days.days))
```

This might look confusing, as the days object has an attribute called *days*. But you'll see when I talk about classes and objects in Chapter 14, this isn't unusual, nor is it a problem. However, it does tend to make you look twice.

To determine how many 30-day cycles that is, you simply do integer division by 30:

```
print("Number of 30-day cycles: {}".format(int(days.days / 30)))
```

The overall output from the program is the following:

```
days = 71
Number of 30-day cycles: 2
```

This makes sense, since the first cycle finishes on day 30, the second cycle finishes on day 60, and the third cycle finishes on day 90.

As you can see, date math really isn't a complicated thing, but it is very important. As a programmer, you will spend a lot of time working with dates, dealing with some of the *edge cases*, and as such, worrying about getting the right date. The following sections detail some date math edge cases you'll likely encounter as a programmer.

DEFINITION

Edge case refers to a condition that isn't normally encountered but could be. For example, consider the following simple equation:

```
X = 2/y
```

This equation looks like it ought to be okay for all values, but it fails when y is equal to 0. That time it is fails is the edge case.

Passing the End of the Year

Let's imagine you are writing a billing program and need to calculate the next date to send out a bill. Today is December 10, and your company bills every 30 days. If you just think about these things as a nonprogrammer, your first thought is probably just to say, "Oh, the next month is January, which is the next year." Unfortunately, computers don't think that way. Fortunately, datetime() functions do, as you can see here (by the way, "eoy" is pretty common in the programming world and stands for "end of year"):

```
>>> import datetime
>>> eoy = datetime.date(2013, 12, 10)
>>> eoy = eoy + datetime.timedelta(days=30)
>>> eoy
datetime.date(2014, 1, 9)
```

So if your company sent out a bill on December 10, 2013, the next bill should be sent out on January 9, 2014, which is correct. Good thing the date classes can do this, or my bills would be way behind!

Leap Years

As I'm sure you are aware, every four years is a leap year, with the addition of one day on the calendar—February 29. Over the years, I have worked with hundreds of date libraries in lots of different languages. You'd be stunned by the number of them that didn't handle one of the weird leap year edge cases properly, which caused problems during the program run over the years. It could be a nightmare—it really isn't every four years, it is every year that is divisible by 4, except those that are divisible by 100, unless they are also divisible by 400. Who dreams up this stuff? Thankfully, it's a lot easier to do it now.

Let's imagine you have something you are doing on February 28 and the next day. For four different years, what would that "next day" be? Let's look at such a case, as shown in Listing 11.5.

```
import datetime

# Case 1: A normal year
d1 = datetime.date(2013,2,28)
d1 = d1 + datetime.timedelta(days=1)
print("Date 1 = {}".format(d1))

# Case 2: A normal leap year
d2 = datetime.date(2012,2,28)
d2 = d2 + datetime.timedelta(days=1)
```

```
print("Date 2 = {}".format(d2))

# Case 3: A century year
d3 = datetime.date(1900,2,28)
d3 = d3 + datetime.timedelta(days=1)
print("Date 3 = {}".format(d3))

# Case 4: A century year divisible by 4
d4 = datetime.date(2000,2,28)
d4 = d4 + datetime.timedelta(days=1)
print("Date 4 = {}".format(d4))
```

Listing 11.5

The confusing world of leap years.

Now, if everything I told you is correct, and the programmer who wrote the date libraries knew what he was doing, you should see two leap years (that is, February 29 dates), and two nonleap years (March 1 dates). Let's see what Python thinks:

```
Date 1 = 2013-03-01
Date 2 = 2012-02-29
Date 3 = 1900-03-01
Date 4 = 2000-02-29
```

Hurrah! You got what you expected.

PROGRAMMING TIP

One of the nicest things about treating dates as "objects" is you don't have to remember the number of days in a given month. The date classes in nearly every programming language know how to figure out whether it is a leap year or a regular year or whether a non-February month has 30 days or 31. Just add the number of days you want, and the date object will automatically figure out what month and day it is.

Working with Time

Time math is very different than date math, for the simple reason that times without dates don't mean a lot. For example, suppose I have a time value of 11:59 P.M., or one minute before midnight. Now, I add two minutes to that. What do I get? The answer is 00:01 on the next day if going by a 24-hour clock. The time value itself makes no sense; I am adding a positive number to a positive number and getting a smaller value. Any mathematician can tell you that isn't right.

To figure out how to work with time properly, you have to begin to think like a programmer. Programmers work with what they have, and extend it by using what they know. So what is it you have, and what do you know, that will help you work with time values?

First of all, you know that dates are really times and dates combined. That is, "January 1, 2014" is really a fully qualified date and time of "1/1/2014 12:00 A.M." That means there is a time value in there somewhere.

The second thing you know, having worked on it all of this chapter, is that date values can be modified with math functions. You can add days to dates, weeks, or even months. You might think, therefore, that you could do something like the following (where 12, 12, 12 means the twelfth second of the twelfth minute of the twelfth hour):

```
>>> import datetime
>>> t1 = datetime.time(12, 12, 12)
>>> t1 = t1 + datetime.timedelta(hours=4)
```

This should simply add four hours to the date you've defined, and all should be good, right? If you try it, though, you'll find out it doesn't work:

```
>>> t1 = t1 + datetime.timedelta(hours=4)
Traceback (most recent call last):
  File "<pyshell#3>", line 1, in <module>
    t1 = t1 + datetime.timedelta(hours=4)
TypeError: unsupported operand type(s) for +: 'datetime.time' and 'datetime.
  timedelta'
```

Well, that's annoying. But what if you fully create the date instead of just using a time object? You can create a fully qualified datetime, which means providing not only the date but also the time portion of the thing. For example, here's what you'd do if you wanted to add five hours to January 1, 2014, at 0:00 (midnight):

```
>>> import datetime
>>> d = datetime.datetime(2014,1,1,0,0,0)
>>> td = datetime.timedelta(hours=5)
>>> print(d+td)
2014-01-01 05:00:00
```

Now, just because you happen to have the date portion of the time field doesn't mean you have to use it. You can simply track the time portion. As you can see from the preceding code, you've added five hours to the beginning of the year, and gotten the same day at 5:00 A.M.

ERROR MESSAGE

As you can see in cases such as working with time, you sometimes have to do things the hard way, because the programmers who wrote the code in the first place didn't really think things through.

So as you can see, there is nothing magical about adding times in Python or any other language. You simply can use your knowledge of dates plus how time works in a 24-hour cycle to get find what you need.

Inputting and Parsing Dates and Times

One common task when working with programming concepts is learning how to get data from the user in that particular format. Certainly, with dates and times, you have learned enough about input and slicing of strings to be able to get a date in from the user in a specific format and then assign the pieces to the datetime structure. One of the most important things a programmer can learn, however, is how not to fall into the "not invented here" trap.

The term *not invented here* (often abbreviated NIH) refers to a corporate or individual culture of not using things that were created by others. While there is often a cost to using someone else's work, you always have to be aware, as a programmer, of what the cost to yourself is to develop something that has already been created by another.

Beginning programmers often find themselves writing code that has been written hundreds of times before. Some of this is simply a matter of doing the same thing to learn how it is done, but a great deal of it is due to not knowing what else is available to them. Experienced programmers know where to go to find existing code libraries and prefer to use them due to their well-tested and well-documented natures.

So with that in mind, let's look at how you might input a date or time from the user and use it in your application. Imagine, for example, you want to enter and save a bunch of people's names and birthdays. You might write a program that works something like this (in pseudocode):

```
While Not Done Entering names
    Enter a name
    If the name is blank, stop
    Else
        Enter a birthday
        Save the name and birthday
```

You can clearly do more with this later down the road, perhaps saving the names and birthdays to a persistent storage device or even allowing the user to edit the dates or names when something changes. For now, though, I'll focus on worrying about getting the data into your little program. The code you will be using is in Listing 11.6.

```python
import datetime
import time


birthdayList = []
while True:
        name = input("Enter a name: ")
        if len(name) == 0:
            break
        else:
            dateStr = input("Enter their date of birth (MM/DD/YYYY): ")
            birthdate = time.strptime(dateStr, '%m/%d/%Y')
            birthdayList.append((name, birthdate))

# Print out the list we got
for i in range(len(birthdayList)):
    print("Name: {0} Birthdate: {1}".format(birthdayList[i][0],
        time.strftime("%m/%d/%Y", birthdayList[i][1])))
```

Listing 11.6

A simple birthday entry program.

This program is interesting because of all of the little components it uses, but it really isn't very complicated. You loop until the user enters an empty string. Within the loop, you input a name and a birthdate (assuming the name wasn't blank) into a list called *birthdayList*. Each date is entered in MM/DD/YY format and converted to a date structure using a built-in function called *strptime()*. While Python is certainly unique in that particular naming convention, there are similar functions to parse dates and times in nearly all programming languages. Finally, you print out the list when you are done so you can see that it really worked.

PROGRAMMING TIP

The general process of inputting a string and converting it to the specific type you are interested in is a standard in programming. Computers can only deal with numbers and strings. Therefore, anything you create to model the real world—like dates and times—has to be somehow converted from a string input. Thankfully, most languages have this conversion functionality, meaning it is very rare that you have to write your own. Always look through the documentation for your language to see what conversion functionality exists.

As you can see when looking at your little program, you have built a working application using all of the pieces you've learned to this point in the book. Programming isn't about leaping in and working on something, it is about building a sold structure from well-constructed "building blocks." As you learn a new technique, component, or language construct, it is important that you work it into your daily activities with the language. Programming is very definitely a "use it or lose it" kind of job.

Working with Timers

How long does it take to run your program? How long does it take for a user to enter a value? How long does it take to run through a loop 10,000 times? The answer to all of these questions is "some period of time." But how can you figure out just how long that "some period of time" is? The answer lies in timers. Timers are another of the core building blocks of programming, allowing you to determine which areas of a program run most slowly or how long users are spending in a particular area of your code.

When you read about timers, you will likely run across two completely different types of them. The first, which I will discuss in this section, is of the stopwatch variety. It is a start, run something, and stop kind of thing that reports on how long it took for something to run. The second kind, which is actually called a *timer* in Python, is a thread-based bit of functionality that allows you to run a given piece of code at a given time; this is more of a scheduler than a stopwatch.

You might be asking yourself, *Why do I care how long something takes to run?* It is a valid question. As programmers, you should be concerned with the *usability* of your programs. And one of the things that users complain about the most is that it takes too long for something to finish. This might be due to the sheer amount of information that needs to be processed; it might also be due to having to look up lots of information across the internet. However, unless you know what part of the program is causing it to be "too slow" (and this is always a subjective measurement), you can't really fix it. That's where the timer comes in.

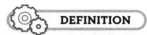

DEFINITION

Usability is a multifaceted term that refers to how easy it is for users to accomplish whatever task they need to do.

So if your goal is to figure out how long something takes to run, how would you go about it? Clearly, you know when something starts, and you can figure out when it ends. If you use the time functions to do math, you can actually subtract the beginning from the ending and display the results in any way you want. This might be in seconds or milliseconds for a very short program. It might be in minutes or even hours for a very long program. You can always look at the smallest denomination of time and work your way upward.

Let's assume you want to calculate prime numbers. You've written a little function that determines if a number is prime or not. The program looks like the one shown in Listing 11.7.

```
import math

def isprime(startnumber):
    startnumber *=1.0
    prime = True
    for divisor in range(2, int(startnumber ** 0.5 + 1)):
        if startnumber / divisor==int(startnumber / divisor):
            prime=False
    return prime

for i in range(2,10):
    if isprime(i):
        print("{} is prime!".format(i))
    else:
        print("{} is NOT prime".format(i))
```

Listing 11.7

A prime number program.

Does the program work? Running it gives you the following output, snipped for brevity:

```
2 is prime!
3 is prime!
4 is NOT prime
<snip>
9 is NOT prime
```

So, yes, it appears to work. The question is, how long does it take for the program to calculate whether or not something is a prime number?

Looking at the code, you see a loop that runs to the number divided by 2. For small numbers—say, those under a million—that loop is pretty fast. Surely fast enough that the time for the program to output its information is slower than the time to compute whether or not it is a prime number. However, for really large numbers, that loop is going to be executed a lot of times. How slow will that make it? You need to find that out.

Let's add some code to your little program to test how long things take:

```
import math
import time

def isprime(startnumber):
    startnumber *=1.0
    prime = True
    for divisor in range(2, int(startnumber ** 0.5 + 1)):
        if startnumber / divisor==int(startnumber / divisor):
            prime=False
    return prime

start = time.time()
for i in range(2,10):
    if isprime(i):
        print("{} is prime!".format(i))
    else:
        print("{} is NOT prime".format(i))
end = time.time()
print("Time to run: {}".format(end - start))
```

Now, if you run the program with a range of 10, you get a time to run of the following:

```
Time to run: 0.0500030517578125
```

Let's increase how many numbers the program processes from 10 to 100, by changing the "10" in the range function to "100." The time is now the following:

```
Time to run: 0.34001994132995605
```

What is interesting is that the time does not increase in a linear fashion. You might have expected that the time to run 10 times the number of values would be 10 times slower, but apparently not. What happens when you change the number to 1,000?

```
Time to run: 3.1721808910369873
```

As you can see, the time to process a thousand values is pretty close to 10 times a hundred values. Does this hold up over time? You can find this out by increasing the range value to something very large—say, 100,000. When you do this, the program runs for a really long time. But the output is the following:

```
Time to run: 305.508474111557
```

The value is approximately 100 times the value for a thousand iterations, which means your code is running about the same no matter how many iterations you put it through. This is very valuable information, since some functions increase geometrically when you increase the size of the input. You could now say confidently that the program will run in the same basic time per iteration, no matter how big the iteration.

The Least You Need to Know

- The gmtime() function returns the time based on Greenwich Mean Time (GMT), which is the standard that's usually returned by programming languages.
- The strftime() function formats a time value into a string and returns it to you as a string.
- The timedelta() function allows you to create a "delta," or change in some unit of time or date, and then apply that to an existing date.
- Doing math using times requires your knowledge of both dates and how time works in a 24-hour cycle.
- Timers allow you to determine which areas of a program run most slowly or how long users are spending in a particular area of your code.

Error Handling, or When Things Go Terribly Wrong

What a wonderful world it would be if nothing ever went wrong. How nice it would be to make plans and have them work out, without ever seeing a problem or issue. Of course, that's not going to happen. Problems occur, things happen that you didn't think of, people do things incorrectly—all the banes of the programmer. Sometimes, I say if there were no users, there wouldn't be such problems. Of course, if there were no users, there wouldn't be anyone to use programs and I'd be out of a job. (Ah, well, I suppose we must put up with the users and their silly mistakes.)

In this chapter, I show you common programming errors and how you can handle them.

In This Chapter

- What are errors?
- Knowing when errors occur
- Handling and raising exceptions
- Working with error codes
- Throwing exceptions or error codes in functions
- Doing type-safe conversions with exceptions

Errors Defined

In the real world, an error happens when something goes wrong. An error might be turning the wrong way on a one-way street or speeding too fast, both of which are things that are under your control and shouldn't happen. An error can also be a tire blowing out on your car or the power going off at work, causing you to lose an hour of typing. (I hate it when that happens.) Similar to these, there are really two kinds of errors when programming: those caused by people doing something they shouldn't be doing, and those caused by simple acts of nature.

When you are designing programs, there are many kinds of errors you can anticipate. People may try to do things in the wrong order, such as trying to delete a file that doesn't yet exist or entering an invalid password for their user name. There are also errors that exist outside of the user space that you can be aware of. For example, you might try to save a file to a drive that is read-only, such as a DVD-ROM, or the user might try to send an email when not connected to the internet.

Let's look at a couple of "normal" errors, or things that you should think about before you write code:

- When saving a file, the user is required to enter a file name. Imagine that she does not. What would you do?

- When logging into a secure system, the user enters a user name and password that are invalid. What do you do?

- A user tries to purchase something on a website, and the credit card she offers you is declined. How do you handle this?

- Asked for a date in "MM/DD/YYYY" format, the user enters "13/01/2013." The month 13 is clearly not a valid one. How would you handle it?

- Playing a set of music from your MP3 player, you hit **Next** for the next song, but you are at the last song in the set. What should happen?

All of these are events that are very easy to anticipate for the software developer. There is absolutely no reason for a program to fail when an anticipatable error occurs. If you don't take care of a mistake that should have been anticipated, it's all on you as the software writer. There are lots of things that can go wrong that you might not be aware of, but handling the things that you know about is an essential part of software development.

PROGRAMMING TIP

Of course, sometimes errors are only obvious in hindsight. Your job as a developer is to identify the kinds of actions and data that should be coming into your program and to ensure that anything outside of that list does not occur. That doesn't mean nothing else will go wrong, but it does mean you are covered for the things you can't handle.

Kinds of Information and Their Relation to Errors

In the software world, there are three kinds of information:

- Things you know

- Things you know you don't know

- Things you don't know you don't know

Examining the list, you obviously have things that you know. From the perspective of errors, you know that people forget passwords or sometimes hit the wrong keys, and that their computers sometimes crash at the most inopportune moment. For this reason, you design programs so they can retrieve lost passwords, ignore invalid keys, and save documents automatically while users work so that even if the computer crashes, they don't lose much.

Things you know you don't know are areas that need to be investigated before you write a program. This usually falls under the category of requirements gathering, although many programmers gather information more on an "as you need it" basis. When you run into something you don't know, there are two things you can do about it. First, you can ignore it and hope someone else figures it out. (Please don't do this; I've worked with more than my share of people who prefer this approach.) Second, you can try to determine what the right thing to do is. This is a much better approach, even if you never find the absolute right answer. It is always better to say "<x> might happen; I don't know what to do, so I'll print an error message and exit the program" than to have the program just ignominiously crash.

Then there are the things you don't know you don't know. Sounds rather strange, doesn't it? Yet you encounter this sort of thing all the time in the form of errors, because not knowing that something is out there to get you makes it very hard to anticipate. For example, say you are driving a brand-new car, one you've never driven before, and a snowstorm pops up. There is a slick spot ahead on the road. What will the car do? Experience tells you that it probably isn't something good, but you really don't know. Now, imagine that when you do hit the slick spot, the car suddenly shifts into reverse, because that's what the designers told it to do. You could never have imagined such a thing, so you didn't prepare for it. This is something you didn't know would happen. Similarly, when it comes to programming, you can't anticipate a major earthquake happening in the middle of someone trying to perform a transaction on your website.

Python supports all of the standard forms of errors that come with these types of information, and uses a more-or-less standard approach to them, so everything you learn here will apply to any modern language you use.

How Are Errors Propagated?

You would think that an error just happens and is either dealt with or the program crashes. Unfortunately, that is not the case. Most errors happen at a fairly low level of code, and then slowly work their way up the chain until they crash in some completely bizarre place. This is challenging for the software developer, because it isn't easy to pin down exactly what is going wrong when you get conflicting reports.

Errors can be handled by code written by the developer, in which case the error can either be dealt with properly or cause problems down the road. I'll talk more about this a bit later in the chapter, but the reality is, you have to actually deal with an error; you can't just recognize that it took place and ignore it. That would be like seeing a giant hole in your roof and thinking, "Gee, there's a hole in the roof, but it isn't raining, so why do I care?" Sooner or later, the rain will come down, and bad things will happen. So it is with errors.

Programs have levels to them, from the low-level code that interfaces to the operating and file systems, to the high-level code that provides a *graphical user interface* (*GUI*) to the end user. An error that occurs at a very low level, such as the file system, works its way up to the GUI level (at least you hope it does). Wouldn't it be frustrating to run out of disk space and never know about it when you tried to save a file? You'd think your file was safe and secure on the hard disk, when in reality it was out in the ether somewhere. Not a very nice feeling.

DEFINITION

A **graphical user interface (GUI)** is a type of user interface that relies on icons, menus, and a mouse, but not typing in commands.

So how do you know an error occurred, and how do you handle it? Let's start out with a really simple example of an error. As we all know, you can't divide by zero. After all, how many zeroes are there in 1? Either a whole lot or none, depending on who you talk to. Because nobody can decide, trying to divide by zero results in an ugly error.

If you enter such an equation into IDLE, you see something akin to the following:

```
>>> x = 3 / 0
Traceback (most recent call last):
  File "<pyshell#0>", line 1, in <module>
    x = 3 / 0
ZeroDivisionError: division by zero
```

Let's take a look at the error message and see just what information you have. First, you get a line that says "Traceback." This is Python's way of telling you there is an error. Knowing that an error occurred is, of course, half the battle. Next, you get a line about what line and module the error occurred in. This is useful under most conditions, but when the line is in immediate mode in the interpreter, you can skip it. You only typed in a single line of code, so it shouldn't be that hard to figure out where the error happened.

Finally, you get the error type (ZeroDivisionError), followed by an English description of the error (division by zero). Okay, well, you knew that. What is important here is that the interpreter is telling you what went wrong and what you would have to do to fix it, in a roundabout way.

Now, if you had this little code snippet running, it would be very hard to fix. After all, the zero is hard coded, so no matter what you do, the division by zero error is going to happen. This isn't exactly a normal turn of events in programming. Much more likely, you have something more like what's shown in Listing 12.1.

```
iVal = int(input("Enter a number: "))
rVal = 10 / iVal
print("The result is {}".format(rVal))
```

Listing 12.1

A simple math program.

If you enter anything other than zero, of course, this program works fine, as you can see in the following:

```
Enter a number: 12
The result is 0.8333333333333334
Enter a number: 2
The result is 5.0
```

However, if you enter a zero for the value, you get a problem:

```
Enter a number: 0
Traceback (most recent call last):
  File "F:/Books/Beginning Programming/Chapter 12/ch12_1.py", line 2, in
  <module>
    rVal = 10 / iVal
ZeroDivisionError: division by zero
```

Now, in programming, when you have a problem like this, there are two ways you can deal with it. You can handle the problem—in this case, an exception (I'll talk about this more in the next section)—in your code. This is a good way to deal with, well, exceptional problems. On the other hand, you can handle the problem by preventing it from happening in the first place. The latter should always be your preferred approach.

So how do you change the program so it doesn't crash? Well, that's simple enough; Listing 12.2 shows you how.

```
iVal = int(input("Enter a number: "))
if iVal != 0:
    rVal = 10 / iVal
    print("The result is {}".format(rVal))
else:
    print("You may not enter a zero value!")
```

Listing 12.2

The updated math program.

Now, when you try to enter an invalid value, the program tells you not to do that:

```
Enter a number: 0
You may not enter a zero value!
```

ERROR MESSAGE

Make sure you know how to differentiate between errors you can prevent and exceptional conditions you can do nothing about. An error that can be stopped before it happens is always preferable to one that requires intervention. For one thing, it is much slower to handle an exceptional case. For another, it is generally sloppy programming practice to not at least do some validation before calling a function or class that might cause an exceptional event to occur.

Exceptions

In the previous section, I mentioned that certain errors are exceptional events. That means all errors aren't considered exceptions. For example, if you are asking the user to enter a number from 1 to 10 and they enter 12, that's hardly exceptional. It is an error, certainly, and you should tell the user about it, but it's not something that requires any special processing. Exceptions are a different class of error, where something "exceptional" has taken place. Good examples of exceptions are division by zero, using an array element that isn't defined, and trying to create a file on a device that doesn't allow writing (like a CD-ROM).

Most modern programming languages have some form of exceptions (errors) and exception handling (how you handle that error in your program). You've seen the rawest form of exception handling to this point, which is simply allowing the program to crash and display an error message.

In Python, as with many modern programming languages, the keyword to handling something that might throw an exception is *try*. With this keyword, you're basically saying to the interpreter, "Try to do this. If something goes wrong, I will handle it." The general form of exception handling in nearly all languages is something like the following:

```
Try
   <statements that might cause an exception>
Except <some exception type>
   <statements that handle the exception>
```

Some languages prefer the word *catch* instead of *except*, but the overall processing is the same. Let's see how this works by rewriting the math program you did earlier in the chapter with exception handling instead of error processing. You can see what that looks like in Listing 12.3.

```
iVal = int(input("Enter a number: "))
try:
    rVal = 10 / iVal
    print("The result is {}".format(rVal))
except ZeroDivisionError:
    print("You may not enter a zero value!")
```

Listing 12.3

The math program with exception handling.

Now, if you run the program and enter a zero, you get the same error you would get if you handled the exception with your if statement:

```
Enter a number: 0
You may not enter a zero value!
```

What is going on here? Well, when you enter a zero, Python attempts to divide by zero. As you've seen before, that generates an exception, which has the name ZeroDivisionException. The interpreter then looks for a handler for that exception, which it finds in the "except" part of the code. What happens if it doesn't find a matching exception? It behaves as if there were no exception handling at all. For example, here's what would happen if you entered letters instead of numbers:

```
Enter a number: asdf
Traceback (most recent call last):
  File "F:/Books/Beginning Programming/Chapter 12/ch12_3.py", line 1, in
  <module>
    iVal = int(input("Enter a number: "))
ValueError: invalid literal for int() with base 10: 'asdf'
```

In this case, you didn't enter a valid number and the interpreter complained about it. Your exception handler wasn't called for two reasons:

1. In order for something to be caught by an exception handler, it has to be within the try block. That's the part from the "try:" to the "except" part of the code.

2. The exception that was generated didn't match anything you had in your list.

Because you can have as many except handlers as you want, you could create one to handle entering letters instead of numbers for your program. Or, as a better option, you could have a blank except handler that handles all errors that aren't caught by some other level. This is called a "blanket handler," because it covers all of the possibilities that aren't handled by something else.

If you rewrite the math program one last time to deal with different kinds of exceptions, you'll see what I mean. In this case, you'll handle all errors that occur anywhere in the program, no matter where they are or what they are. Listing 12.4 shows you the new look of the program with those handlers.

```
try:
    iVal = int(input("Enter a number: "))
    rVal = 10 / iVal
    print("The result is {}".format(rVal))
except ZeroDivisionError:
    print("You may not enter a zero value!")
except:
    print("Got some kind of other error")
```

Listing 12.4

The final math program with exception handling.

Now, if you run your program with different inputs, you'll see you handle every possible case of error, along with all valid cases:

```
Enter a number: 0
You may not enter a zero value!
Enter a number: asdf
Got some kind of other error
Enter a number: 5
The result is 2.0
```

In the preceding code, you handle the case of the division by zero explicitly. However, if the error is something else—in this case, entering a non-numeric string—you handle it by default in the "other kind of error" case. And of course, if you enter a valid number, you get the results you expect.

When it comes to the structure of your code in relation to exception handlers, what is most important to understand is that you are looking at code that appears to be in a straight line but isn't. If you don't get an error, the except blocks aren't called. If you get an error, however, the code that is inside the try block isn't called past the point of the error. Here's an example of what I mean:

```
try
     <some statements>
   1
   2
   3
except <some exception>
   4
   5
   6
Except
   7
   8
   9
10
```

If all goes well, statements 1 through 3 are executed, and then statement 10 is executed; everything after statement 3 and before statement 10 is ignored.

But what if you have a case where <some exception> arises? Let's say, for arguments sake, that the exception happens on statement 2. In this case, your program executes statement 1 and 2 and then 4, 5, and 6 before going on to 10.

On the other hand, you might get a case where an exception occurs but is not a <some exception> type of error. Let's say it happens on the same statement, line 2. In this case, your program executes statement 1 and 2 and then 7, 8, and 9 before finishing with 10.

Handling Multiple Exceptions

As you've seen, you can handle one exception in an except block, or you can handle all remaining exceptions in an except block that has no exception types (like DivisionByZeroException) defined for it. Generally, types for exceptions are found in the type library that uses them (in this case, "math"). But what if you want to handle multiple exceptions the same way? You can use the default handler for exceptions and do them all, but that might not be appropriate in all cases. Thankfully, Python does provide an alternative, which is handling multiple exceptions within the same block.

ERROR MESSAGE

There is often a lot of "stuff" going on behind the scenes. When a program is running, the compiler or interpreter is constantly looking at the context of the code rather than simply reading one line at a time and executing it. Python, for example, needs to know about exceptions and exception handling, as well as finding functions you've written and loading them when they are called. It isn't as simple as it looks, and forgetting that will always cause you problems in the end.

The syntax is fairly simple:

```
except(ExceptionType1, ExceptionType2, etc):
    block of code to handle exceptions.
```

This is really just some syntactical sugar that allows you do a bunch of things in multiple cases without copying code. What it points out, however, is how aware you have to be of what can go wrong when you are writing code.

How do you know what sorts of exceptions can occur? Some of them, such as division by zero or invalid list indexes, can occur anywhere you are doing division or working with lists. For example:

```
>>> x=(1, 2, 3)
>>> for i in range(0, 4):
    print(x[i])


1
2
3
Traceback (most recent call last):
    File "<pyshell#8>", line 2, in <module>
        print(x[i])
IndexError: tuple index out of range
```

In this case, the error is that you are trying to use more elements than exist in the tuple.

You could handle this by exception handling, but why would you really need to? Every slice-able element has a length property to it, which you can get at using the len() function (see Chapter 6). Rewriting that bit of code as the following will always produce the proper result, with no exceptions to worry about:

```
>>> for i in range(0, len(x)):
    print(x[i])
1
2
3
```

Yet had you not known the possibility of an array index out of range, you might not have thought through the better way to write the code.

The else and finally Blocks

There are two cases in exception handling you need to consider. First of all, what happens if nothing goes wrong? Second, what happens when you've dealt with whatever it is that did go wrong? Most languages have constructs to deal with both of these cases, and Python is no exception.

If nothing goes wrong, under normal conditions, the code will simply drop past all of the except handlers and continue on with the program. Sometimes, however, you want to be quite sure that things worked properly and not simply that an error was caught and swallowed. For this purpose, Python offers you the else statement (see Chapter 5). Let's take a quick look at how this works, as shown in Listing 12.5.

```
try:
    iVal = int(input("Enter a number: "))
    rVal = 10 / iVal
    print("The result is {}".format(rVal))
except ZeroDivisionError:
    print("You may not enter a zero value!")
except:
    print("Got some kind of other error")
else:
    print("Everything went great!")
print("Continuing on with the program")
```

Listing 12.5

No errors here!

Now, even if an error occurs, you are going to handle it, so the last thing this program will always print out is "Continuing on with the program." But sometimes, you want to know if you entered a valid value or got some sort of exception, such as processing the string badly. In that case, one of the except blocks will be called. For issues, you want to have an except block called with a flag or something to indicate that while you can continue, the data is invalid; in Listing 12.5, those are "You may not enter a zero value!" and "Got some kind of other error." However, if the data is perfectly valid, you want to trigger the else statement:

```
Enter a number: 2
The result is 5.0
Everything went great!
Continuing on with the program
Enter a number: asdf
Got some kind of other error
Continuing on with the program
```

As you can see, in the first case with the preceding code, you hit the else statement, indicating that all went well. In the second case, an error occurred somewhere and you didn't get through all the processing in the try block. This can be important, since you might have been doing something that will be needed later in that block.

Exception handling is normally done around blocks of code that are doing something that has to be either completely finished or not done at all. In the programming world, this is called *transactional processing*.

 PROGRAMMING TIP

Transactional processing is an all-or-nothing situation—either the full operation takes place, or the operation doesn't happen at all.

Now that you've looked at how to know whether nothings goes last wrong, let's look at what to do once exception handling is done. This is where the finally block comes in. When you handle exceptions, particularly when you are working with a resource like a file or internet connection, you often have to clean up your mess whether it works or not. That is, if you open a file or create a connection to the internet, you have to close it when you are done, whether your code worked or not. Failing to close resources when you are done with them results in "resource leaks" which eventually cause your computer to crash. (And you really don't want to be responsible for anyone's computer crashing, do you?) The finally block is called after all that exception handling is complete, whether or not there were errors encountered.

In code, there can be both an else block and a finally block; they may both be called, or only the finally block may be called. If they're both called, it means the exception handling was done and there were no errors. If only the finally block is called, it means the exception handling was done, but errors were encountered. Listing 12.6 shows the usage of the finally block in Python.

```
try:
    iVal = int(input("Enter a number: "))
    rVal = 10 / iVal
    print("The result is {}".format(rVal))
except ZeroDivisionError:
    print("You may not enter a zero value!")
except:
    print("Got some kind of other error")
else:
    print("Everything went great!")
finally:
    print("Finally block called")
print("Continuing on with the program")
```

Listing 12.6

Using the finally block in exception handling.

To give you an idea of how it all fits together, let's look at two different sorts of output from the math program. In the first case, everything goes right; in the second case, there is an exception in the code:

```
Enter a number: 12
The result is 0.8333333333333334
Everything went great!
Finally block called
Continuing on with the program
Enter a number: asfadsfd
Got some kind of other error
Finally block called
Continuing on with the program
```

As you can see, the finally block is always called when there is exception handling defined and there is a finally block in the code. It will be the last thing done before the program continues.

PROGRAMMING TIP

Exception handling is often one of the hardest things for a new programmer to understand because it isn't really linear. Things happen in a defined order, but that order isn't always reflected in the order of the code you are reading. Once you get a handle on what is happening in each of the examples in this chapter, though, there aren't that many things that will be harder to learn!

Raising Exceptions

Exception handling isn't just for the interpreter or for the writers of the system functions. In Python or any other language that supports exceptions, you can raise exceptions as easily as anyone else. Exception raising is a two-step process: deciding on the exception type to raise and adding a message to the exception to let someone know exactly what went wrong.

Statement for Raising Exceptions

The general form of the exception raising statement is the following:

```
raise (exception-type, description)
```

As an example, let's go back to your little math program one last time and deal with error conditions via the exception mechanism. The results are shown in Listing 12.7.

```
try:
    iVal = int(input("Enter a number: "))
    if ( iVal < 0 ):
        raise Exception("BadNumberInput", "You entered a negative number")
    rVal = 10 / iVal
    print("The result is {}".format(rVal))
except ZeroDivisionError:
    print("You may not enter a zero value!")
except Exception :
    print("You entered a BAD number. Not good. Bad")
except:
    print("Got some kind of other error")
else:
    print("Everything went great!")
finally:
    print("Finally block called")
print("Continuing on with the program")
```

Listing 12.7

Raising an exception in Python.

The line marked in bold shows a way you can raise your own exceptions. You can raise any of the defined exceptions in Python, or you can create your own. In any case, you may opt to send zero, one, or more arguments to the Exception class. This is the second argument to the raise statement; for this program, the second argument is "You entered a negative number." This information is not relevant to Python; it is solely for the programmer to reveal more information about why the exception was thrown. In the case of something simple, like division by zero, there is clearly no reason to add more information. What else are you going to say, really?

In cases where you want the additional information, though, you can use the "args" attribute of the Exception class. When you catch an exception, you can specify an object of that class that is to be used to store the information that was passed along. Up to this point, I've had you ignore any additional information, but in Listing 12.8 I will show you how to catch an exception and print out the information that the programmer—in this case, us—wants you to know about.

```
try:
    iVal = int(input("Enter a number: "))
    if ( iVal < 0 ) :
        raise Exception("BadNumberInput", "You entered a negative number")
    rVal = 10 / iVal
    print("The result is {}".format(rVal))
except ZeroDivisionError:
    print("You may not enter a zero value!")
except Exception as msg:
    print("You entered a BAD number. Not good. Bad {}".format(msg))
except:
    print("Got some kind of other error")
else:
    print("Everything went great!")
finally:
    print("Finally block called")
print("Continuing on with the program")
```

Listing 12.8

Exceptions with arguments.

The number of arguments for an exception vary, depending on the exception and what the programmer sent back. In this case, you send a single argument—the string "You entered a negative number"—which you then print out for the user. You can send any information you want in an exception, the only point being that you must document what they are so the calling programmer knows what he is getting back. When the code receives a message of text, it knows to print out "You entered a BAD number. Not good. Bad." This is because the error propagated upward to the calling program.

> **PROGRAMMING TIP**
>
> The difference between hobby programmers and those who write code that will be used by real people is often in the handling of errors. While many people simply allow the program to crash in their hobby programs, this isn't an optimal solution for the average user.
>
> Try to think through what might go wrong and at least tell the user what the problem was when your code fails.

When and When Not to Raise Exceptions

You might see exceptions as the way to indicate any problem that occurs. If you recall from earlier in the chapter, though, exceptions are for, well, exceptional events. The implication of an exception is that something bad has happened that prevents you from moving forward. If there is a warning or just information that you want to pass back to the calling program, there are better choices than exceptions. Remember, if an exception is not handled by the calling program, it will crash and display an ugly dump on the screen of all the pertinent and nonpertinent data associated with that exception. This can be rather scary for the end user.

To help you differentiate, consider the following events and try to decide which are really "exceptional" events, and which are simply things that you can handle without having to do much beside possibly informing the user:

- The file the user wants you to load is empty.

- The file the user is trying to save can't be saved for some reason.

- The user entered an invalid value.

- The connection to the internet failed.

The first one is not an exceptional event. The fact that a file is empty just means there is nothing to process. You can inform the user, if you like, or simply say that nothing was done because no data was found.

The second one is definitely an exceptional event. The user expected her data to be saved to some sort of persistent storage, such as a hard drive or flash drive, and it wasn't. Data loss can occur, and this is certainly a bad thing. Therefore, you can raise an exception.

The third event is not an exceptional event. If you threw exceptions every time the user typed something wrong, you'd spend all of your time handling exceptions. Inform the user that her input is invalid and retry.

The fourth event may be exception, depending on why it happened. If, for example, you are periodically checking to see if you have a connection to the internet, this is clearly not an exceptional event. If, on the other hand, you are testing the user's user name and password to connect to a website and you can't get to the internet, that's an exceptional event that can be raised.

Understanding when something is really bad versus something that can be handled is knowledge that comes with experience. It won't hurt you to be overcautious and raise too many exceptions, but it will make your code harder to read and the overall system a little slower.

Using Error Codes

From what you've just read in this chapter, you might think that the only way you can communicate errors is by raising and catching exceptions. That couldn't be further from the truth. In fact, most programmers rarely raise exceptions at all and only catch the ones they are required to catch from library functions in the system. Whether this is a good thing or a bad thing is debatable, but the simple fact is exceptions are difficult to understand.

Error codes, on the other hand, are pretty simple. When I call a function, it returns a value to me. That value can be whatever it is I asked for from the function, or it can be an error code indicating that something went wrong. Error codes are easy to understand, easy to program, and easy to work with. However, they are losing popularity amongst the programming elite, because they are also easy to ignore.

Consider the following little snippet of Python code in Listing 12.9. In it, you prompt the user to enter a string and then search for the substring "help" within the string. If the string is found, you print out the position in the user input string where you found it; otherwise, you tell the user that she didn't enter a string containing "help."

```python
s = input("Enter a string that contains the word help: ")
idx = s.find("help")
if idx == -1 :
    print("Help not found!")
else :
    print("Found help at position {}".format(idx))
```

Listing 12.9

A simple Python search program with an error code.

As you can see, the find() function in the string library looks for the given substring within the context of the bigger string. If it is found, that offset is returned, indicating the index of the substring in the larger string. So if you enter a string that says "There is no help for you," you would get back the index of help within that string, or position 12. If, on the other hand, you enter a string that doesn't contain the word "help," you get back -1.

The signal value -1 is an error code indicating that the function found an error. In this case, since the only possible error is the substring isn't found, it is pretty simple to work with the returned error code.

Compare this to the index() function of the string library, which does the same thing but raises an exception if the substring isn't found, as shown in Listing 12.10.

 PROGRAMMING TIP

Why have two functions that do the same thing? Welcome to the world of programmers. If a function doesn't work exactly the way one programmer wants it to, the programmer naturally creates another that does the same thing but with a slightly different approach. Sigh—this is why learning about exceptions can be complicated.

```
s = input("Enter a string that contains the word help: ")
try:
    idx = s.index("help")
    print("Found help at position {}".format(idx))
except ValueError:
    print("No help for you!")
```

Listing 12.10

The same search program with exceptions.

Is the latter code more readable than the former? I would argue no, but most programmers seem to think it is. The world is moving toward exceptions and exception handling, however, so you need to understand both to work with modern programming languages. Pretty much all languages have constructs like this, so you aren't hurting anything by learning the way Python does it in the long run.

Dealing with Errors in Functions

Exception handling and error codes are really much more important when you are designing functions (see Chapter 10) than when you are dealing with them in simple straight-line code. To this point, I've really only dealt with raising exceptions as a curiosity and returning error codes as something someone else did. In this section, however, I want take a much more serious look at these two items in relation to writing your own functions.

Throwing Exceptions

When you write a function, there are always things that can go wrong, such as bad input, math errors, file errors, or whatever else. Some of these errors have to be dealt with by the code of the function itself; otherwise, what is the point to having a function? However, some of it cannot. For example, if you are expecting a valid input value and the function receives bad input, it cannot—and should not—continue.

Let's look at an example in Listing 12.11, so you can see what I'm talking about with respect to exceptions.

```
def calc_average(list_of_values):
    if len(list_of_values) == 0:
        raise ValueError("No values input")
    total = 0
    for i in range(len(list_of_values) + 1):
        total = total + i
    average = total / len(list_of_values)
    return average


try:
    list_of_values = (1, 2, 3, 4, 5)
    avg = calc_average(list_of_values)
    print("First average: {}".format(avg))
    other_list_of_values = ()
    avg = calc_average(other_list_of_values)
    print("Second average: {}".format(avg))
except ValueError:
    print("Function didn't like our input!")
```

Listing 12.11

A simple function that throws an exception.

The ValueError exception is built into Python (you'll learn how to build your own exception classes in Chapter 14). In this case, your function is trying to calculate the average of a list of numbers. Clearly, if there are no numbers in the list, bad things would happen, since you divide by that number. More importantly, what is the average of an empty list of numbers? You could simply return zero, but that would not indicate to the end user of the function that she has done something wrong. As a result, your program receives the "ValueError" object with the message "No values input."

 ERROR MESSAGE

Always make sure that the programmers using your code are aware of when they have made a mistake. Don't just "swallow" the problem and return a "reasonable" value.

Therefore, you really need to think through the kinds of errors you want to return to the calling program. For example, if your function calls another function, and that other function raises an exception, you should catch it and either deal with it or translate it into something that makes sense for the guy that called your function in the first place. This is much akin to working with a contractor in your home. You don't really care that the contractor is having an issue getting part number 123,456 for the whosit that goes into the basement; what you care about is that your gas oven isn't working. In the same way, translating the error into something the caller cares about makes it much more likely that the problem will be fixed quickly.

Returning Error Codes

When it comes to errors, functions can also return some sort of status code indicating whether or not the functionality requested was performed. This can be a tad difficult sometimes, since functions also tend to return values that are computed or input within them.

There are numerous solutions to this in the programming world. The first is called an *output parameter*. In this case, the function accepts a variable that is set to a value inside the function. Python does not support this method, but many other languages do.

Another alternative, which is the one I'll discuss here, is to return multiple values from a function. This is pretty much a Python-only sort of solution; however, it is a very nice feature that will likely be adopted by other language designers in the future.

It is actually a lot easier to show an example of returning multiple values than to discuss it, so let's look at some code! Listing 12.12 shows you a function that returns multiple values.

```
def myFunction(input_value):
    input_value = input_value * 2
    ret_val = 0
    if input_value < 100:
        ret_val = 1
    return input_value, ret_val

inp = 20


inp, oup = myFunction(inp)
print(inp, oup)
```

Listing 12.12

A function returning multiple values.

Now, obviously, this is a pretty contrived example. The function in Listing 12.12 accepts a single input, multiplies it by 2, and checks to see if the result is less than 100. If the result is less than 100, the function returns a value of 1 in the status code; otherwise, it returns a value of zero. The interesting thing is in these two lines:

```
return input_value, ret_val
```

and

```
inp, oup = myFunction(inp)
```

The first statement, which is within the function, tells the Python interpreter to take the two values (input_value and ret_val) and return them to the calling program. The second statement assigns the two values, in order, to the inp and oup variables. This is kind of the equivalent of writing the following:

```
inp = input_value
oup = ret_val
```

If you look at the output from this function, you'll see that this is exactly what happens:

```
>>>
40 1
```

As you can see, the value of input_value has been multiplied by 2, while the return value is set to 1 because the value is less than 100. The ret_val, on the other hand, is the error code returned by the function.

PROGRAMMING TIP

If you don't get the setup of the return values in the code, walk through the code a few times. While returning multiple values is not an important part of learning to program, working through the logic of functions and code is definitely a major part.

Should You Use Error Codes or Exceptions in Functions?

The decision to use error codes or exceptions is, ultimately, up to you the developer. Nobody can tell you absolutely that one way is better or worse in any given situation. One of the great powers of programming is that you can decide what you want to do and how you want to do it. In general, you should use exceptions if you possibly can, unless your program is extremely sensitive to time. (Exceptions do take more time to process than return values.)

With that said, there are a couple guidelines I can offer you to decide what works best:

Be consistent! It might annoy other developers if you choose a method they aren't accustomed to using, but they will be furious if you do it six different ways throughout your code. If you do things the same way each and every time within a given set of code, you will make the person that has to pick up your code later much happier. And if you aren't a professional programmer, the chances are good that you are the one who has to pick up the code later. (Believe me, you'll appreciate my advice then!)

Consider what you are trying to accomplish. If you are doing a calculation in a function, it doesn't really make a lot of sense to return an error code. Imagine, for example, that you're writing a function that calculates the average of a group of values. You decide to use a return code of -1 when there is an error in the input. Now, imagine that you pass in the values -3, -1, 0, 0 for the list of values. When you add up these values, you get -4; when that number is divided by 4, you get, you guessed it, -1. Is that an error? Nope. In this case, exceptions would have been much clearer and would not have interfered with the value returned. So be careful when selecting error codes, especially in a function that returns some sort of calculated values.

Type-Safe Conversions Using Exceptions

I've shown you how exception handling is done in functions, but I haven't shown you how exception handling is used to do real work. One of the most common uses for exception handling in Python or any other language is to do type-safe conversions.

For example, consider the case where the user enters a date you want to use in your program. The user can't actually enter a datetime value, nor would you really want them to be calculating ticks in their head and entering them in the program. Instead, the user enters some kind of a string representation of the date, which then needs to be converted (see Chapter 11 if you need a refresher). Unfortunately, entering a value in an invalid format or entering an invalid date will cause the program to crash when you try to convert the string and use it as a date.

Type-safe conversion functions are the type of tricks all programmers should have in their toolbox. Because these functions are independent of what the program actually does, they can be used in any program that needs a string converted to something else, like a date.

PROGRAMMING TIP

Building a toolbox of reusable functions is something every beginning programmer should strive for. The less code you have to write to support all of the underpinnings of the program, the more time you have to work on the actual business logic associated with the program—and the happier your end users will be (most of the time).

Listing 12.13 shows a date conversion function that is very usable in the real world.

```
from datetime import datetime

def parse_date(s, fmt):
    try:
        ret = datetime.strptime(s,fmt)
    except ValueError:
        ret = datetime.now()
    return ret
```

Listing 12.13

A simple date parser in Python.

In this example function, you try to parse the date using your old friend the strptime() function from the datetime library. If the date is in the format you pass to the function, the parsed date is returned to the calling program as a valid datetime object. If the string is not in a valid form, or the format doesn't match, the function simply returns the current date and time.

You can test your function by giving it a few entries, both valid and invalid:

```
>>> parse_date("12/31/2013","%m/%d/%Y")
datetime.datetime(2013, 12, 31, 0, 0)
>>> parse_date("31/12/2013", "%m/%d/%Y")
datetime.datetime(2013, 9, 27, 7, 30, 23, 738981)
>>> parse_date("02/29/2013", "%m/%d/%Y")
datetime.datetime(2013, 9, 27, 7, 30, 45, 23198)
```

As you can see, when you pass the function a valid date, you get back the date parsed properly. When you pass the function an invalid date, such as 2/29/2013 (2013 is not a leap year), or in an invalid format, such as 31/12/2013, you get back the current date and time from the function.

Does it work? It seems to. Does it work perfectly? Actually, no, it does not. Consider the following input to the function:

```
>>> parse_date("", "")
datetime.datetime(1900, 1, 1, 0, 0)
```

This is actually expected behavior from the strptime() function. If you give it an empty string, it returns the beginning of the epoch (1/1/1900), otherwise known as the earliest date it knows how to deal with. Is this an error? No, it really isn't; that's just how Python works. However, your end user may not want an empty string turned into a date over a century in the past. This is why you need to work with users to decide what happens in cases like this.

Suppose your user says if the person entering data into the program came up with a date before, say, 2000, it should be ignored and the current date used. You could to modify your program to do so, or you could modify this function to handle it. Neither of these is really optimal.

However, there is another choice. You could write another function specific to this program that does the same job and reuses the parse_date() function with some additional error checking. Listing 12.14 shows you how to do it.

```
from datetime import datetime

def parse_date(s, fmt):
    try:
        ret = datetime.strptime(s,fmt)
    except ValueError:
        ret = datetime.now()
    return ret

def parse_date_after_2000(s, fmt) :
    ret = parse_date(s, fmt)
    if ret.year < 2000 :
        ret = datetime.now()
    return ret
```

Listing 12.14

Reusing your conversion function.

Now, you can call your modified function and see if it works:

```
>>> parse_date("", "")
datetime.datetime(1900, 1, 1, 0, 0)
>>> parse_date_after_2000("", "")
datetime.datetime(2013, 9, 27, 7, 39, 22, 905819)
```

Of course, being good programmers, you also want to make sure you didn't break anything for current dates, right? So let's test that, too:

```
>>> parse_date_after_2000("12/31/2013", "%m/%d/%Y")
datetime.datetime(2013, 12, 31, 0, 0)
```

As you can see, you are reusing your function to do conversions, taking advantage of the fact that it does all the error checking for you, and then simply adding a small amount of logic to validate dates after the millennium.

The Least You Need to Know

- Programs can cause errors and inherit them from existing code.
- Exceptions are the Python way of handling errors in your code.
- You can raise your own exceptions in your code for others to see.
- Using error codes, functions can return multiple values in place of throwing exceptions.

Files, Directories, and Other Things That Persist

One of the nicest things about computers is that they can do calculations lightning fast. They can crunch numbers and determine in milliseconds if you are going to be over-drawn on your checking account come the end of the month. However, all of these calculations are pretty much worthless unless you can save them and bring them back up. Otherwise, you'd have to enter all of your checks and deposits every month and then find out in a millisecond you were going to be short at the end of the month.

Storing data on computers is done via a persistent storage mechanism. In this chapter, I discuss the different concepts related to persistent storage and how to use them.

In This Chapter

- Understanding files and directories
- How to create and put data in a file
- Finding files
- Reading and writing files
- Moving around a file
- How to store preferences

Persistent Storage

Up to this point, all the data you've worked with has been transitory, meaning that as soon as the program ended, the data went away. The computer doesn't care where data comes from; it simply has it in memory and does what you want it to do with that data.

So what is *persistent storage?* Basically, storage is persistent if it can survive the computer being turned off. There are lots of forms of persistent storage, such as hard drives, flash drives (or thumb drives as they are sometimes called), and CDs or DVD-ROMs. Cloud storage, which is simply data stored on a network somewhere outside the computer, is also persistent.

The point of persistent storage is that, well, it persists. You can save things like your checkbook data to a disk and later bring it back up.

Of course, there is some danger with persistent storage. For example, if I tell you to enter a credit card number, do something with it, and then terminate the program, that credit card number vanishes at the same time. But if the credit card number is persisted, you run the risk of someone stealing it and misusing it, as in credit card fraud.

This is an important part of persistent data—it has to be protected. Whether that means encrypting the data—which is turning it into an unreadable set of characters that can only be recovered with the proper "key"—or protecting your file system with passwords and the like, security of data in persistent storage is a major concern for you as a programmer.

 ERROR MESSAGE

I'm not going to discuss protection in this chapter, but it really is an important aspect to programming. Whether shielding your data from snoopy people in the company or hiding important financial data in your databases from hackers, protection is something that needs to be considered from the ground up. Never try to "bolt on" an encryption or data hiding scheme—build it in from the initial program design.

Another issue you should think about as a programmer with respect to persistent data is size. Up to this point, I have merely talked about storing data in memory, and with the size of the data you've created, that would never end up being a problem. However, when you start writing data to a persistent storage device—particularly when you have a large number of users—you have to be concerned about running out of space.

All of these issues make persistent storage more than a simple problem. Fortunately, I'm now going to take you through what makes up persistent storage and show you how to avoid these issues.

Files

When people talk about computers, they often talk about files and file systems. But what is a file, really? Files are the very basis of persistence. If you are just writing a simple utility, like a calculator or a mortgage payment scheduler, you don't care about long-term storage. You enter some data, you get back a value, and you move on. There is no need to store that information and no need to worry about what someone might have entered in the past.

Of course, if your program involves files that will be used over again, like a tax return, your budget, or even just a word processing document, you can't possibly avoid storing data. Can you imagine if you had to type a word processing document from scratch every time in order to format and print it? It isn't very likely a user would opt to use that program for very long!

You can think of a file as a persistent variable or set of variables. Like a variable, a file has a name (known as the *file name*) and contains data. Does that mean you can do all the things with a file that you can do with a variable? Surprisingly, the answer to that is yes. You can assign a file values by writing data into it. You can also remove data by deleting it from a file. You can even put a file in a list structure by moving it into a directory.

Also similar to variables, files come in two varieties: text and binary. A text file is one you can read with any sort of editor without interpretation; in other words, it is in plain text. Figure 13.1 shows a Python source file in text.

Figure 13.1: *A Python source file shown in Notepad.*

As you can see, the file is very readable and easy to understand (well, if you read Python.) Because this is a text file, it shows only textual characters. It is also easy to modify.

On the other hand, binary files usually require a specific program to manipulate or view them in any way. Figure 13.2 shows a binary file as shown in the Windows Notepad application.

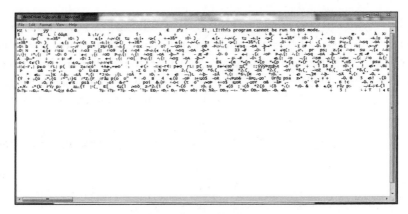

Figure 13.2: *A binary file shown in Notepad.*

As you can see, there is little to understand here. All the characters are weird looking and certainly can't be made into words or even programming constructs. As it happens, this is an image file displayed as if it were text, which is all Notepad knows how to display.

ERROR MESSAGE

Some standard document types—such as JPG, DOC, or PDF—can be displayed by a multitude of different programs, but they are still binary files that can't be directly edited by the end user.

Of course, files aren't variables. The biggest difference is that files can be accessed and used not only by the program that created them, but also by any other program that knows how to read and interpret the data within the file. And unlike variables, which only "live" inside a program while it is running, files are persistent. They stick around until they are deleted or moved to another place, or the device on which they exist is destroyed in a cataclysm. (Let's hope the last one doesn't happen too often to you.)

Directories

If files are like variables, then directories are more like lists in Python. A directory is simply a storage area for files or other directories; they don't actually do anything on their own, but they contain variables that do something. You can iterate over the directory and get back each file within it. Like other kinds of lists, the directory can contain other lists within it, which are simply other directories.

Directories are known by names such as "My Files," "Temp," or anything else you like. Most operating systems allow you to have directory names or filenames over 200 characters, though is unlikely you'll ever use that many. However, there are some limits on what you can call a directory. For example, you can't use the backslash (\) character in a directory name, nor may you use an asterisk (*) or question mark, because these characters are used for special purposes by the operating systems.

So now that you can see files and directories from the perspective of a programmer, where do you go from here?

Creating Files

Before you can do anything with a file, clearly it has to exist. Creating a file is a matter of specifying where you want it to "live," and what the name of the file will be.

In Python, as with most languages, there are various ways to create a file. You can create a brand-new file, or you can "overwrite" an existing file, which truncates its data and allows you to write whatever you want into it.

To create a new file, Python uses the open() function. Listing 13.1 shows you the simplest possible file creation routine.

```
f = open("fred.txt", "w")
f.write("This is a test")
f.close()
```

Listing 13.1

Creating a file in Python.

If you then open the file in a file editor like Notepad, you would see the output string, as shown in Figure 13.3.

Figure 13.3: *The output file shown in Notepad.*

You may be wondering where to find the file. This brings up a good point to remember. If you don't specify a directory path (something like "C:\Temp") in the file name you try to open or create, the operating system will use the current path. When you launched the IDLE editor in Chapter 1, you actually assigned the current path.

On my machine, I used the default of C:\Python33. Therefore, when I want to find the file, I look in the default Python directory, and there it is, as shown in Figure 13.4.

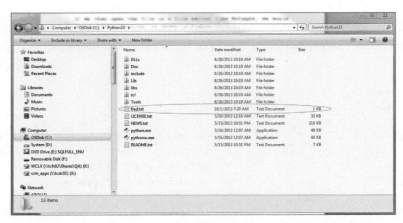

Figure 13.4: *The Python directory showing your newly created file.*

Saving Data to Files

If you notice, you did a little more than create a file in the previous example. That was simply so that I could show you the file actually had something in it that you put there. However, when I first wrote the code, I was in a hurry, and just wrote:

```
f = open("fred.txt", "w")
f.write("This is a test")
```

Imagine my surprise when I launched Notepad and opened the file to find it blank! This is caused by the way in which I opened the file. The open() function actually takes three arguments:

```
open(filename, openmode, buffering)
```

The openmode specifies how you want to open the file. In this case, I opened the file for write, meaning it would overwrite the existing file if it existed. You'll look into some of the other modes here next, but for creating a file this works fine. The buffering flag, however, is used for determining whether the operating system immediately writes data to the file or buffers it in memory, writing it when the file is closed or when enough data has been accumulated to make the write efficient. Back in the dark days of computer technology, this actually made a lot of sense, since disk drives were very slow to write and writing small chunks of data repeatedly could take a lot of time. Today, well, we are stuck with it for backward compatibility.

If you don't set the buffering flag to zero (0), the system will buffer writes. Until the file is closed, the data won't be written to the file. Now, as soon as I close IDLE, the file would be closed automatically and the data would appear in the file on disk. But until that time, or until I wrote sufficient data to the file, it would look blank if you opened it in Notepad or any other editor.

 PROGRAMMING TIP

Files are much more dynamic than they appear on disk. The operating system loads and writes files in "chunks" so when you issue a read or write command, you may or may not actually hit the disk drive. If you find your data is not being saved properly in a file, check to see if you have buffering set on and are failing to close the file.

Putting Data into Files

Earlier, you did a little more than create a file; you also wrote some data in the file. You can write any kind of data to a file, but you have to tell the interpreter what sort of data you want to write there. There are two different sorts of opening modes you can use for a file, as shown in Table 13.1.

Table 13.1   Opening Modes

Mode Letter	Meaning
w	Open a file for writing, using text as the basis.
wb	Open a file for writing, using binary as the basis.

So, for example, when you open a file in text mode, all data that is written to the file is in just that—textual format. What if you try to write data to a file that is not a text string when in text mode? You can see in Listing 13.2 that numbers are being used in a text file.

```
f = open("fred.txt", "w")
i = {1,2,3}
f.write(i)
f.close()
```

Listing 13.2
Writing binary data to a text file.

When you run this little program, the output is the following:

```
Traceback (most recent call last):
  File "F:/Books/Beginning Programming/Chapter 13/ch13_2.py", line 3, in
  <module>
    f.write(i)
TypeError: must be str, not set
```

As you can see, you aren't allowed to write nontextual data to a text file. How can you write out the data then? The str() function enables you to include binary data in a text file. You can change your code to read like what's in Listing 13.3.

```
f = open("fred.txt", "w")
i = {1,2,3}
f.write(str(i))
f.close()
```

Listing 13.3

Writing binary data as text.

If you do this, the new output of your file looks like this:

```
{1, 2, 3}
```

This is pretty much what you'd expect a set to look like in textual format.

PROGRAMMING TIP

If you wonder what something is going to look like in a file, you can simply use the print() function to write it out to the console first, since that function uses the same formatting engine as the write() function.

Where Was That File Again?

Say after you've worked on the programs from earlier in this chapter, you go off and do something else for a bit. Perhaps you write a document for your boss, play a game, or whatever strikes your fancy. You then come back, write another program, and go to look at the output. It doesn't look right; it looks like the last program you wrote. You look at the file in Windows Explorer or the Unix ls command, and the date and time aren't correct—they look the same as when you ran the program earlier in the day. Why is this? The answer lies in the "current directory."

In any operating system, each process has a current directory. It might be the directory from which the program was run, or perhaps it's the default output directory in which files are going to be stored. Whatever it is, it can be changed, either from within the program or by the user running a different program and your program not updating it to where it wishes its data to be written. How are you to know where the file is going now?

In Python, there is a function that exists within the os module called *getcwd()*, for "get current working directory." You can use this function to look for your file by printing out the current working directory after you close your file, as shown in Listing 13.4. Now, by looking at the output from the program, you know where your file is!

```
import os
f = open("fred.txt", "w")
f.write("This is a test")
f.close()
print("You will find the file at: {}".format(os.getcwd()))
```

Listing 13.4
Printing the current working directory.

Naturally, you can also set the current directory within your program to ensure your files get written to the right place. The chdir() (change directory) function takes a single argument, which is the directory you want to set your output to go to.

PROGRAMMING TIP

If you happen to be or have been a Unix programmer, you will probably notice that the os functions map nicely to the Unix command line commands. This is no accident, since the majority of directory functions in all languages come out of the Unix world. Most of these functions also work in Microsoft Windows, although some have slightly different names.

Listing 13.5 shows you how to change the current working directory to C:\\TEMP using the chdir() function.

```
import os

os.chdir("C:\\TEMP")
print("The new directory is: {}".format(os.getcwd()))
```

Listing 13.5
Changing the current directory.

Running the program in IDLE results in the following output to the console:

```
The new directory is: C:\\TEMP
```

As you can see, it works!

Reading Files

Clearly, if you can write data to a file, it is useful to read it back. And not only data that you have written—data that other people have created for you to use can be read into your application. Reading data from a file really isn't any different than writing it to a file, except you have to be able to understand what it is you are reading and apply some sort of logic to it.

In most programming languages, you can read data in one of two ways. First, you can simply read a block of characters and interpret them any way you see fit. This is called *free-form reading.*

In the second method, you have to read the data as it was written, because it consists of specific information. This information can be in textual format or in binary format.

The easiest way to test your file reading, of course, is to first write out the data in the format you want, and then read it back and verify it is correct. In Python, this consists of several different steps:

1. Open a file for write access.

2. Write the data you want into the file.

3. Close the file.

4. Reopen the file for read access.

5. Read in the data you want to read.

6. Process the data.

7. Close the file.

 ERROR MESSAGE

The last step is technically not necessary, since if you don't change a file, closing it won't make any difference. As I mentioned earlier in the chapter, however, if you don't close a file you have written to and the data in that file is buffered, you will likely lose anything you write.

Let's walk through these steps. First, create a file and write out the data you want to read back in later. Listing 13.6 shows the code you will be using; it is really nothing new, except it shows how to write a datetime value to a file.

```python
import datetime
import os

# A free form text example
# First, create a new file and write out the date and time to it
f = open("MyTextFile.txt", "w")
f.write("Todays Date is: {}".format(datetime.datetime.now()))
f.close()
print("Wrote the file to {}".format(os.getcwd()))
```

Listing 13.6

Writing a simple file in Python.

Okay, so you have the date and time that the information was stored into the file persistently saved to disk. How do you get back that information? You now use the read() function. Let's read in a string from Python and see what is what here. You can either add this code to the end of the code in Listing 13.6 or create a brand-new script to use it:

```python
# Reading a free form text file
# Now, let's read it back in
f = open("MyTextFile.txt", "r")
s = f.read(256)
print("I read in {}".format(s))
f.close()
```

PROGRAMMING TIP

Python, like most languages, has a correlation between read() and write() functions. They can rarely be used on the same file at the same time, although you can if you really want to.

If you run the script in Listing 13.6 to generate the text in the file and follow it by running the preceding script, you get the following output from the IDLE console:

```
I read in Todays Date is: 2013-10-03 07:54:15.456910
```

No surprise there; that's what you wrote out. However, how did Python know to read in only that amount of text? In fact, it didn't. If you notice, in the read() function call, you pass in a constant value of 256. That is the maximum number of characters that the read() function will input before terminating. If there are less characters than that in the file, only the ones present will be returned and the rest of the length will be ignored.

So what does this mean exactly for you as the programmer? Say you have a file that has characters in it:

```
123456789012345678901234567890
```

This would be a fixed form text file. In this case, you can see that you have 30 characters. You might ask the read() function to return 15 of them, giving you back "123456789012345." What happens to the rest of the characters? They are still in the file, waiting to be read. If you then read five more characters, you'd get back "67890" in your read() function call. This is called the *file pointer*.

Moving Around Files

Most of the time, you read a file from beginning to end, the same way you might read a book. However, once in a while, you need to skip back and forth, referring back to older sections or jumping forward to find something. Reading files in programming languages is the same process—you can simply allow the underlying code to move through the file in sequential order, reading the file as you need to, or you can change where you want to read or write in the file.

Reading from files is a function of two variables: the position and the length. The position is where a file pointer exists in the file for the file object. This pointer tells the read() function where to start reading. Normally, when you open a file, that pointer is reset to 0 or the beginning of the file; however, you can move things around if you want.

In order to report where you are in a file, you use the tell() function. Tell returns you the off-set, in characters, from the beginning of the file to where the pointer is reading or writing at the moment.

If you want to move the file pointer to a new position, you use the seek() function. The seek() function takes a single argument—the position you want to move to.

ERROR MESSAGE

If you give the seek() function an invalid number, such as a negative value or a value beyond the end of the file, it will generate an error and not move.

Let's take a look at the seek() and tell() functions and see how they work. Listing 13.7 shows you the code.

```python
import datetime
import os
import random

# Create a text file, and write out a bunch of lines.
f = open("MyTextFile2.txt", "w")
for i in range(0,100) :
    f.write("This is line {}".format(i))
f.close()
print("Wrote the file to {}".format(os.getcwd()))

# Now, re-open the file for read access
f = open("MyTextFile2.txt", "r")


# Now, let's jump around to various lines
for i in range(0,5) :
    position = random.randrange(0, 1000)
    f.seek(position)
    s = f.read(30)
    print("At position {} read characters[{}]".format(f.tell(), s))

f.close()
```

Listing 13.7

Random access to a file in Python.

The output from the Listing 13.7 code when it is run is the following:

```
At position 492 read characters[ line 31This is line 32This is]
At position 488 read characters[s is line 31This is line 32Thi]
At position 275 read characters[This is line 17This is line 18]
At position 761 read characters[s line 49This is line 50This i]
At position 797 read characters[ 51This is line 52This is line]
```

What is going on here? There are some interesting bits in the code, moving the file pointer to a random location using the random number function in Python. While random numbers are a fairly complicated subject, basically, you can get a number in a given range using the random functions (which are found in the math library in Python). The randrange() function accepts two numbers, a starting and an ending value—in this case, 0 to 1,000—from which it generates a pseudo-random number that lies between the two. That number is then passed to the seek() function, which positions the file pointer in the file to that position. You then read in a block of characters at that position and print them out for the user to see.

As you can see from the output, the file pointer is not particularly bothered in going back and forth from the front to the end of the file, as you get lines from both the beginning and the end of the file.

PROGRAMMING TIP

You might wonder why you work in terms of file pointers, seeking and telling. The history of programming files comes mostly from the magnetic tape world. With magnetic tapes, you actually had to physically rewind a tape to move backward or fast-forward it to move forward. These concepts have stuck around, in spite of the fact that random access has been a part of the file system for decades.

Finding and Identifying Files in a Directory

Remember our discussion about finding files (see "Where Was That File Again?")? At the time, I said there were issues to understand that you really couldn't "get" without understanding the way files work. It is now time to address those underlying operating system issues.

Now that you understand how to work with the internals of files, including reading from them and writing to them, the next big thing is to understand how to work with the overall file system, including directories and file management.

One of the most common functions in the computer world is obtaining a list of files in a directory. Users use this function all the time to find the file they were working on, to remember where something was stored, or simply to look at what files were created by some program. Files take up space on the persistent storage devices, after all, and sometimes you just need to get rid of some space.

Most modern programming languages provide a direct interface to the file system, and Python is no exception. You can easily get back a list of the files in a given directory using the code in Listing 13.8. Let's take a look at it, and then dig a little deeper to understand what is going on and how you are most likely to use this kind of function.

```python
from os import listdir
from os.path import isfile, join
import os

mypath = input("Enter a directory to list: ")

for f in listdir(mypath) :
    print("File: {}".format(f))
```

Listing 13.8

A file lister in Python.

As you can see, there isn't much to the program: It prompts the user for a directory and then lists all of the files in the directory. Actually, it lists everything in the directory, whether it be a file or a subdirectory, since those can exist, too. A directory is really just a special kind of file that can contain other files, so it will show up in your list. If you run this on the main Windows directory (c:\windows), you should get something like the following:

```
Enter a directory to list: c:\windows
File: $Reconfig$
File: addins
File: AppCompat
File: AppPatch
File: assembly
File: atiogl.xml
File: ativpsrm.bin
File: authtest.txt
File: bfsvc.exe
File: Boot
File: bootstat.dat
File: Branding
File: cfgall.ini
File: cfgwtp.ini
```

But what if you just wanted the files in the directory instead of the directories, subdirectories, and such? Fortunately, there are ways to do this, too. A file can't contain other files, whereas a directory can, so it is important to know if something is an ordinary file or a directory. The operating system keeps track of this with attributes to the file entry in the file system, indicating whether it is a file, a directory, a hard link (something that points to another file or directory), or a system entry. Of all of these, all you really care about are the files, so you'll use the simple isfile() function of Python. Listing 13.9 shows you just how to do this.

```
from os import listdir
from os.path import isfile, join
import os

mypath = input("Enter a directory to list: ")

for f in listdir(mypath) :
    filename = os.path.join(mypath, f)
    if isfile(filename) :
        print("File: {}".format(f))
```

Listing 13.9

Listing only files.

When you run this little script, you get a much smaller list of entries, which looks something like this:

```
Enter a directory to list: c:\windows
File: $Reconfig$
File: addins
File: AppCompat
File: AppPatch
File: assembly
File: atiogl.xml
File: ativpsrm.bin
```

As you can see, a lot of the previous entries from the Listing 13.8 code are missing, as they were directories in the c:\windows main directory.

Obtaining File Information

Once you have the name and complete path of a file, you might wonder what sort of information you can get back about them. A complete path, by the way, is the full drive letter, directory path, and file name, like "C:\MyDirectory\MyFile.txt." You can split this complete file down into pieces, if you like, using the Python functions; you can see how this is done in Listing 13.10. (Naturally, it isn't quite as straightforward as you might like it to be, but welcome to dealing with programmers.)

```
from os import listdir
from os.path import isfile, join
import os

filename = input("Enter a file to parse: ")
drive, path = os.path.splitdrive(filename)
path, filename = os.path.split(path)

print("Drive: {}".format(drive))
print("Path: {}".format(path))
print("FileName: {}".format(filename))
```

Listing 13.10

Splitting a file name.

So if you enter a standard file name, like "C:\Matt\Fred.Txt," the snippet of code will split the file into its standard components. In this case, the components are the drive letter assigned to the file (C:), the path on that drive in which to find the file (the Matt directory), and the actual name of the file (Fred.txt).

PROGRAMMING TIP

You might be wondering why you have to do the splitting in two steps, and the answer is, nobody has a clue. The path.splitdrive() function, however, only returns you the drive and the path of the full file name, whereas the split function only returns you the path and the file name.

You can get more information about the file using some of the other functions in the library as well. For example, you might care about the size of a file. This can be obtained by the stat() function, which is a standard part of most operating system libraries for most programming languages. To use it, you need the full path of the file, as shown in Listing 13.11.

```python
from os import listdir
from os.path import isfile, join
import os

f = input("Enter a file to parse: ")
drive, path = os.path.splitdrive(f)
path, filename = os.path.split(path)

print("Drive: {}".format(drive))
print("Path: {}".format(path))
print("FileName: {}".format(filename))

sz = os.stat(f)
print("Size of the file: {}".format(sz.st_size))
```

Listing 13.11

Getting a file size in Python.

As an example, you might run the program in the Windows directory that exists on every Windows machine:

```
Enter a file to parse: c:\windows\winhelp.exe
Drive: c:
Path: \windows
FileName: winhelp.exe
Size of the file: 256192
```

As you can see, you get the drive (the main drive on my machine, c), the directory or path (\windows), the name of the file you are examining (winhelp.exe), and finally the size of the file in bytes. Doing a directory listing in the c:\windows directory, you see that this is the number of bytes the file occupies on disk.

Storing Preferences

Now that you have some sort of clue as to how to work with files and directories, you might be wondering why you would do such a thing. After all, files are a part of the operating system and really belong to it, right? You shouldn't have to worry about drives and directories and paths and file sizes. The problem is, as a developer, these are the things you should worry about most.

If you are working with most real-world projects, you have to worry about what the user entered. Things like "most recently used file lists" have become a standard in the programming world.

You take for granted the ability to store things like your "preferences" in a program, such as the language in which to display things, the last project you were working on, or even the positions of the parts of the screen you work with. You don't have to do this, of course, but your users will expect it and will whine and gripe about it if you don't.

Rather than go on and on about how you might use this kind of thing, suppose I give you a concrete example of how you would use files to store preferences. In this case, you are going to use something very simple—the format of the date to display in a program. Nothing complicated here, but it will take you through the process you will need to consider when storing things like preferences for your own programs.

First of all, you need to understand the possible "states" of the program. A program state is a set of conditions that exist at any given time. In your preference program, you have two real states to worry about:

- The program has not yet run, meaning there are no preferences set.
- The program has run at least once, meaning that a preference value has been set.

There is a third state, which is when a preference value is changed, but realistically that is no different from the second state.

When the program hasn't run, meaning that the preference data isn't set, you need to decide on a reasonable default value for the preference. Once the program has run, the user may select a preference, and that preference will be saved to the preference file. Finally, the program may be run a second or third (or more) time and the preference modified. Every time the user changes the preference, you need to save it to the persistent storage device and read it in the next time the program runs.

Let's take a look at the code that implements the simplest possible case of a preference storage. The code to implement your storage and retrieval of preference information is shown in Listing 13.12.

```
import datetime

# This is the date format number
dateformat = 0
# Try to open the preferences file
try :
    f = open("prefs.txt", "r")
    # Read in the value
    dateformat = int(f.read(2))
except :
    # The file doesn't exist, use a default
    dateformat = 0

today = datetime.date.today()

print("The date format is {}".format(dateformat))
if dateformat == 0 :
    print("Current date: {}".format(today.strftime("%m/%d/%y")))
elif dateformat == 1 :
    print("Current date: {}".format(today.strftime("%d/%m/%y")))
elif dateformat == 2 :
    print("Current date: {}".format(today.strftime("%y/%m/%d")))
else :
    print("Unknown date format: {}".format(dateformat))

dateformat = int(input("Enter date format. 0 = MM/DD/YY, 1 = DD/MM/YY, 2 = YY/
    MM/DD: "))

# Save the format
f = open("prefs.txt", "w")
f.write(str(dateformat))
f.close()
```

Listing 13.12

Setting and saving preferences.

As you can see, you first *default* the date format. This is important since it is assumed that you will always have a valid date format to work with. You should think carefully when setting defaults, since most users never bother with them until it is something important to them.

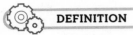

DEFINITION

Defaults are the program setting if the user does not select anything for that value. It is the programmer's responsibility to make sure that all persistent settings for a given value have a default value.

The next step in the process is to try to open the preferences file. Remember, if this is the first time you are running this program, the file isn't going to exist. So you need to test for that by opening it for read access. Opening a file for read access will fail if the file isn't there, whereas opening it for write access will almost always succeed.

If the file exists, you read in the dateformat the user has previously selected and use it to display the value of the current date. If the file does not exist, you use your default value to display the date. Whatever the case, when you are done, you save the current value of the dateformat variable back to the file so that it will be there next time.

That should be it, right? Except that it really isn't. You've considered the "happy path" (nothing going wrong) case of when the file does not exist. What you haven't looked at yet is what happens when the file does exist. In this case, the value will be read from the settings file and loaded into the variable and then the value display. What happens if the data is invalid or the dateformat is somehow wrong?

Notice the if-elif-else block in Listing 13.12. You do handle the case where the date format is outside of the range. You do not, however, reset it to something valid, so all the user gets is an error message. That's hardly very friendly. You might try modifying the program so that the user can't enter an invalid date format value. The ideal way to do this is to use the datetime class to try to parse the string, catching any errors that might pop up. For example:

```
from datetime import datetime

d1 = input("Enter a date (mm/dd/yyyy): ")
date_object = datetime.strptime(d1, '%m/%d/%Y')
print("Month: {0}. Day: {1}. Year: {2}\n".format(date_object.month, date_
    object.day, date_object.year))
```

Now you can test the input to see if it is valid:

```
Enter a date (mm/dd/yyyy): 12/31/2005
Month: 12. Day: 31. Year: 2005
Enter a date (mm/dd/yyyy): 12/32/2005
Traceback (most recent call last):
  File "J:/Python3_3/datechecker.py", line 4, in <module>
    date_object = datetime.strptime(d1, '%m/%d/%Y')
  File "J:\Python3_3\lib\_strptime.py", line 500, in _strptime_datetime
    tt, fraction = _strptime(data_string, format)
  File "J:\Python3_3\lib\_strptime.py", line 337, in _strptime
    (data_string, format))
ValueError: time data '12/32/2005' does not match format '%m/%d/%Y'
```

So if you want to test a date, you could write code that looks like this:

```
from datetime import datetime

try :
    d1 = input("Enter a date (mm/dd/yyyy): ")
    date_object = datetime.strptime(d1, '%m/%d/%Y')
    print("Month: {0}. Day: {1}. Year: {2}\n".format(date_object.month, date_
object.day, date_object.year))
except ValueError:
    print("Invalid Date!")
```

The Least You Need to Know

- Files are an essential part of programming, as they store data between runs of a program.
- Directories are just a "special" kind of file that can contain other files.
- Files can be enumerated, created, deleted, and modified within your Python code.
- You can read a file either sequentially or by moving about it in a random fashion.
- Preferences for a user can be stored in persistent files so they can be loaded for each run of the program.

Programming with Class(es)

Back in the early days of programming, we had what was commonly referred to as *linear programming*. That is, a program started at the top, ended at the bottom, and followed all of the steps along the way, only detouring for conditions and exceptional events. In other words, all programs out there looked a lot like the little program snippets you've been writing in this book.

However, when you write straight-line code like this, it is very hard to reuse it. The reason for this is you have lots of variables that are tied to the program state and to the specific inputs that the program uses.

Objects are a way to solve this problem. An object "encapsulates" a certain amount of functionality devoted to a specific subject. Classes are the foundation of object-oriented programming. In this chapter, I'll tell you more about them and their relation to object-oriented programming.

In This Chapter

- The four object-oriented programming principles
- How a class object works
- Public versus private accessibility
- How to derive child classes
- Ways to embed classes
- Adding attributes to a class at runtime

The Principles of Object-Oriented Programming

In the programming world, nothing is complete unless it has a set of principles that guide it and best practices that help you implement it. The principles are often rather vague and more ideological than concrete, but at least you can get something out of them. Object-oriented programming has four basic principles, or tenets, that make it up. Let's take a look at them and try to make some sense of them.

ERROR MESSAGE

Please understand, there is absolutely nothing wrong with writing a little program to accomplish a specific task and not loading it down with a lot of esoteric concepts just because "that's how it is done." The reality is, that's not how it is done. Programs below a certain size and level of criticality rarely need a lot of design and thought before they are written. If all I want is a script to change the names of a bunch of files, I hardly need to have a full requirements document with a bunch of defined objects and other "cool" stuff just because that's how we do it. I can just write my script and use it. That's the power of programming.

Encapsulation

Encapsulation means putting things into capsules. In the programming world, it means keeping things protected from outside interference.

For example, let's say that you had an object that modeled a car. The object might contain attributes (internal variables) for the state of each tire, the state of the engine, the current speed, and so forth. If the speed were a simple variable that anyone could change, you would be able to have a car go from, say, 100 miles per hour forward to 50 miles per hour in reverse instantly. While the math works out fine, it is hardly realistic to have a vehicle do this.

Therefore, you protect the speed variable and provide "accessors" to allow you to change the speed. For example, you might tell the car to decelerate to 50 miles per hour from 100 miles per hour. The object would then take care of doing the proper physics to determine how long this would take.

Abstraction

The notion of abstraction is, well, abstract. The idea is to take away the details that distract you from the essential "thingness" of the object and focus on what really matters.

Continuing with the car example, you have certain attributes (color, weight, number of cylinders, and so on) and certain functionality (accelerate, decelerate, turn, and so on) you care about. The rest of the car doesn't really matter to you from a programming perspective and frees you to look at the car as a simple object you can manipulate. The real thing to take away from this is that you don't care how a car is implemented—all you care about is the functionality and attributes that the car provides to you.

Like a file object, you don't care about how the actual implementation "talks" to the operating system—what you care about is that your file gets created on disk and that the data you write to it is saved there when you close the file.

Inheritance

Like people inherit traits from their parents, objects can have parents and inherit traits from them. To use the car example again, you might have a base model car that has a certain type of very basic functionality, such as accelerate and decelerate or turn and stop. Now, you might have a deluxe version of the car that can also fly. (I want a flying car; why shouldn't I be able to create one? Well, at least in code.)

The notion here is that your flying car can do everything the basic car can do and more. That means that your flying car is a car, just with more functionality. Similar to this, there is another concept called *composition,* whereby an object has a relationship with another object; I'll talk about that idea later in this chapter.

In any case, think of inheritance the same way you do with parents and children, and you'll do fine.

Polymorphism

Once you understand inheritance, polymorphism makes a bit of sense. It's an insanely big word that means "works the same as" (which makes you wonder why people find it necessary to use big words when little ones work just as well). The idea of polymorphism is that if a given function or method works on an object of type "base," it should work fine on an object of type "derived," so long as derived inherits from base.

To understand the problem a little bit, let's go back to the car example. Imagine you have your base car and your flying car that is "inherited from" the base car. Now, let's imagine that you have a function you've written that accepts a single argument, a car object.

That function tells the car to accelerate to twice its current speed. To do this, it calls a "method" on the car object, which I will talk about in just a little while. For now, think of a method as a function that knows a little more than a regular function.

Whether the car is a flying sort or a regular sort, it uses its own internal accelerate functionality to increase the speed of the car. That means the function works on either a regular base car or a flying one, hence the term *polymorphic*.

PROGRAMMING TIP

The tenets of object-oriented programming are neither complicated nor onerous. Understanding why they exist makes you a better programmer and makes your programs easier to understand and debug. It also makes the code you write easier for other people to use.

Classes and Objects

Now that you understand the basics of object-oriented programming, you may wonder, what an object is. Before I tackle that question, however, I'd like to first define class for you.

Python defines a class as "a user-defined prototype for an object that defines a set of attributes that characterize any object of the class." Oh, well, that's clear.

Here's a simpler definition you can use for now; it isn't exactly 100 percent accurate, but it works out well enough to understand the concept: A class is a template from which you can create concrete objects. So really, a class is a cookie cutter or a blueprint.

When you are creating a class, think of it as creating a blueprint for a bunch of objects of a given type. Let's say, for example, your program's job is to keep track of stock prices for a dozen different securities. Clearly, you could simply have a list of security names or identifiers, as well as a list of stock prices and another of dates, but that doesn't really make a lot of sense. What you really want is a list of stock price objects. A stock price object would contain the date the price was entered, the value of the stock in whatever units you choose, the stock symbol, and whatever other information you might want to track for a given stock (perhaps the industry or sector of the stock). Those parameters for what should be included in the object make up a single class.

An object, which is really just a variable in Python and any other programming language, is a concrete instance of a class. So while a class has a blueprint that says it contains a stock name and price, the object contains the actual values for the name and price.

While there is only ever one class definition, there can be hundreds of object definitions for a given class. This isn't really any different from the way you program regular variables. Consider the following little program snippet:

```
a = 1
b = 2
c = 3
```

In this case, you have three variables: a, b, and c. These variables happen to be integers, mostly because you stored integer values in them. The "class" for these objects is *integer,* while the objects themselves are just instances of the integer class. Integers don't have any cool attributes or methods, so all you can really do with them is math and printing.

The idea here, though, is to see that there is a template for the integer class, which happens to be prebuilt in Python (and all other languages). Instances of the class are called *variables* and contain values.

The Life and Times of a Class Object

Although I've said that class objects are just normal variables like integers or strings, that isn't quite true. A class object has a lifetime, just as the others do, called the *scope* of the object. However, unlike a string or a numeric value, the class object contains functionality that is called at specific times during the lifetime of the object. Specifically, there are two important states of functionality: start-up and shutdown.

Constructors and Destructors

Like a program, a class object is started up, during which time it is initialized using whatever values the programmer wishes to set and defaults used for other values. The process of starting up a class object is called *construction,* and the initial method that is called is known as the *constructor.* (The actual name of the method varies from language to language, but thinking in terms of constructors will do you just fine with object-oriented programming.)

Likewise, at the end of the lifetime of the object, it is destroyed. Unlike a typical variable, however, the class object can do some work when it is being destroyed. Classes contain a "destructor" that is called at the end of the lifetime of the variable.

PROGRAMMING TIP

Understand that while the methods constructor and destructor are part of the class definition, they are invoked for the object being created or destroyed.

How Class Objects Work

Realistically, the only way I can really discuss this in any detail is to show you a code example, which you can find in Listing 14.1. Please don't be terrified by all the new things in here; I promise I will examine and explain them one at a time.

```python
class Point:
    def __init__( self, x=0, y=0):
        self.x = x
        self.y = y
        print("Class Point object created")
    def __del__(self):
        class_name = self.__class__.__name__
        print("Class {} object destroyed".format(class_name))
    def print(self):
        print("X = {}".format(self.x))
        print("Y = {}".format(self.y))

p1 = Point(10,10)
p2 = Point(20,20)
p1.print()
p2.print()
del(p1)
```

Listing 14.1

A Python class.

Just to give you an idea of what is going on, you can run the little program snippet and get the following output:

```
Class Point object created
Class Point object created
X = 10
Y = 10
X = 20
Y = 20
Class Point object destroyed
```

PROGRAMMING TIP

When trying to understand a given program or class or simple piece of code, break it down into the smallest units you can grasp and then slowly work through them until you understand the entire module. This method, called *decomposition,* works with virtually all programming models.

Alright, let's start out by looking at the code in Listing 14.1 piece by piece. The first piece of the equation is the definition of the class itself. The "class" keyword, which is pretty much the same in every programming language, indicates you are going to be defining a new class. Remember, this isn't a variable; this code will not be executed until you instantiate (or create) a variable of the type of this class. A class has a name—in this case, Point—that illustrates what the class is to do. In this code, you are modeling a graphical two-dimensional point, so the name makes a lot of sense. Choosing your names carefully will help those trying to find and use your classes.

Once you have defined the name of the class, the next step is to define the functionality that goes with it. This class is going to be extremely simple so you can build on it as the chapter goes along. For now, it only has three methods, which are functions that can be called for that class object.

The first method is a special one in Python; it is called *__init__()*. This method is called when the object is first instantiated and is equivalent to the "constructor" I talked about earlier. The __init__() method takes three arguments. Two of them are just the initialization values for the x and y attributes of the point and really aren't too interesting. The third argument, however, is very interesting. The "self" argument is the object being operated on. As you will notice when you use the methods of the class, you don't actually pass anything for the self argument; the interpreter does that for you when you use the "dot" notation of the class object. Take, for example, the following:

```
p.print()
```

This is the equivalent of saying Point.print(p). You are telling the interpreter which object you want to print, because each object is different and contains different data. So whenever you see the "self" parameter (called *this* in some languages), just think of it as "the object for which I am working."

Within the __init__() method, you assign some attributes to the self parameter:

```
self.x = x
self.y = y
```

You will notice that x and y aren't defined anywhere. That is because Python is interpreted and allows you to add new attributes anytime and anywhere you like. However, from a strictly object-oriented programming viewpoint, your objects should contain consistent lists of attributes.

In this case, you are assigning the values of the passed-in arguments x and y to the self object attributes x and y. These are not the same things. Once you leave the __init__() method, the self object will be modified to hold onto these values. The print() method of the class verifies this.

The next method defined in your class is the __del__() method. Like all other methods that begin and end with underscores, the __del__() method is internal to the interpreter. You can often call these methods directly, but it is considered bad form to do so. When the object goes out of scope and the memory is reclaimed for that object, the __del__() method will be called as the last action for that object. This gives you a chance to log information, clean up files, or do whatever needs to be done when the object is destroyed. Look at the method:

```
def __del__(self):
    class_name = self.__class__.__name__
    print("Class {} object destroyed".format(classname))
```

As you can see by the output, the program is simply printing out the class name of the object that is being destroyed (in this case, Point). You don't have to implement a destructor, and quite often they serve no useful purpose. Some people use them to keep track of the number of objects of a given class that are created or destroyed, but realistically, unless you have resources that you are using in your application (such as files that are open), you don't need to worry about the destructor method.

 PROGRAMMING TIP

Most of the methods that Python provides for you are automatically created when you define a class. It is important to know about them; however, you don't have to implement much of anything for a class. You can create one that just stores your data, if you like.

Our final method of the class at this point is a method called *print()*. This simply displays the data for a given object of class Point. It looks like the following:

```
def print(self):
    print("X = {}".format(self.x))
    print("Y = {}".format(self.y))
```

As you can see, the self keyword is used to extract the proper values from the object you are working on to print. For the preceding code, it prints out the x and y values for the object. There isn't much to the method, but it does what it is supposed to do.

The print method is a decent example of encapsulation, in that it accesses internal variables in the object only within the scope of that object. In Python, all variables are, by default, "public"—that is, anyone can access them. For example, given the Point class, you can write the following:

```
p1 = Point(20, 30)
Class Point object created
>>> p1.x
20
```

As you can see, this does violate the principle of encapsulation a bit. This is due to accessibility.

Class Variable Accessibility

One type of accessibility available in an object-oriented application, as you have seen, is *public* accessibility. In a public scenario, anyone can read or write to a class variable. That means that in your Point class, anyone can change the internal data of the class anytime they want. This is usually not an optimal solution, but it is the default access model in Python.

Another sort of accessibility is called *private*. In private access mode, only the class itself can touch the internal member attributes (or variables) that are defined. Python does allow for private access, but it isn't quite as straightforward as in some other languages.

If you preface your attribute name with a double underscore, the interpreter treats that value as private. That means that others will not be able to access the value from outside of the class and can only use the methods defined for the class to change the value. Listing 14.2 shows how you accomplish this.

```
class Point:
    def __init__( self, x=0, y=0):
        self.x = x
        self.y = y
        self.__mult = x * y
        print("Class Point object created")
    def __del__(self):
        class_name = self.__class__.__name__
        print("Class {} object destroyed".format(class_name))
    def print(self) :
        print("X = {}".format(self.x))
        print("Y = {}".format(self.y))
        print("Mult = {}".format(self.__mult))
    def getMult(self):
        return self.__mult
    def setMult(self, val):
        self.__mult = val
```

Listing 14.2

A full implementation of the class Point.

Now, if you create a Point object in the interpreter and try to access the __mult attribute, you will get an error:

```
>>> p = Point(1, 1)
Class Point object created
>>> print (p.__mult)
Traceback (most recent call last):
  File "<pyshell#12>", line 1, in <module>
    print (p.__mult)
AttributeError: 'Point' object has no attribute '__mult'
```

You can still access the __mult attribute, but you have to do it through accessor methods, which are defined in the class now:

```
>>> p.setMult(200)
>>> print(p.getMult())
200
```

This is private access, because only the class itself can access the variables defined within it.

PROGRAMMING TIP

There is a third form of access called *protected access,* in which only the class and all classes inherited from that class can access the attributes defined in the base class. However, you won't have to worry about that one too much.

Deriving Child Classes

If you recall from earlier, I talked a bit about deriving child classes from base classes. Like all object-oriented languages, Python allows you to derive classes from other base classes. This permits you to inherit all the functionality of the base class while extending it to allow the end user even more functionality.

Normally, the way this works is that you have a very generic base class that is then subsumed into more specific child classes. For example, you might have a base class that defined a vehicle. Vehicles have a few basic attributes—they have some number of wheels, perhaps a color, and a maximum speed. Clearly, real vehicles have a lot more than that, but that's really enough for now.

Listing 14.3 shows what you have for a base class Vehicle.

```
class Vehicle:
    def __init__(self, name, wheels, color ):
        self.name = name
        self.wheels = wheels
        self.color = color
    def print(self):
        print("The {} vehicle has {} wheels and is {} color".format(
            self.name, self.wheels, self.color))
    def getName(self):
        return self.name
    def getWheels(self):
        return self.wheels
    def getColor(self):
        return self.color

    def setName(self, name):
        self.name = name
    def setWheels(self, wheels):
        self.wheels = wheels
    def setColor(self, color):
        self.color = color
```

Listing 14.3

The base Vehicle class.

Now, clearly, the base class Vehicle is pretty generic. You have the number of wheels, the color of the thing, and so forth. You might also have methods to calculate the miles per gallon of gas, the top speed, or whatever you want to calculate for all vehicles; however, it requires a lot of inputs for something like a car. We all know a car is a vehicle, that it has four wheels, and so forth.

You might define a subclass of vehicle called Car that sets the defaults for all of the items, so the end user doesn't have to worry about them; Listing 14.4 gives you the setup.

```
class Car(Vehicle):
    def __init__(self, color):
        super().__init__("car", 4, color)
```

Listing 14.4

A derived class.

Taking a look at the derived class, it doesn't look very complicated, does it? It isn't, and that's how things should be. Object-oriented programming is supposed to make things easier, not more difficult. In fact, all your derived class does right now is initialize the Vehicle class with the rational defaults for a Car object. You still have to specify a color, since all cars are not the same color, but the remainder of the attributes are set to valid default values for you.

One of the important things about deriving child classes is you can use all of the functionality of the base class within that child class for free. Consider the following code in Listing 14.5, which relies on the classes you've defined in the previous code listings.

```
c1 = Car("blue")
c2 = Car("red")
c1.print()
c2.print()
```

Listing 14.5

Using base class functionality in a child class.

The output from this little code snippet is as follows:

```
The car vehicle has 4 wheels and is blue color
The car vehicle has 4 wheels and is red color
```

The important thing here is that the print() function is not defined in the Car class; it is defined in the base Vehicle class. By the way, in case you missed it, you "told" Python the Car class was derived from the Vehicle class in the very first line of the definition of the Car class in Listing 14.4:

```
class Car(Vehicle):
```

By placing the name of another valid class name within the parentheses following the name of the class, you have indicated to the interpreter you want to derive from that class. This is important, since the interpreter needs to know exactly what functionality is available to it when it goes to instantiate an instance of the class at runtime.

The next interesting part of the Car class is in the constructor (the __init__() method) of the class. It is this line:

```
super().__init__("car", 4, color)
```

The super() function is interesting, because it figures out what the class this class is derived from and invokes methods at that class level. In your case, the preceding line is the equivalent of saying the following:

```
Vehicle.__init__("car", 4, color)
```

This would call the __init__() method of the Vehicle class within the constructor for the Car class. This allows you to reuse the initialization and checking methods of the base class within the derived class.

PROGRAMMING TIP

When you call the _init_() method of the Vehicle class, it is kind of like you created a Vehicle object, which is really exactly what you are doing. First, you create the base class object (Vehicle), and then you create any derived classes and initialize all of their data. Again, you are getting all of the initialization functionality for free!

Overriding Functionality in a Child Class

Now you might be wondering, *What if I want most of what a base class has to offer but need to change some of it?* You can write new functionality into your child class that does what the base class did. If you remember your introduction to object-oriented programing, however, you'll know you need to be able to write a function that can accept any base or derived class and treat them the same way. Suppose, for example, you wrote a function to display a vehicle:

```
def DisplayVehicle(v):
    print("Displaying vehicle:")
    v.print()
```

Right now, this would simply call the base print() method of the Vehicle class and would be the same for all Vehicles, whether they are base or Cars. However, you can change this functionality by adding to the Car class:

```
class Car(Vehicle):
    def __init__(self, color):
        super().__init__("car", 4, color)
    def print(self):
        print("I am a car and I am {}".format(self.color))
```

Notice that you've implemented a new method in the Car class. Well, it isn't a new method; it is the same named method as in the Vehicle class. If you look at the entire set of code, as shown in Listing 14.6, you'll see what's being done here.

```
class Vehicle:
    def __init__(self, name, wheels, color ):
        self.name = name
        self.wheels = wheels
        self.color = color
    def print(self):
        print("The {} vehicle has {} wheels and is {} color".format(
            self.name, self.wheels, self.color))
    def getName(self):
        return self.name
    def getWheels(self):
        return self.wheels
    def getColor(self):
        return self.color
```

```
        def setName(self, name):
            self.name = name
        def setWheels(self, wheels):
            self.wheels = wheels
        def setColor(self, color):
            self.color = color

    class Car(Vehicle):
        def __init__(self, color):
            super().__init__("car", 4, color)
        def print(self):
            print("I am a car and I am {}".format(self.color))

    def DisplayVehicle(v):
        print("Displaying vehicle:")
        v.print()

    c1 = Car("blue")
    c2 = Car("red")
    c1.print()
    c2.print()
    DisplayVehicle(c1)
    DisplayVehicle(c2)
```

Listing 14.6

The updated classes with overridden method.

As you can see, you are implementing the same method (print) in both the base class and the derived class, Car. When you call the function that ends up calling that method, what happens? As always, the easiest way to find out is to run the code:

```
I am a car and I am blue
I am a car and I am red
Displaying vehicle:
I am a car and I am blue
Displaying vehicle:
I am a car and I am red
```

The derived class does call its derived method. What happens if you use a base class?

```
>>> v1 = Vehicle("semi", 18, "white")
>>> DisplayVehicle(v1)
Displaying vehicle:
The semi vehicle has 18 wheels and is white color
```

Once again, the proper method was called—in this case, the base class print() method. So, as you can see, Python definitely supports the object-oriented paradigms for polymorphism and inheritance.

PROGRAMMING TIP

In the preceding example, you can also see how the abstraction paradigm comes into play with your wrapping of attributes for "objects" like cars and other vehicles.

Multiple Inheritance

Depending on how you build your classes, sometimes it would be very nice to be able to use more than one of them in a derived class. For example, suppose you have one class that supports saving an object to disk and another class that supports displaying objects using their individual attributes. You want to create a third class that does something but has the ability to save itself to disk and to print out its attributes. For this, you need to inherit from both the base classes. This is called *multiple inheritance.*

Many object-oriented languages support multiple inheritance in one form or another, and Python happens to be one of them. Let's take a look at how it works, without getting too involved in the nitty-gritty details.

Listing 14.7 shows a multiple inheritance structure, along with a little bit of code to show you what could be done.

```
import datetime

class SaveToDisk:
    def __init__(self, filename):
        self.filename = filename

    def save(self, obj):
        # open the file
        f = open(filename, "w")
        # write the object to the file
        f.write(str(obj))

class PrintOutAttributes:
    def print(self):
        for a in self.__dict__:
            print(a, self.__dict__[a])
```

```
class MyObject(SaveToDisk, PrintOutAttributes):
    def __init__(self):
        self.myname = "MyObject"
        self.mytime = datetime.date.today()
        self.value = 123
        self.randomstring = "1asdfadf"
```

Listing 14.7

A multiple inheritance structure.

As you can see by the class definition line for MyObject, the class derives from both
SaveToDisk and PrintOutAttributes. That means it can use methods from either or both
classes, as well as any that are defined within the child class itself. This is an extremely
powerful technique in object-oriented programming—combining unlike things to form a
stronger class with the best of all worlds.

Of course, things like this come with a price. One such price is that if you inherit from two
classes that have a method with the same name, you have problems.

Consider the following code in Listing 14.8, which can be duplicated in any language that
supports multiple inheritance.

```
class A:
    def doit(self):
        print("A::doit")

class B:
    def doit(self):
        print("B::doit()")

class C(A,B):
    def didit(self):
        B.doit(self)
```

Listing 14.8

A multiple inheritance snafu.

Now, when you create a C object and call the doit() method, which one gets called? In
Python, the problem is dealt with by the interpreter, which simply selects the first one available and calls it. However, other languages don't have that kind of intelligence and cause
serious errors.

You can specify which doit() to call, as shown in the didit() function in Listing 14.8. Take a look at some output from this code and you'll see what I mean:

```
>>> c = C()
>>> c.didit()
B::doit()
>>> c.doit()
A::doit
```

As you can see, calling doit() by itself calls the class A version of the method. Calling didit() by itself specifies the class B version. What happens if you pass this class to a function?

```
def func1(cObj):
    c.doit()
>>> c = C()
>>> func1(c)
A::doit
```

Again, the interpreter is smart enough to use the first version. Python has no notion of "casting" a class to a subclass, but the concept does exist in many other languages. In those cases, you will see the C object "cast" (or changed to) a B or A object within the code to get at specific functionality. You can accomplish the same thing in Python on a method-by-method basis by doing things like this:

```
def func2(bObj):
    B.doit(bObj)
```

This will directly call the class B version of the doit() function.

ERROR MESSAGE

While multiple inheritance can be an awfully cool thing, it is also rather confusing to the beginning programmer and leads to unexpected results and problems. You should be aware of the technique in case you see it in code, but there is really no reason to use it in your own code unless absolutely necessary. Always try to keep your code as simple as possible; remember, someday you will have to maintain it.

Embedding Classes

When you are working with multiple classes, you'll naturally want to combine them. You've read earlier in this chapter how you can combine two classes using inheritance in order to get all of the functionality from one class into another. However, there is another way of doing things that is quite common as well and much more useful to programmers. That is the embedded class, or the "has a" relationship.

When you derive one class from another, you give the end user of your class access to all of the functionality of the base class. This is often exactly what you want, so it is a good thing. But what if you don't want them to be able to use all of that functionality? Say, for example, your class requires access to configuration information for the program. If you derive your class from a configuration class, the end user will be able to not only read all of your configurations but change them as well, since that's what the configuration class does.

Quite often, you don't want the end user even knowing about things like configuration; because it is a part of the application and is set in the base classes that you have created, you don't want anyone messing with them. Yet you might have a class that needs access to that information. You reconcile the two problems and allow your own code access while denying the end user that same access with an embedded class.

Let's imagine you have a configuration class that manages certain information in your application. The code for the class is shown in Listing 14.9.

```
class Configuration:
    def __init__(self):
        self.numusers = 1
        self.bkgdcolor = "green"
        self.filename = "myfile.txt"
    def getNumUsers(self):
        return self.numusers
    def setNumUsers(self, numusers):
        self.numusers = numusers
    def getBackgroundColor(self):
        return self.bkgdcolor;
    def setBackgroundColor(self, color):
        self.bkgdcolor = color
    def getFileName(self):
        return self.filename;
    def setFileName(self, filename):
        self.fileName = filename
```

Listing 14.9

The Configuration class.

Clearly, you don't want some of this information changed. For example, the file name in the Configuration class needs to stay at what you set it to; if it changes, you would have no idea where the configuration information went! This wouldn't be a good thing, particularly when you are trying to track down a problem in your application later on.

If you were to create our own Program class and derive it from Configuration, you would be allowing the end user access to all of the information in the configuration file. A better alternative is to allow the Program class to have a "has a" relationship to the Configuration class. Consider the following code:

```
class Program:
    def __init__(self):
        self.config = Configuration()

    def getFileName(self):
        return self.config.filename
```

In this case, you have a Program class that has an attribute called *config*, which is a valid configuration file. You can then expose only those portions of the configuration you want—for example, allowing the user to see what the name of the configuration file is. If you run this little program script, you'll see what I mean:

```
>>> p = Program()
>>> p.getFileName()
'myfile.txt'
```

Users can get back the information they want, but they have no direct way to change it.

Dynamic Attributes

The final topic in class definitions is that of dynamic attributes. This is a subject that applies more to Python than other languages, although you can certainly implement the same thing in virtually any programming language.

The biggest advantage to an interpreted, rather than compiled, language is that things aren't evaluated until the line of code comes into focus—that is, you can change the code or the data at any time, so long as it isn't currently being evaluated by the interpreter. This is important, since it means you can add attributes to a class at runtime.

There are two ways to add attributes to a class at runtime. One involves some fairly complex methodology using the set_attr() and get_attr() functions of Python. Because this is so very specific to the Python language and really has nothing to do with programming as a whole, let's skip that one.

PROGRAMMING TIP

Just because I say that something is a bit more complex than I want to handle in this book doesn't mean you shouldn't check it out for yourself. The only way you will ever really learn about programming is to explore it on your own and learn new techniques and technologies by playing with them.

The second method for adding attributes is to add them to the class object rather than the class itself. For example, you might do something like this:

```
class MyFoo:
    def __init__(self):
        self.name = "Fred"

f = MyFoo()
f.mynewattribute = "irving"
```

Now the "mynewattribute" attribute or property does not apply to the class MyFoo. Rather, it only applies to the instance of the MyFoo class called *f*. You can show this easily enough, as illustrated in the following code:

```
class MyFoo:
    def __init__(self) :
        self.name = "Fred"

f = MyFoo()
f.mynewattribute = "irving"
print(f.mynewattribute)

g = MyFoo()
print(g.mynewattribute)
```

The output from this little snippet is the following:

```
>>>
irving
Traceback (most recent call last):
  File "Q:/Books/Beginning Programming/Chapter 14/ch14_10.py", line 10, in
  <module>
    print(g.mynewattribute)
AttributeError: 'MyFoo' object has no attribute 'mynewattribute'
```

As you can see, the object *g* doesn't have the new attribute. This shows how you can add your own personal "tags" to objects.

PROGRAMMING TIP

You can also add properties to the class dynamically, but that is beyond the scope of this book. If you wish, check out online resources about the set_attr() and get_attr() methods of objects to understand how the process works.

The Least You Need to Know

- Classes are "templates" for variables you want to create.
- A class may implement many methods or just a very few—it is up to you.
- Every instance of a class is a different variable that can contain different information.
- You can derive a class from an existing class (known as a child class via single inheritance) or from several existing classes (known as a child class via multiple inheritance).

Working with the Python Environment

With the Python environment, you can produce quality software and find problems in your code. In this part, you learn about the programming editor and the integrated debugger, which will allow you to determine why your program is not behaving as it should be. You also learn the process of designing applications, as "real" programmers do. I also cover collaboration with users, as well as requirements gathering, testing, and improving programs through iterative development.

Graphics and Python

We've all seen pretty works of art on computer screens. Many of us have worked with charts and graphs to provide information to our bosses in an easy-to-understand way. All of these presentations are forms of graphics. Whether you are drawing a line or bar graph, an image displayed on the screen, or a fractal image that just looks gorgeous for no apparent reason, you are presenting a graphical display.

Python, like many languages, does not have any sort of built-in graphics functionality. Graphics are too machine- and operating system–dependent to make it possible for compiler or interpreter writers to create independent graphic components that work across the board. Fortunately, there are third-party graphic libraries that work across many, if not all, machines and operating systems. The Python distribution contains one of these libraries: the turtle graphics module. In this chapter, you'll learn about this module and how you can use it to make graphics in Python.

In This Chapter

- Turtle graphics explained
- Drawing simple shapes or random displays
- How to fill in shapes
- How to write and display text on the graphics screen
- Creating fractals
- Making charts and graphs

What Are Turtle Graphics?

Turtle graphics are based on the simplest concepts in graphical programming. The turtle library is intended to provide an easy-to-use and easy-to-learn approach to drawing graphics on a screen for the user to view. The underlying concept, believe it or not, is that your cursor is a turtle moving around on the screen. Based on the commands you give, the "turtle" will move to that location. This may seem odd, but it is actually quite easy to work with and even easier to produce simple graphics displays for the end user from your Python application.

> **PROGRAMMING TIP**
>
> Turtle graphics concepts did not originate with Python; in fact, you can find them in many other programming language libraries running on most machines and operating systems. Understanding the underlying concepts of how turtle graphics work will aid you in learning graphical programming in Python and many other programming languages.

How Do Turtle Graphics Work?

Behind the scenes, the turtle graphics library does a lot of work in setting up a screen and drawing to it so that it works properly on all settings. The turtle graphics library uses the Tkinter library, which is a cross-platform library that allows applications to be written that run on any machine using any operating system. Fortunately, you really don't need to know any of this. All you do need to know is that the turtle graphics routines will create their own display window. That means you can't easily embed graphics within your own program. This is not normally a problem, since graphics tend to be separate from any sort of information you wish displayed in text.

In any case, the process for using turtle graphics is the same. You set up a "screen" that the graphics code will use to display its data. Next, you do whatever work you want to do to display graphics on the screen. You might process some data from an external source or draw a pretty fractal or graphic primitive like a box or a circle. In any case, you process the graphics until you are finished and then either wait for the user to close the graphics window or simply close it yourself after some period of time elapses.

Turtle graphics work pretty simply. You start at a given position and move to a new position on the screen. You can either have the "pen" down or up during a move. If the "pen" is down, a line is drawn between the old position and the new one. That's all there is to it, for the most part.

Of course, there is some setup involved before you can do any drawing. You first need to import the turtle graphics module, which fortunately imports all of the modules it needs by itself. You only need to type one of the following in the Python interpreter:

```
import turtle
```

or

```
from turtle import *
```

Next, you need to create a "screen" that will handle the display of the drawings. To create a turtle, you just instantiate (that is, create an instance of) the Turtle class:

```
myTurtle = turtle.Turtle();
```

Finally, you need to create a "turtle" that will do the moving for you. You can create as many turtles as you want, and each will move independently of the others.

To set the position of the turtle, use the goto() function; the x and y are where you place the coordinates in pixels:

```
goto(x,y)
```

For example, "goto(100,50)" will move the turtle to a position 100 pixels from the left side and 50 pixels from the top. The following are some other common pieces of code you'll use when making graphics:

- **turtle.forward(***pixels***)** tells the turtle to move forward the number of pixels you want it to move.

- **turtle.right(***pixels***)** tells the turtle to turn right and go the number of pixels you specify.

- **turtle.left(***pixels***)** tells the turtle to turn left and go the number of pixels you specify.

 PROGRAMMING TIP

Turtle graphics seem pretty easy, right? There's a reason for that. Turtle graphics were actually originally designed for kids to create graphics programs, so they were made to be as simple as possible. However, when people realized it made as much sense for beginning programmers to use, the library was extended a bit and included in most distributions of programming libraries.

Creating a Simple Graphic Display

Now that you know the terms associated with creating graphics, let's try them out. Listing 15.1 shows a simple turtle graphics program that will create a rectangle on the screen.

```
import turtle
wn = turtle.Screen()
myTurtle = turtle.Turtle()
myTurtle.forward(150)
myTurtle.left(90)
myTurtle.forward(75)
myTurtle.left(90)
myTurtle.forward(150)
myTurtle.left(90)
myTurtle.forward(75)
turtle.exitonclick()
```

Listing 15.1

Drawing a simple rectangle using turtle graphics.

As you can see from the code, the sides are 75 and 150 pixels, and the angles of each corner are 90 degrees. The output is pretty simple—just a rectangle in the middle of the screen. Figure 15.1 shows you how the image is displayed on the screen.

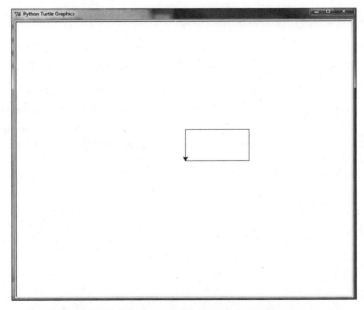

Figure 15.1: *The output of the rectangle display program.*

Creating a More Random Graphic Display

While it is nice to be able to draw a rectangle, it really isn't all that exciting. Suppose you want to draw circles, and you want the system to make them as randomly placed as possible on the screen. This would provide a different viewpoint every time you ran the program and would produce a much more interesting graphical display for the end user. Listing 15.2 shows how you can do just such a thing.

```python
from turtle import *
import random
color("green")
up()
goto(0,-50)
down()
circle(50)
for x in range(0,5) :
    up();
    x = random.randint(-200, 200)
    y = random.randint(-200,200)
    goto(x, y)
    down()
    circle(50)
exitonclick()
```

Listing 15.2

Code for creating random circles on the screen.

As you can see, you can integrate turtle graphics with pieces of programming you've learned to this point, such as random numbers and looping and range functions.

The output from this program, at least for a single run of the thing, is shown in Figure 15.2. Note that your output is very unlikely to look exactly like mine, since the coordinates for each circle are generated by random numbers. As a result, the circles will appear in different places each time you run the program, which is kind of cool for the end user to view.

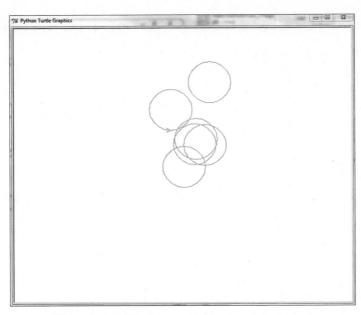

Figure 15.2: *The output of the random circle program.*

Filling in Shapes with Color

In order to fill a shape with color in the turtle graphics library, you need to take three steps:

1. Tell the library that you want to fill the shape with begin_fill().

2. Set the color for the shape you want to use to fill the shape with color("*color*"). In place of *color*, put in the color of your choice.

3. Draw the shape and tell the library to stop filling it. In this case, you put in code for a circle with a radius of 50, or circle(50), and write end_fill() to tell the program to stop filling.

Listing 15.3 updates the code from Listing 15.2 with those changes so you can have filled circles.

```
from turtle import *
import random
color("green")
up()
goto(0,-50)
down()
begin_fill()
color("green")
circle(50)
end_fill()
for x in range(0,5) :
    up();
    x = random.randint(-200, 200)
    y = random.randint(-200,200)
    goto(x, y)
    down()
    begin_fill()
    color("red")
    circle(50)
    end_fill()
exitonclick()
```

Listing 15.3

Filled circles in Python graphics.

Figure 15.3 shows the output of the program.

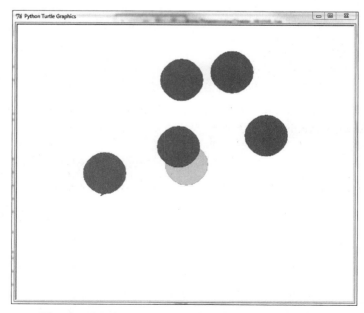

Figure 15.3: *The output of the random filled circle program.*

Running the program shows you get one green circle and a quartet of red circles. Why? Because the code specifies the color green for one circle while using the color red for circles in a general area. You could change the code to select a color randomly from a list of defined colors and fill each circle that way. It is the call to the color() function that sets the current drawing and filling color. The color is independent of the graphic shape being drawn or filled.

> **PROGRAMMING TIP**
>
> What if you want to change the color randomly from a list of defined colors and fill each circle with that random color? You already know how to set the fill color of the circle, so creating a list of colors is easy enough:
>
> ```
> # Add whatever colors you like
> Colors=[red, blue, green, yellow, black, white]
> ```
>
> You also already know how to create a random number:
>
> ```
> #Select a random color
> import random
> # use the range 0 to the number of colors, incrementing by one.
> idx = random.randrange(0, length(Colors)-1, 1)
> ```
>
> Once you have the color, changing it is simple:
>
> ```
> color (Colors[idx])
> ```
>
> As you can see, you haven't really done anything new—just put together the pieces that you've learned throughout the book.

Adding Text

With turtle graphics, you can also put text on a graphical display. You could do this to tell the user just what he is looking at. It can also be useful to display text headings to indicate what sort of data the user is looking at or to simply to indicate the title of your piece of art. Whatever the case, you want the ability to not only display the text, but to do so in a way that allows you full control over what the text appears like, how big it is, and where it appears on the screen.

With write(), you can specify the text, the font and size, and its attributes (such as bold, italic, or normal). Listing 15.4 shows the basics of displaying text on a graphical display.

```
from turtle import *
up()
goto(-50,50)
write("This is some text", font=('Arial', 12, 'normal'))
up()
goto(-50,150)
write("This is some more text", font=('Arial', 24, 'bold'))
exitonclick()
```

Listing 15.4

Displaying text on the turtle graphics screen.

As you can see, the first text specified is 12-point Arial font in a normal setting, meaning no bold or italics. The second line is in a much larger font, 24-point Arial, with bold attributes.

The output looks like Figure 15.4. As you can see, the text aligns along the left side, which makes sense since you set the output *x* coordinate to be the same in each case, -50.

Figure 15.4: *The output of the turtle graphics text display.*

Drawing Fractals

Fractals are definitely one of the cooler aspects of graphics, whether you are using turtle graphics or high-res, high-power graphical modules in high-end programming languages. Fractals are simply mathematical equations that produce eye-catching and fascinating displays in patterns resembling trees, seashells, or other images. But fractals aren't always made just to look pretty; they can also help people solve some very complicated math problems.

The nicest thing about fractals is they are remarkably easy to produce. Listing 15.5 shows the very simple code needed to produce a fractal image using turtle graphics in Python.

 ERROR MESSAGE

The fractal algorithm itself will work in any language. However, the actual graphics may need to be modified to work with that language.

```
from turtle import *

# A simple fractal display
def fractal(l, d):
    # If we are at the end, just move forward
    if d == 0:
      forward(l)
    else:
      fractal(l/3, d-1)
      right(60)
      fractal(l/3, d-1)
      left(120)
      fractal(l/3, d-1)
      right(60)
      fractal(l/3, d-1)

up()
goto(-100,-100)
down()
fractal(500, 4)
exitonclick()
```

Listing 15.5

A fractal display program in turtle graphics for Python.

The output from this little program snippet creates an enchanting moss display on the screen, as shown in Figure 15.5.

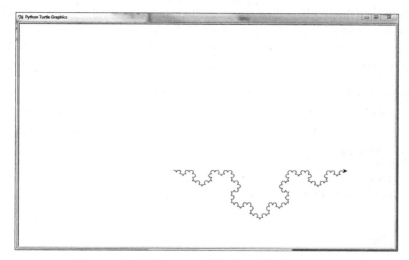

Figure 15.5: *The output of the fractal display program.*

To understand more about fractals tends to require a math degree, but using them is pretty easy. In this case, you are using a predefined fractal algorithm to draw a single fractal, moving around within the drawing area until you have filled the pieces you want. Once the area is filled, you stop.

Drawing Charts and Graphs

There are few things quite as annoying as looking at a column of numbers without being able to understand the relationships between the values you are looking at. Say you are given a list of numbers that represents the sales of individual salespeople in a region:

48, 117, 200, 240, 160, 260, 220

The numbers aren't very useful in their current format. What can you do with them? The clear answer is to present the information in a way that can help you and others understand how the salespeople are doing in their individual regions.

Numerical reports don't give you a way to compare and contrast the various values you are looking at; therefore, a much better way is to display the information in a graphical fashion, so people can immediately grasp how the data matches up. A bar chart provides information in a very simple manner and is particularly easy to implement in turtle graphics.

Let's take a look at some easy code to create a bar chart out of the salespeople data provided earlier. I'll start out simple by just showing you how to draw the individual bars that show off the relationships between the data elements and the overall sales. For this, you create a new function in our code called *doBar()* that draws a single bar with a given height. The function assumes that you have moved the turtle to a position horizontally, which it will do automatically as it draws the bars. Listing 15.6 shows you the code that will draw the bars, as well as some simple add-on code that sets everything up and does the drawing.

```
from turtle import *

def doBar(height):
    setheading(90)
    forward(height)
    right(90)
    forward(40)
    right(90)
    forward(height)

# a list of values to graph
values = [48, 117, 200, 240, 160, 260, 220]

# move tess to position the bar chart
up()
goto(-300, -200)
down()

# loop over the values in the list, calling draw_bar to graph each one
for value in values:
    doBar(value)
exitonclick()
```

Listing 15.6

A simple bar chart application in Python turtle graphics.

If you run the little program in IDLE, you will see output similar to Figure 15.6, showing the bars for each of the data elements requested. As you can see, you have a set of values for the chart (in the values array) that simply represent whatever data you are trying to draw a bar chart of. These values might have been entered by the user or read from a file, database, or anywhere else.

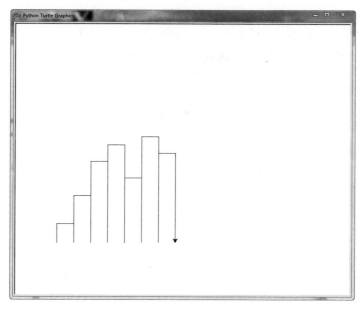

Figure 15.6: *The output of the bar chart program.*

As you can see, you get a different-sized bar for each entry in the data list based on the sales numbers. This allows users to get a good idea of the sales of each person without really having to get into the heavy-duty math of the problem. People understand that larger bars mean bigger sales, and that's really all you care about.

Of course, the problem here is that the boxes don't really indicate much with respect to who is who in the sales hierarchy. It would be a lot better if you could use color to indicate which of the boxes belongs to which of the salesmen and thus make it easier to understand who is doing the best work.

PROGRAMMING TIP

People respond much better to colors and graphics than they do to simple numbers. Therefore, by using those to indicate different pieces of the story you are trying to display in your graphical output, you will make it much easier for the end user to understand quickly what you are trying to say.

How do you accomplish this? Well, you've looked at how to fill shapes earlier in this chapter, so it isn't any harder than selecting the colors and filling the shapes properly. However, you need to create an array of colors you can use in conjunction with the list of values. There should be a one-to-one relationship between the color and the value, so users can easily match up the data on the screen and see at a glance which salesman has which sales by the color used to fill the bar on the bar chart.

To see how this works, you'll modify the existing code to add the fill colors and do the actual work of filling the bars, which you can see in Listing 15.7.

```python
from turtle import *

def doBar(height, clr):
    begin_fill()
    color(clr)
    setheading(90)
    forward(height)
    right(90)
    forward(40)
    right(90)
    forward(height)
    end_fill()

# The values to plot
values = [48, 117, 200, 240, 160, 260, 220]

# The colors to use
colors = ["green", "blue", "red", "yellow", "orange", "purple", "black"]

up()
goto(-300, -200)
down()

# loop over the values in the list, calling draw_bar to graph each one
idx = 0
for value in values:
    doBar(value, colors[idx])
    idx += 1
exitonclick()
```

Listing 15.7

A filled bar chart.

The output from your final bar chart is shown in Figure 15.7. As you can see, each of the bars is now filled with a different color (a shade of gray in this book, but a bright, vivid color on the screen). This allows you to quickly and easily match up a color to a salesman, and to understand easily who is doing what in terms of sales.

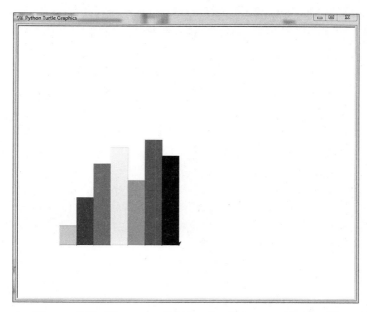

Figure 15.7: *The output of the bar chart program with color fill.*

Hopefully, this shows you the value of displaying things graphically, rather than in simple lines of numbers.

 PROGRAMMING TIP

When you consider displaying any sort of content on the screen, and that content is of a consistent type (such as numeric columns), you should seriously consider using a graphical display rather than a textual one to make things clearer to users.

The following are some basic tips you should keep in mind when displaying information in a chart or graph:

1. Always make it abundantly clear what it is you are displaying. If it is a bar or line chart, make sure the data is identified and easily picked out on the screen.

2. Use color to highlight the differences between elements on the screen. If you are displaying data that belongs to different people or programs, make sure the color is consistent across multiple graphs to map directly to those people or programs.

3. Keep it simple. Ornate graphics with hundreds of little icons and textual displays do nothing to help users understand the data they are looking at. Remember, it is always about comprehension, not about looking pretty. It is nice when a graph looks nice, but it is much more important that you understand what it is the graph is trying to tell you.

4. Make it as easy as possible for users to get the information they need from your graph. If you are trying to show who is selling the most, a bar chart is an excellent choice. On the other hand, if you are trying to show trends for a given salesperson, then a line chart showing the sales over time is a much better choice, because it indicates exactly what you are trying to say.

The Least You Need to Know

- Graphics are an important way to display information in a simple yet intuitive manner.
- Python provides the turtle graphics library to do simple graphics display.
- Always make it as simple as possible to get the information that users want from a display, whether it be text or graphics.
- Graphics can be used to generate mathematical formulae representation in the form of fractals or business representation in the form of charts and graphics.

Packages and Modules

Every modern programming language provides methods for sharing code amongst application developers. Whether that code is in binary (that is, compiled) form or in source code form that can be included in your application, modern languages promote reuse of code. That's where modules and packages come in. They are reusable chunks of code you can import into new or existing code, so you don't have to "reinvent the wheel" each time to you code.

In this chapter, I discuss creating modules and packages, as well as the importance of reusing code.

In This Chapter

- Why it's essential to reuse code
- How to create modules
- Putting together packages

Reusing Code

Reusing code is what programming is really all about. In the "bad old days" of programming, developers would always write their own code, regardless of how many times the same code had been written. There were date classes that had been written a hundred different times, always doing the same things but never doing them exactly the same way. Every time a new developer came onto a project, he would either have to learn the way in which the original coders had written the system or have to rewrite the code yet again. Programs would have dozens of the same classes, with slightly different bits that worked slightly differently.

In the real world, this would be like every automobile having a different sort of steering wheel or different pedals in various places, or having to relearn the way in which the car parts were laid out and how to control them every time you drive. Wouldn't that be just a bit insane? Of course it would. It's not like cars haven't changed over time, with automatic transmissions replacing standard ones and high and low beams replacing headlamps. However, the changes didn't occur just because they were different—they were actual improvements over existing technology. So it is with software. While modules or packages may be updated and changed, the logic behind them will likely remain the same, making them integral to your programming.

 ERROR MESSAGE

Just because a given module exists does not make it the best possible software. Once upon a time, we used time and date modules that worked with dates having two-digit years. Then the "Y2K" problem came along, meaning programmers had to learn and change the code to handle it. Newer modules will always replace existing ones—we simply learn by testing and using code.

Why Write or Use It?

Given all of the background about reusable code, you might be asking yourself, "How do I write reusable code?" You might also be wondering why you would even bother in the first place when you can't create something that lasts. While there are few things that really last in life, the underlying ideas behind them stay the same, to the point most people never really notice the difference. That is why programmers create reusable code—because people will use it over and over throughout the years, never knowing that the code changes constantly to fix problems, to extend the functionality, and to change the behavior underneath.

The purpose to creating reusable code is to reuse functionality in order to provide a single way to accomplish tasks. It is to the programming world what the assembly line was to the manufacturing world. You don't have to assemble the same thing every time, but you do have to use the same approach to creating new things that you did with old things.

Of course, there is another reason why code should be reusable, and that is because you want developers to reuse it. By understanding what code is out there and what functionality that code offers, you and other developers can always reuse what exists, rather than creating it from scratch.

What About New Code?

As you may have noticed in this book, I've focused on making sure you are aware of the functionality that exists in the Python import libraries. You've used the file functions, the date and time functions, and other functions that provide basic functionality to you as a developer. You are being trained in how to use code, not necessarily how to write it.

Does this mean you should never write any new code or release any new modules? Of course not. If nobody were to write new modules or packages, there would be no code to reuse. What it does mean is that you should always look to see if an existing module does what you need, and whether it is well documented and tested. Just because a module exists does not mean you should use it. It might be poorly written; it might not have the functionality you need; it might be poorly tested. All of these elements come into play before you can decide whether to write your own.

Obviously, there will be times when there are no modules in existence that fit your needs. This is particularly likely when you are looking for code that fits specific business needs, pertains to specific business logic, or does things that nobody else in the world does. If your company doesn't do something that nobody else in the world does, congratulations! Keep them. But the odds are good that you aren't in that fraction of a percent of corporations.

Creating a Module

So how do you decide whether to create a new module? Realistically, you have to answer three questions:

- **Does the functionality exist somewhere else?** Clearly, if there is already an existing module or package out there that does what you want, there is really no reason to create a new one, unless the existing one is so error prone it is causing more problems than it cures.

- **Does the existing code meet my needs?** This is always a difficult decision. Sometimes, a module will be out there that almost does what you want. Unfortunately, in the programming world, "almost" is a long way from "does," which can cause you to want to write your own module that accomplishes the same tasks. Before you do, however, consider the idea of extending the module, which allows you to add only those pieces you really need, rather than rewriting it from scratch.

- **Will anyone else gain from using this code?** Naturally, if you want to reuse code, it only makes sense you write code someone else might want. That can be hard to really know, particularly if you are working in an area that is proprietary or fairly new. In either case, if the module doesn't exist and you clearly need the functionality in your own program, it only makes sense to write your own.

PROGRAMMING TIP

Modules are important for two reasons. The first is they gather up the code you want to save for future use. If you learn to do the work of extracting and saving specific functionality now, you will be way ahead of the game later. Most programmers learn this the hard way—by having to dig through reams of old code, looking for a function or method that did something useful.

The second reason for writing modules is to make people aware of your skills. As a beginning programmer, the more you contribute to others, the more likely you are to get a job in the industry when you are ready for it. Never put down the value of a job!

Rather than go on and on (or is it too late for that?) about when you should write your own modules versus when you should not, it might be easier to look at an example of an actual module created and used in your application so you have an idea of what it is you are really doing here.

First of all, let's create a very simple function and put it into a Python source file. In this case, your function is going to accept a string and reverse it, returning the reversed string to the calling program. You'll store the function in a file called *stringfunc.py*, as shown in Listing 16.1.

```
def func1(stor):
    s = ""
    for c in range(len(stor)-1, -1, -1):
        s = s + stor[c]
    return s
```

Listing 16.1

The stringfunc.py file containing a string reversal function.

Now let's imagine you want to use this function in your own program. Because the function exists in a file in your current directory, you might think you could easily do something like the code shown in Listing 16.2.

```
s = input("please input string to be reversed: ")
sr = func1(s)
print("Reversed, string = {}".format(sr))
```

Listing 16.2

Using the reverse string function.

However, if you try to run the program shown in Listing 16.2 in the IDLE editor, you will get the following error:

```
please input string to be reversed: fred
Traceback (most recent call last):
  File "F:/Books/Beginning Programming/Chapter 16/revstr.py", line 2, in
  <module>
    sr = func1(s)
NameError: name 'func1' is not defined
```

So how do you go about using the function you have defined in your new file? The answer is, just like any other function in any other module. You need to import the module so the IDLE editor and Python know that you are using it, and then indicate that the function exists in that module. Listing 16.3 shows the updated file.

```
import stringfunc
s = input("please input string to be reversed: ")
sr = stringfunc.func1(s)
print("Reversed, string = {}".format(sr))
```

Listing 16.3

The updated calling file.

Does it work? Running the updated code in the IDLE editor shows that, in fact, it does:

```
please input string to be reversed: fred
Reversed, string = derf
```

As you can see, the proper function is located in the module and called, and the returned string is printed out as you expected. So why do you need to qualify the name of the function? After all, there it is, right in the stringfunc.py file; the interpreter can easily find it and call it, right?

Not quite so easily, as it turns out. For one thing, what if you had a func1() already defined in your code? Which one would the interpreter call when you asked for that function? It is very unclear and makes for a difficult problem. To find out, suppose you update your main program to look like what's in Listing 16.4.

```
import stringfunc

def func1(s) :
    return "{} isn't reversed".format(s)

s = input("please input string to be reversed: ")
sr = func1(s)
print("Reversed, string = {}".format(sr))
```

Listing 16.4

A new function in the main program.

If you run the program now, you will get a very different output:

```
please input string to be reversed: fred
Reversed, string = fredisn't reversed
```

Clearly, the interpreter is calling the local function, func1(), in the same file as the rest of the code and ignoring the imported function even though it has the same name. This is called a *matter of scope* and is there for a reason. If you want the function in the imported module, you have to specifically tell the interpreter that. You can think of the main program as the module <blank> so that any function called without a module operator, such as func1(), can be thought of as <blank>.func1(). If you want the module stringfunc's version of the function, even though it has the same name, you need to specify it as stringfunc.func1().

It is important to always clarify exactly what code you want the interpreter or compiler to use so you get what you want when you want it. You can never be too clear, whether in writing code for people or implementing code for an interpreter or compiler.

What Else Can I Do with My Module?

You might think, "Okay, modules are interesting, but what good do they really do for me?" You can actually do an amazing amount with a module. For example, you can specify data values that are used within a module, make the name of the module as simple as possible to work with, and create a local name for a long name within the module.

Specifying Data Values

One thing you can do with a module is specify data values in the module that can be used by other code. Let's say, for example, you want to specify a maximum length for strings that were processed in the reverse string function. You could code that into the module, and the value could be used by other modules, as shown in Listing 16.5.

```
Stringfunc2.py:
def func1(stor):
    s = ""
    for c in range(len(stor)-1, -1, -1):
        s = s + stor[c]
    return s

maximumlength = 20
revstr4.py:
import stringfunc2

def func1(s) :
    return "{} isn't reversed".format(s)

s = input("please input string to be reversed: ")
if len(s) > stringfunc2.maximumlength:
    print("The string is too long!")
else:
    sr = stringfunc2.func1(s)
    print("Reversed, string = {}".format(sr))
```

Listing 16.5

Defining a constant for a module.

As you can see, you have defined a variable to be used as a constant in the stringfunc2 module (I've renamed the module so you can see the progression between the various bits of code). You can test for that value in your main program by scoping the variable to the module using stringfunc2.maximumlength. Now, if you try to reverse a really long string for whatever reason, you get an error:

```
please input string to be reversed: This is a really long string that needs
    to be reversed
The string is too long!
Naturally, if I input a string that is shorter than the maximum length, I get
    the output I expect:
please input string to be reversed: fred
Reversed, string = derf
```

So as you can see, you can add variables to the module, as well as functions. What else can you do with a module?

Getting Rid of the Clarifying Name

You may recall I said that you could only use module functions if you clarified, or scoped, the name using the module name, as in <module>.function(). That's not entirely true. You can, in fact, use the name directly. Going back to your stringfunc module with the func1() function in it, let's imagine you don't want to write stringfunc.func1() every time you want to use the function; instead, you'd rather write the code shown in Listing 16.6.

```
from stringfunc import func1
s = input("please input string to be reversed: ")
sr = func1(s)
print("Reversed, string = {}".format(sr))
```

Listing 16.6

The updated main program.

Notice that you haven't changed the stringfunc module at all. Instead, you've changed the import statement in the main program to read as follows:

```
from stringfunc import func1
```

What this tells the interpreter is you want to "globalize" the func1() function from the stringfunc module so you can use it as a function without having to specify the module in which it exists.

ERROR MESSAGE

There are dangers to globalizing the function, of course, such as the fact that if you have a function of the same name, you will create problems in your code. However, when the names of the module functions, classes, or variables are mostly unique, it is a nice way to avoid having to type out the name of the module over and over.

Assigning Local Names to Modules

There is one other thing you can do with module functions that is worth mentioning, because it exists in so many different programming languages. You can assign a local name to a module function and use that in your code. This is called *creating a function pointer*, meaning something that points at an existing function name. For example, let's go back to your stringfunc module as it was in Listing 16.1 and import it without overriding any local naming conventions. Now, let's assume that I'm a grouchy programmer who doesn't like the names you gave something.

If I don't like your naming conventions, I can use my own, as shown in Listing 16.7.

```
import stringfunc
reverse_string = stringfunc.func1
s = input("please input string to be reversed: ")
sr = reverse_string(s)
print("Reversed, string = {}".format(sr))
```

Listing 16.7

Renaming a function locally.

This permits me to override what you called a function but does not in any way change the functionality you have implemented. Kind of the best of both worlds, when you think about it. No more grumpy programmer, and no more making the nice programmer make changes to code just to please the grumpy programmer.

Module Limitations and Issues

There are, of course, limitations to anything you do within a programmatic environment. With respect to modules, you may only have a single module with a unique name. That kind of goes without saying, since if you had two modules named "foo" and each had a function called "bar," what would the following line of code be interpreted as?

```
foo.bar()
```

Clearly, you are asking the interpreter—Python, in this case—to make an impossible choice, and interpreters don't like to do that. Instead, it will throw the problem back at you with an error message saying the name is not unique.

Okay, so you can't have nonunique module names. That doesn't seem like a tragedy—after all, very few people would want to do such a thing. There are, however, other implementation details you may or may not want to be aware of.

 ERROR MESSAGE

All programming languages have limitations, whether for security reasons or simply because they were never intended to be used for general purposes. Python is intended to be as general purpose as possible, but its implementation does cause side effects you need to be aware of.

Therefore, when you are writing your own code, always document any limitations or assumptions that are present, so anyone using the code will be aware of them up front and not curse your name later.

First of all, like all languages that allow the inclusion of "foreign" or external code, Python will only load a module once, no matter how many times it is included in your program. That is, you might have three different Python files—called py1.py, py2.py, and py3.py—and they look something like this:

```
py1.py:
import datetime
print("Today is: {}".format(datetime.today())
py2.py:
import datetime
Print("The current time is {}".format(datetime.now())
py3.py:
import datetime
# Do something with the date time object
```

Only the first datetime import really makes any difference. This doesn't really matter in the case of the datetime functionality, since it is all either static or relies on system functions to retrieve the information for which you ask. However, let's consider a module that you write.

Imagine you have a module called ch16_module_1, just to be unique and fit in with the chapter in which you are working. This module is in its own file and contains the following code:

```
print("Entering module 1")

def mfunc1(s) :
    s += " module 1 "
    return s
```

Nothing very special here, except notice that the module has a print() function that is sitting all by itself. In a "normal" Python program, that print() function would be executed as soon as you ran the program. Let's import that module into the IDLE interpreter:

```
>>> import ch16_module_1
```

You would expect that nothing would happen. After all, you are simply loading the code into the interpreter, right? Yet something does happen. When you get the function mfunc1() loaded, the print() function is also executed!

As you can see, importing a module is exactly the same as running it. Let's write a little program like the one shown in Listing 16.8 and see just what happens when the thing runs. After all, that's the best way to figure out how things work, isn't it?

```
import ch16_module_1
s = "hello world"
print(s)
s = ch16_module_1.mfunc1(s)
print(s)

import ch16_module_1
print(ch16_module_1.mfunc1("Hello"))
```

Listing 16.8

A simple program using a module.

Running this little program, you would expect to see it print out "hello world," followed by the string "hello world" modified by the function in the module. You would then expect it to reload the module and do the same thing with the string "Hello," right?

Surprise! Here is the output from the program:

```
Entering module 1
hello world
hello world module 1
Hello module 1
```

Not quite what you would expect, now is it? For one thing, you do get the initial print() function telling you that module 1 has been loaded in the first import. You also get the modified "hello world" string, as expected. Yet when you then import the module the second time, you don't get the string "Entering module 1," which indicates that the interpreter didn't load and execute the module as expected. What is going on here?

When you load a module the first time, the interpreter loads the code and executes it, which causes the print() function to be run in the case of our module. However, once the module has been loaded into the memory of the interpreter, it will check to see if the code has changed when you try to load it a second time. If the code is the same, it will simply use what it has in memory and neither load nor execute it.

While this might seem very simple and straightforward, it does have some side effects that you will want to consider when writing or loading a module:

- Always assume your code is loaded once and only once—that is, do not rely on the current time, date, or other system value to be set each time the code is loaded. If you must gather such information, create an initialization function that the user must call.

- Do not put code the end user (the programmer, not the user of the program) does not want executing in his program. For example, in your case, it might be quite ugly to suddenly have a print() function appear in the middle of the output from a programmer's code.

- Write modules so they have independent parts to them. If you need several functions that work with the same data, pass the data to them rather than storing it in a local or, worse, global variable for the module.

If you follow these simple rules, your code will become much more usable, and programmers will be much more likely to reuse it. Reuse is kind of the ultimate reward for a programmer—you get to point at something that someone else is using and proudly say, "Hey! That's my code you are using."

PROGRAMMING TIP

Modules are one of the best ways there is to package code in Python and other languages. You can save the code for reuse in your own programs or for use by other programmers in your company or the world. Every time you write a new component that accomplishes a specific task, ask yourself whether this could be something that would appeal to others, and if so, make it into a module or package.

Creating a Package

You might wonder why a language would have both modules (which are supposed to be reusable code chunks) and packages (which are, well, reusable code chunks). The difference is really one of scope and size. A module is almost always a single file that contains a single bit of functionality. It may be that the functionality is spread over a set of functions or classes, but it is always pretty much restricted to a single topic.

Packages, on the other hand, are broader in scope. They can consist of multiple files and multiple classes, all of which are related in some way but are much more "loosely coupled," means that the individual pieces of a given set of functionality have no real dependencies on other individual pieces. A good example of this is the math package in Python. All of the pieces of the math package have something to do with math, whether it be statistics, trigonometry, or algebra. Some will rely on basic bits of math, but few actually require that pieces outside the basics of math are involved.

ERROR MESSAGE

Coupling in software is a much more important issue than I can get into here. Just know that the stronger the coupling between pieces of your program, the less likely it is that it can be reused by others. In addition, the stronger the coupling, the harder it is to make changes to the underlying structure of the code.

A package shares a common name across all of the modules within it. Unlike modules, packages have a structure to them, whereas a module is just a single file. Packages have a directory structure, as well as an internal structure to them.

Let's start by creating a simple package and using it within your program. This particular package will eventually be capable of validating and using various credit card numbers and will have modules for each of the major credit card packages.

Making a Directory

The important thing about packages is they need to be structured properly, so you are going to create a directory structure to handle your code. I am going to create the files in a directory called "PythonPackages," but you can create them wherever you want to (just remember to change "PythonPackages" to whatever you called your directory in the code that follows).

First, let's create the subdirectory. For now, I'll simply assume that the package directory is at the root level; if you want to change that, by all means do so. From Windows Explorer (or File Explorer, or whatever version of the file manager your version of Windows has), navigate to the root directory of the file system on the main drive (in my case, C:). You should see something like the display shown in Figure 16.1.

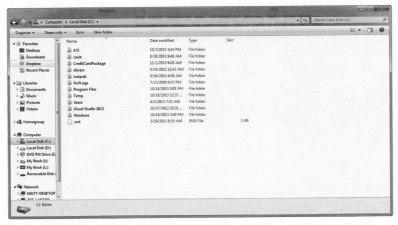

Figure 16.1: *Windows Explorer showing the root directory.*

Right-click anywhere in the right window pane and select **New Folder**. You should see a new folder appear in the listing, as shown in Figure 16.2, called, appropriately, "New folder." (Quite the imagination those programmers at Microsoft have, isn't it? Ah well.)

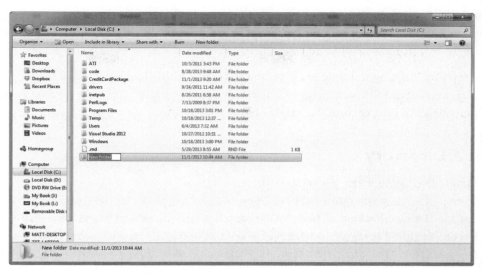

Figure 16.2: *The new folder in Windows.*

The directory is highlighted so you can type a name into the box. Type **CreditCardPackage** into the box and hit **Enter**. You should see the display shown in Figure 16.3.

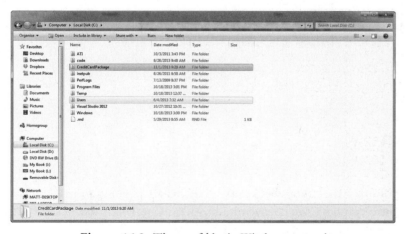

Figure 16.3: *The new folder in Windows renamed.*

Putting Files into the Directory

Packages are hierarchical structures that have files in a directory, with special files that indicate which ones are significant. So now that you have created the folder, you need to put some files in it that will define the functionality of your package. Let's start with a utility class that does some validation for all credit card types. The Luhn checksum algorithm, which has been released to the public domain, does the work of computing the proper checksum for a credit card.

PROGRAMMING TIP

If you are unaware, a credit card number consists of a 12- to 16-digit number. The last digit is called a *checksum digit* and does the job of verifying that the other digits are in the correct place. It doesn't determine if the actual credit card is valid, only that the format of it is valid.

Let's implement the algorithm in Python code. Listing 16.9 shows you the code.

```python
# The luhn checksum, available freely on the web and most Python sites,
# checks the checksum digit (the last digit in the credit card string)
def is_luhn_valid(card_number):
    digits = [int(d) for d in str(card_number)]
    odd_digits = digits[-1::-2]
    even_digits = digits[-2::-2]
    checksum = sum(odd_digits)
    for d in even_digits:
        checksum += (int(d) * 2) % 10
        if int(d) * 2 > 10:
            checksum += 1
    return checksum % 10 == 0
```

Listing 16.9

The Luhn checksum algorithm.

This code goes into the luhn_checksum.py file, which is going to reside in your package directory. Once you have the checksum file, let's create your credit card validation function—in this case, for MasterCard. (Realistically, it can be any credit card, as they all use the same formula for determining the validity of the number; they simply have different lengths of numbers.)

Listing 16.10 shows the MasterCard.py file, which you should put in the CreditCardPackage directory on C:, just as you did with luhn_checksum.py.

```
def validate(s):
    "Validates a MasterCard number"

    # Mastercards have 16 digits
    if len(s) != 16:
        return False

    # Make sure all of the characters are digits
    for i in range(len(s)):
        if s[i].isnumeric() == False:
            return False

    # The Luhn algorithm checks the checksum value
    if luhn_checksum.is_luhn_valid(s) == False:
        return False

    return True
```

Listing 16.10

The MasterCard checker file.

As you can see, the actual validation at this point is pretty simple. You make sure that the number has the proper number of digits and that each character in the string is a valid number. Finally, you call the checksum function to validate that it has a proper checksum when you are all done with the credit card number.

Making a Constructor for the Package

Now you have to deal with the issue of how Python "knows" what goes into the package and how things are found in the program that uses the package. The first issue is actually dealt with via a "special" file called *__init__.py*. If the name looks familiar, it is similar to the __init__() function that is the constructor of a class. This is not by accident, since the constructor for a package is very similar to the one for a class. It does the work of associating files and classes with the package and exposes them for the end user to use. Let's try creating one and putting it in the CreditCardPackage directory, as shown in Listing 16.11.

```
from . import luhn_checksum
from . import MasterCard
```

Listing 16.11

The __init__.py file for your package.

If you have done everything as instructed, your directory for the CreditCardPackage should look like the one shown in Figure 16.4.

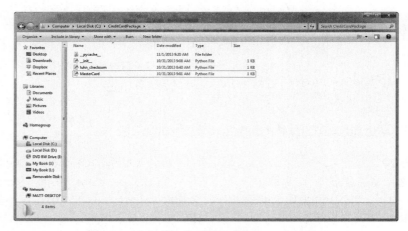

Figure 16.4: *The CreditCard directory structure.*

(**PROGRAMMING TIP**)

Directory structures are very important in some programming languages. Files have to have certain names and be stored in certain places. For other languages, the files can be stored anywhere and named anything. Therefore, one of the first things you should check when you start out with a new programming language is what the requirements are for file naming and placement.

Associating the Package with Python

Once you have the files in the directory where you want to use them, you need to associate them with Python. There are very good tools out there to install packages in Python, but most of them require a fair amount of knowledge of the language and the operating system, and all of them require you to add files in very bizarre formats. To make this easier, I am going to skip those things. If you really decide to get into Python programming, by all means read a good book on the subject and use the tools that are out there for Python people. What I am going to show you will work and is always available to you but won't make your package available to all the rest of the world. All things considered, that's probably not a bad thing.

So what is involved in adding your package to Python? Well, you are going to have to issue some pretty strange commands in the IDLE editor. Rather than explain them all at once, let's just look at what is involved:

```
>>> import sys
>>> sys.path.append("c:\\CreditCardPackage")
```

The sys module deals with the Python system as a whole. What you are doing here is telling Python to look for your module along all of the standard paths (that's what the path part holds) along with the c:\CreditCardPackage directory. Once it has found the package, you can then import it the same way you would import any other Python module:

```
import MasterCard
MasterCard.validate("12356")
```

IDLE responds with "False," because the number given is not long enough. I'm not going to put any valid credit card numbers into the book for obvious reasons, but if you have a credit card, go ahead and type the number in. (I promise, it will not secretly send it to anyone in Eastern Europe to let them buy things on the internet.) If you type in the full number correctly, you will get back a True. If your number is incorrect, not long enough, or doesn't have a proper checksum value, you will get back a False.

Believe it or not, that is all you need to do to get a package working with Python. It may seem like a lot of work initially, but once you have done it a few times, it will become easier and easier.

What Is in a Package?

One thing you might wonder about is how you find out what is in a package, what methods and classes you can use, and what they look like. Fortunately, Python and most other languages have a way of "reflecting" the information in a module, package, or class to show you what is available to you. The function is called *dir()* for directory and provides you information about the item you pass to it. For example, you might want to know what methods the MasterCard module has in it:

```
>>> dir(MasterCard)
['validate', '__builtins__', '__cached__', '__doc__', '__file__', '__
    initializing__', '__loader__', '__name__', '__package__']
```

This assumes, of course, you have imported the MasterCard module at some point in the IDLE editor, by the way. As you can see, you have a bunch of items that begin and end with the double underscore (__). These are all built-in system-level functions that aren't really important to you. What is important is the one function that doesn't have the double underscore, called *validate()*; this is the function you use to validate the credit card number. Of course, this module isn't terribly exciting, as it only contains one method.

Let's look at something a bit more complicated and involved:

```
>>> import math
>>> dir(math)
['__doc__', '__loader__', '__name__', '__package__', 'acos', 'acosh', 'asin',
  'asinh', 'atan', 'atan2', 'atanh', 'ceil', 'copysign', 'cos', 'cosh',
  'degrees', 'e', 'erf', 'erfc', 'exp', 'expm1', 'fabs', 'factorial', 'floor',
  'fmod', 'frexp', 'fsum', 'gamma', 'hypot', 'isfinite', 'isinf', 'isnan',
  'ldexp', 'lgamma', 'log', 'log10', 'log1p', 'log2', 'modf', 'pi', 'pow',
  'radians', 'sin', 'sinh', 'sqrt', 'tan', 'tanh', 'trunc']
```

Once again, ignoring the system-level functions, you can see the math module contains all sorts of interesting functions.

How Do I Use the Function?

One thing you might notice in the functions that ship with the standard Python library is that when you use them, a little yellow pop-up comes up in the IDLE editor showing you the usage of the thing. For example, if you type the following:

```
math.atan2(
```

Python kindly responds by popping up a small yellow box that shows that atan2 takes two arguments: y and x. You might wonder where it gets that information from. After all, none of the functions you have written that take arguments show you the arguments when you type their names in IDLE.

The answer is in "document string." Python provides a built-in way for the writer of the function to show end users how to use their function and, if they so choose, tell them more information about the function.

Let's take a look at how this works. Many other languages have the same functionality, called variously *Intellisense* or *functional documentation*, depending on the language and system you choose.

When you create a function, you have the option of including documentation for the function in the definition. You do this using a documentation string, which appears below the name and parameters for the function. For example, your validate() function could look like this:

```
def validate(s):
    "Validates a MasterCard number"
```

If you then use the function in IDLE, you will notice that once you type **Validate** followed by the opening parenthesis, you will see the pop-up indicating the documentation for the function, as shown in Figure 16.5.

Figure 16.5: *A pop-up showing the documentation in IDLE.*

As you can see, Python allows you to do everything they do in the system in your own applications. This is a good model to follow.

> **PROGRAMMING TIP**
>
> When writing large-scale applications, such as something like IDLE, always allow users to extend your program and provide methods to allow them to do anything you do in your program.

The Least You Need to Know

- Packages are an important way to gather code in Python.
- Modules are a great way to keep related code together for later reuse.
- Packages require a specific structure in order to be used by the Python system.
- Creating reusable code will make you happier in the long run and get your name out into the industry.

Designing Programs

Program design is one of the hardest parts of good programming. A well-designed program is not only easy for the user to use and understand, but it is also easy for the programmer to read and understand. A good program is also easy to extend and maintain, which is one of those areas programmers rarely talk about or consider but accounts for quite a large amount of time spent by programmers.

Design a program correctly, and all of the pieces fit together like a jigsaw puzzle. Design the same program incorrectly, and the pieces still fit together, but they stick out in all sorts of odd ways with strange side effects each time you use one of the pieces. In this chapter, I teach you about the best ways to design programs, as well as some common hazards to watch out for.

In This Chapter

- What is program design?
- Requirements and requirement paralysis
- Working with users
- Considering the program layers
- Design guidelines for complex applications

The Art of Program Design

Imagine, for example, you are constructing a building using blocks. You might stack the blocks on top of each other in a haphazard way, shifting them this way and that when they threatened to fall. When it comes to building the thing taller, you would have to shore up parts of the existing building by holding the lower blocks together while you put bigger ones on. The building might lean a little, but it would hold together. You would then build yet another layer and hold together the bottom, but it would eventually reach the point where you couldn't hold the bottom together well enough for you to add more to the top; at this point, the tower would eventually collapse. Programs are a lot like that tower.

The art of program design is that of creating blueprints for programs, both now and into the future. Architects create blueprints for buildings based on physical laws and well-known building processes and procedures. Software, sadly, has no physical laws or rules that govern what software can do or how it can be put together. There are, however, well-known principles upon which software can be built into a stable structure like that tower.

 PROGRAMMING TIP

Like anything else, software design has evolved over the years as developers have discovered "best practices" that result in better designs and more bulletproof programs. It is in your best interests to learn at least some of those practices, and put them in place when you are designing your own software. After all, we don't design programs just for fun!

There's No "Perfect" Program

While the majority of what programmers focus on in software design is in the negative—what can go wrong, how we can adapt to problems, how the software can recover from serious errors, or other issues that crop up during the design of programs and systems—no program can anticipate or handle every possible error.

Programs will crash or get into unanticipated states. The point isn't that you can make the system bug proof (that is, not have any errors), but rather that when a bad error occurs, the user is not left in a state that makes them throw up their hands and uninstall the program completely.

Program Design as a Whole

Program design is all about visualizing the system as a whole. Call it a gestalt, if you like, or a holistic view of the system you want to write—whatever you call it, make sure you understand that it is everything from the top to the bottom.

One of the biggest aspects of program design is in understanding the relationships and separations between the layers of the application. I'll talk about what the layers are in just a bit, but for now, understand that programs have separate pieces that interact with other pieces but should not have tight coupling with those other pieces.

For example, imagine that you are writing a graphical user interface that represents a calculator. Now, we all have a pretty good idea of what the actual user interface looks like; it has buttons for the numbers and the mathematical functions (plus, minus, and so forth), as well as a display that shows you the current value.

There are numerous ways to design a calculator-style program. The worst, by far, would be to put all the calculations and math functions into the handlers for the actual function buttons on the screen. Why? Because that removes any way of replacing functionality for one or more pieces without having to replace the entire thing.

What you want to do is create a layer that handles the user interface, knowing what buttons are valid in what state. Below that, you want a layer that handles the interface between the user interface buttons and the lower-level math functions. This interface would keep track of the current values of the system (for example, the current entry in the calculator) and would understand how to apply whatever math button that was hit to that value. Finally, the bottom layer of the system would have the actual math functionality—the ability to add two numbers, subtract them, and so forth. It wouldn't know anything about the user interface, or even the numbers that were stored in the "calculator" memory; it would simply know how to do math on whatever numbers were passed to it.

Hopefully, you can see the advantages of doing things in a layered approach. Not only does each layer allow for individual testing and use, but each layer could easily be reused with different sets of back-end code. For example, you might replace the display module with one that handles scientific notation or add buttons to handle specialized kinds of math. You could change the middle layer to allow for the storage of multiple values, rather than just two, so you could have multiple memory keys at the top that fed into these memory slots. You could even add new mathematical functions to the bottom layer and allow for things like linear equation solving and the like.

PROGRAMMING TIP

If you don't know what half these things are, that's really okay. What I am trying to get you to understand is that dividing an application up into layers that are completely divorced from one another is an excellent way to start out designing a program.

Requirements for Program Design

While there are no physical laws or rules for designing programs, requirements are a major part of system design and program creation.

First of all, what is a "requirement"? Put simply, a requirement is something the program absolutely must do. Now, this isn't usually something like "don't crash when you start it up," although it certainly could be. Requirements can cover things as diverse as what colors and fonts to use to what pressing the plus button in the calculator example will do.

The Qualities of Requirements

A requirement has two basic qualities that need to be true:

It has to be implementable in a way that can be identified by the user. For example, writing a requirement that a program be "easy to use" is worthless, because "easy" is too subjective a term. On the other hand, writing a requirement that says "the system shall allow the user to exit the program at any time, automatically saving any work in progress" is very implementable and can be observed by the user. You can test it by trying to exit the program at various points and in various ways and verifying that coming back in saves whatever you've done to that point.

It must be testable. Being testable means a tester (I'll talk about them later, I promise; for now, just think of them as evil people that make your life as a developer difficult [just kidding]) can verify the program does what it is supposed to do for that individual requirement. For example, a requirement for your calculator program might say, "If the user enters a single number and presses the plus button, the value of that number shall be added to the current total."

Requirements do not state how a system will do what it is supposed to do; they only state what it has to do in order to satisfy the end user. This is really the important point to you, the developer. You do not write requirements (at least you usually don't)—you write code that satisfies requirements. Someone outside your development group (probably the person who asked for the program in the first place) gives you a list of requirements that your program needs to satisfy. Starting with that list, you begin your program design.

Why You Need Requirements

Now, the next question, of course, is why do you need requirements? For example, if someone comes up to you and says, "I need a calculator program, write me one," you sit down and write it, right?

Back in the bad old days of programming, that's exactly what you would do. You know what happened next? You'd get comments like this:

- "No, I wanted a scientific calendar."
- "But it doesn't run on my web browser!"
- "It should allow me to take the square root of negative numbers."

And so forth, and so on, and so it goes.

This is why you need to meet with users and define requirements. A lot of it is for the user, so she gets what she wants. A fair amount of the reason, however, is simple self-defense for the programmer. If you and the user agree that button <x> will do <y> and put that agreement in writing, the end user can't then come back to you later and say, "But button <x> should do <z>."

The important part about requirements is they must be agreed upon, and understood, by both sides. Too often, requirements are written either in technical computer jargon, or in the language of the business field for which the application is written. Neither is optimal. Just write the thing in English and make sure everyone understands it.

Breaking Down Requirements

One of the most confusing things about working with requirements is they are almost always at a high level. A requirement might say something like "The plus button shall add two values." Okay, that's good to know, and certainly makes sense. But then the questions start:

- "Where do the values come from?"
- "What if there aren't two values to add?"
- "Where does the result of the addition of the two values go?"

The process of determining what really needs to be done from the high-level requirements is called *decomposition*. You may recall I discussed this very topic in Chapter 1 when I talked a bit about breaking down a program from high-level concepts (enter a value) to the pieces for doing so (get a keystroke, determine if it is valid, determine if it fits into the scope, and add it to the current value).

All of this probably sounds like some massive process that only takes place at major corporations that develop software for a living, but that couldn't be further from the truth. Whether you are developing software for someone else or writing it for yourself, knowing what you are doing is the number-one thing that needs to happen to develop something usable.

 ERROR MESSAGE

> Writing code might seem simple and straightforward, but once you get past writing the simplest of programs, that's definitely not true. You need to fully understand all aspects of the programs you write—the larger they are, the harder this becomes. Only by documenting the requirements and sticking to them in the code can you hope to create a program that can be maintained and updated in the future.

How to Decompose a Requirement

So how do you decompose a requirement? Really, the answer is the same as decomposing a programming problem. You take a requirement and break it down into the steps that are necessary to implement it. You then look at each step and see if it is necessary to decompose that step further, or whether there is already code in place to accomplish that task. When you reach the point where there is nothing left to break down, you are done.

Consider, for example, a website that requires you to log in. The requirement might say something like the following:

"To access any private data, the user must be logged in."

The first part of the requirement states there is private data, as opposed to public data. This can be decomposed into whether any of the content on the current page is private. Each piece of content (menus, text, links to preferences, and the like) would need to have some sort of indicator as to whether it was private. (Web pages aren't quite as simple as you thought, now are they?)

 PROGRAMMING TIP

I'll skip some of the more complex requirements, such as whether you can "jump" into the middle of a private data page by bookmarking it; that's really well beyond the scope of the book. However, it is a good thing for you to think about when decomposing a programming issue.

The second part of the requirement states the user must be logged in. Now, this really entails two separate things. First of all, there must be a method to log in to the website. This is typically accomplished via some sort of login page, which is probably already in existence in this case, so I'll skip it. The second part of the problem is knowing the user is logged in, which means maintaining some state in your web application that tells you whether the user is logged in.

Is that really all you need to worry about? Well, no. In a professional web page, you'd also worry about time-outs—that is, how long before the user is logged out when she hasn't done anything on the site. And you'd worry about changing passwords, and forgotten passwords, and how many times a user can retry her login before she gets locked out.

This is what typical programmers think about when they decompose a simple requirement. Notice that I've broken the requirement down into the following elements:

- Is the page public or private?

- How does a user log in to the website?

- How do you maintain the state of the user in the website?

But how far do you go with this? How far do you break down a requirement before you feel comfortable with it?

Requirement Paralysis

There comes a point when you must stop looking at and breaking down requirements in order to decide what sort of program you are writing and then to start actually writing code. The process of decomposition can quickly turn into a state of paralysis, whereby you get so caught up in making sure you have everything documented and correct that you never get around to writing the code for the system. This problem is referred to as *requirement paralysis*.

There are numerous solutions to the requirement paralysis problem. The latest and most well-accepted one is called *agile programming*. Essentially, the idea is that you come up with requirements for a small segment of the program (usually, a high-level segment) and then implement them as best you can in code. That solution is then presented to the user, along with whatever issues came up during the implementation, and the requirements are further decomposed or added to. Using these new rules and requirements, you then extend the code you've written and add a new piece based on other requirements. You then go back to the user and present the new piece and continue this process in an ever-widening circle.

Agile programming favors working code over documentation, which is both a good and bad thing. No documentation means more time to write code. However, no documentation also means someone new coming onto the project has no information about why things were done the way they were.

Therefore, even if you follow the agile programming method, make sure to balance documentation against code. Documentation does not give the user anything she needs to do her job, but it does provide a basis for new programmers to come in to maintain the existing code. Always consider whether you need to document code when you write it. Documentation doesn't explain how the code works; it explains what the code was meant to do. Comments in your code explain how the code works and makes the code easier to understand and maintain.

Working with Users on Designing a Program

So far, I have discussed programs designed, developed, and tested by you. Unfortunately, that isn't really the case for most programmers. We are at the mercy of users, who will use our programs. These users might be simply internal folk at the company we work for, using the little utilities that we write, or they might be people that buy our programs and use them for their own purposes. Whatever the case, there is one absolute guarantee: they will never be 100 percent satisfied with the systems you write.

Users might complain about the layout of a user interface. They might complain about the number of steps they have to perform to accomplish something. Quite often, users complain the program doesn't do enough to guide them through the process of accomplishing a task. It is this last issue that I would like to talk about now, because it is really the one area that programmers can most help the end user.

The art of program design is in making the program easy to use and easy to do things right. If something is easier to do right than wrong, users will flock to your program. If it is clear what needs to be done first, next, and so forth, users will use the program. If, on the other hand, you build a program the way programmers build programs—building individual components and expecting other developers to figure out how to assemble them in the proper order—your program will never be used.

In general, processes within a system are pretty simple individually—you do x, y, and z and the system responds with a, b, or c as a result. The problem comes in when you have multiple processes that have to work together. For example, suppose your system must first load an existing file (or create a new one) and then add a series of filters to the file before finally applying the file to a task. Many systems require you to do one task at a time, assuming you know the order and required list of tasks to complete. Such systems give you wonderful feedback, such as "Filters not applied. Unable to continue." The simple fact is, users don't like this. (Heaven knows I don't like this, and I'm a programmer.)

How do we design systems that fix this problem? That's really what program design is all about. Thinking through the problem, talking to users about what needs to be done, and then implementing solutions that make it easy to do the task correctly and difficult to do the task incorrectly.

The easiest and best way to work with users is to have them present when you are developing the software. Unfortunately, this rarely works out. Many so-called "software development processes" assume the end user has infinite time to work with the developers. Of course, most end users have real jobs that occupy the majority of their time and can't just drop it all to work with you. Still, you should try to put together a quick user interface and have them look at it, make comments, offer suggestions for change, and so forth.

Users can help you to develop task "patterns," or lists of things that need to be done for given solutions. For example, a user can tell you that to edit a given file, you need to find the file, open it for editing, and find the position in the file you want to start editing. If you have previously edited a file, most of this should be automatic. If you have not opened this particular file before, the system should aid you in checking to see what you want to do. If you specify you want to edit the file to add <some entry> to it, it should locate the section of the file containing those entries and probably pop up a little dialog box that allows you to fill in the data you want to add, before inserting the data into the file and saving it.

PROGRAMMING TIP

Believe it or not, there was a time (and still is, in some places) when files didn't automatically save when you made changes. This meant you could write an hour's worth of documentation that disappeared because the program or computer crashed and didn't write the data back to persistent storage. If you have ever been around someone who has had this happen to them, you will have learned a whole new set of interesting vocabulary that you likely can't use in public. Users can help you identify issues like this, so you can add them as requirements to your program.

It is important to always consider your users. They can help you design your application, work through specific functionality, and debug your program. Work with them as cohorts and coworkers, not as evil users that make your life more difficult, and you will have a much easier time designing and writing programs.

The Layers of a Program

No, layers are not the hens that create golden programs. Instead, layers are the tiers the program creates. Some of these tiers are ones the users work with directly, while some are not. Differentiating the tiers, as well as understanding how they should be isolated from other tiers, is an important part of designing an application.

From a high-level view, the layers are most easily identified as follows:

- The highest layer, which is the user-facing layer

- The middle layer, which is usually business logic

- The back-end layer, which normally interfaces to persistent storage

Using your calculator program from earlier as an example, the top layer is the actual user interface that contains your buttons and the total display. The middle layer contains the business logic, which in this case is the functionality to do addition, subtraction, and the like. Finally, you have the back-end layer, which may or may not exist in this case. For transient calculations, this refers to calculations that are done, displayed, and thrown away, so there is no reason to store anything. You could use the back-end layer to store partial sums or something (the memory key on a typical calculator), but it is more likely that the back end simply does nothing for this program.

Identifying Layers

Designing a program means figuring out what pieces you will need to write or reuse, and then putting them in the layer "buckets" so they can be fleshed out. When you are implementing a system, it is easiest to create a little "skeleton" of each layer, so the other layers have something they can use to call into without necessarily doing any real work. (In the software world, we call this *stubbing* the code.)

What does this mean to you as a developer? Generally, it means you need to identify where each piece fits into a layer and create some access to that piece. Let's say you have the requirement to add two values. You will do this via the plus button on the user interface, so you know there will be both a visual element (the button) and some code behind the button to handle the functionality of that button. The art, however, is not to have the functionality to do the actual work of adding the numbers, but rather to validate the numbers are present and valid (if necessary). That information is then shuffled off to the middle tier or layer, and the actual business work is done.

 ERROR MESSAGE

It is often difficult for the beginning programmer to separate the code into layers, because it is so much easier to just put the code where the work is invoked in the first place. This is a mistake for two reasons. First, if the code changes for a given bit of functionality, you need to change it all over the program. Secondly, you can't reuse business logic that has visual elements in it. Always separate the functionality from the visual aspects.

Why Separate the Layers?

You've already looked at one reason to separate the layers, which is to be able to reuse the business logic. But there are other reasons which are just as important, if not more so.

For one thing, consider a web application. Your user interface for the web application is, of course, the browser display of the visual elements. However, the actual work is done on the server side of the application, so it needs to be physically separated from the visual part, since it is on a completely different machine. The back end, if present, needs to be behind a firewall to protect the data from hackers.

Another reason you need to separate the pieces of an application is so each one can be tested in isolation, by "mocking" or "stubbing" the other pieces (I'll talk more about testing in Chapter 18).

Designing a Complex Application

Up to this point, obviously, your applications have been very simple—more examples of how to use individual functions in programming than how to design a real-life application. It is well beyond the scope of this book to show you how to build a system that supports hundreds of users using databases and web services and the like, but it is also important for you to understand exactly what is involved when you want to get to that point.

When you are designing a complex application, the first thing you need to think about are the pieces that go into it. Let's take as an example a system that will store and recall data about employees at a given company. Now, this particular application will be designed for multiple companies to use at the same time. This is called a *hosted application*, since a single hosting company can support multiple outside companies at the same time.

The data you are going to store in the system includes employee personal contact information, Social Security numbers and tax information, and pay rate details. Clearly, this information is personal and should require users to verify they are entitled to view it.

This time, rather than look at the layers of information, let's break down the components you are going to need. Because you are working in an object-oriented language, you will break the components down into classes. As you may remember from Chapter 14, classes are basically templates for data and functionality related to a single real-world idea. You looked at classes that modeled things like cars and such; now you will look at them as related to real-world nonphysical entities, like addresses and financial information.

PROGRAMMING TIP

You might notice that all of the pieces of the software development process follow a similar pattern—start with a big picture, break it down into smaller areas, and then assemble the small pieces into the overall design. In design, you take a user "story," or need to accomplish a specific task, and then break it down into smaller tasks. In development, you take a single bit of functionality to implement a user story and break it down into smaller components that are used to make it all work. In testing, you test the big picture, and then work on the smaller pieces of the code until it has all been tested. Follow this pattern with your own work, and you will be much happier and more successful.

Breaking Down Classes

Now that you know you want to create classes based on the entities you need to model from the requirements, how exactly do you go about it? There are numerous methodologies for modeling in the real world, but the easiest is the "extract noun" process. In this case, you take the description of what you are building, take out all of the nouns, and make them into classes. It doesn't always work out perfectly, but it is an excellent and easy way to start.

To see how this works, let's look at a paragraph of the description text for your application and see what you can extract from it:

> "The data we are going to store in the system includes employee personal contact information, Social Security numbers and tax information, and pay rate details. Clearly, this information is personal and should require users to verify that they are entitled to view it."

If you look at only the nouns in the paragraph, you get the following list:

- Employee personal contact information
- Social Security numbers
- Tax information
- Pay rate details
- User verification

Okay, the last one isn't directly in the paragraph, but it is clear that it is an element you are going to model. Sometimes, you just have to accept a few things that don't fit the process perfectly.

Defining the Classes at a High Level

Once you have the list of classes you are going to be defining, the next step is to assign the attributes and functionality you are going to be building into each class. Note that you aren't really writing code here; you're simply making a list of the stuff that needs to go into each class, and potentially what functionality that class will need to provide to the outside world of the program.

For the personal contact information, you'll need things like the following:

Name

Address

City, state, and ZIP code

Phone number (home)

Phone number (mobile)

Phone number (work)

Next of kin

It should be noted that while you are representing these things as numbers and names, it may not be that way at all. You might, for example, store the phone numbers in their own objects and persistent storage and then reference them by some sort of unique key. That, however, is for the implementation section, not the design portion.

ERROR MESSAGE

There is a major difference between design and implementation. As a designer, you are indicating what needs to be done, what the rules are for the processes, and what the relationships are between data in various places. You should not, however, be specifying the way in which the programmer implements that data or those relationships, even if you are going to be that programmer. Design is code independent.

An Example of Software Decomposition

You might think the Social Security number would be a simple string, but that is really not the case. For one thing, you want a class wrapped around it for validation of the number itself. After all, a Social Security number (SSN, please, not SSN number) must consist of exactly nine characters, each of which must be a valid digit in the range of zero to nine. In addition, there are certain SSN values which are invalid, as you can find via the Social Security Administration's website. Finally, there is the possibility that the user does not have an SSN or does not have a valid United States SSN (a foreign national, for example). Your SSN class should handle all of these possibilities without the program using it needing to know or understand them.

Tax information is likely to consist of two separate kinds of classes. First of all, you need to know what tax rates the employee is subject to and what the ranges of salaries are for those rates. You then need to know how much she has paid for each one of the rates so you can calculate both her total taxes for the year, as well as the taxes for each tax rate. All of this information goes into both her federal tax form, as well as the monthly salary stub that she receives with her paychecks.

Pay rate details includes such information as the type of pay (regular, overtime, sick, vacation, and so forth), the rate at which that pay was administered, and the number of hours of pay that she receives for each type. You can see where this class might break down into separate pieces, such as individual pay type classes.

Finally, you have the user verification class or classes. What is the purpose of this class, after all? It is to provide security for the other information. If I want to look at my own data, for example, I am always free to do so. Similarly, if the head of the Human Resources department wants to look at pay salaries, she should certainly have that ability (after all, she writes the checks). But what if my co-worker suddenly decides she wants to know how much all of the other members of her department are making? That would clearly be a violation of ethics, if not company policy, and should not be allowed. Therefore, it is the purpose of the verification classes to check and make sure someone has the rights to look at the specific data she is requesting.

Determining the Needed Functionality

Once you have the data for the classes you want to define, you also need to know what potential methods or functionality the classes will implement. For most of your classes, the functionality is pretty simple—read functions to retrieve the data in the class, or write functions that update the data in the class, verifying it as necessary before updating the actual persistent data.

For "pure" data classes, such as the SSN class, you aren't really going to need any functionality. There will be stuff to do validation of input, but from the perspective of the programmer using the class, it simply stores data and returns it to you. For other classes, such as the personal contact information class, there might be a bit more to do. For example, there is the notion of contact information for the employee. Do you restrict this to a single contact, or are there multiple contacts? In the real world, there are almost certainly multiple contacts.

At this point, you are beginning to discuss relationships between data objects. Each employee clearly only has one SSN. However, they can have multiple personal information blocks, since they might have several living spaces and have numerous people associated with them.

This kind of information is called *data modeling* and is usually done by an expert in the database world called a *DBA (database administrator)*. You would rarely have to do the design of a data model as a developer, but you would be responsible for writing the code that holds onto that data.

Finally, you might look at the tax information. Taxes are a very serious business (as the IRS is so fond of telling us) and require you do things properly. As a result, you need to make sure that each tax "bracket" is properly computed, and that the data for withholding (that is, the money that is sent to the government for annual taxes) is properly computed and sent to the right place.

One thing that becomes clear when you talk about keeping track of money sent and withheld is that there will be a need for reporting in your system. You will need to report on an individual's withholding, their taxes and pay, the overall withholding for the company, and what needs to be sent to the government on a monthly or quarterly basis.

Reporting, you might notice, did not come up on the original list of functionality needed; however, most systems do require reporting. The need for ancillary functionality is quite common in systems. Another area where this is likely is in auditing. "Who looked at my taxes? Who ran this report? Who changed what data in my personal contact information?" Auditing is something that you don't need, well, until you need it. When something suddenly changes and you need to know why, the audit log or audit report is where you look.

Final Thoughts on Design

As you can see, determining all of the pieces of a design for a system like this is hard work, and comes with experience. The best way to work through things like this is to first decompose the requirements into objects, as you've done previously. You should then consider what those objects will be used for and see when reports, auditing, security, and the like will need to be applied.

 ERROR MESSAGE

The surest way to fail at designing a system is to assume you know up front everything that is going to be needed. Leave time to examine the pieces once you have created them in order to build a system that is extensible and covers all of the needs of the users. Go through the current process the user uses to implement whatever it is the system does in order to make sure you are handling all of the pieces.

Probably the most important thing to consider when designing a system is that the work of design is rarely ever truly finished. Systems change and adapt to the workflow the users using the system create and use. That means your system must adapt and change to handle new workflows and new processes. It is important that you provide a way to do things that the user needs, or your system will not be used and you will have wasted a lot of time and energy.

This sums up the design process. I realize there is no code here to show you how to turn design into coding, but you can apply these processes to anything you write. Next up, I'll talk a bit about testing and making sure your system does what it is supposed to do.

The Least You Need to Know

- Programs have requirements and must satisfy those requirements in order to make the users happy.
- Requirements map directly to program design and must be decomposed in order to ensure they are properly handled.
- Working with users is key to making sure all the requirements are properly understood and the program design does what the user needs.
- Programs have "layers" that need to be independent of each other yet provide the functionality needed by other layers to implement requirements.
- Design is done first at a high level, and then broken down into lower and smaller components.

Testing

A program is only as good as the code behind it and the process by which it is created. Testing is intended to find defects or "bugs" in the system before they reach the end user and are serious problems in the workplace.

Both developers and testers are responsible for finding defects—developers are supposed to find them as they write code, testers are supposed to find them once the code is put together. In this chapter, I discuss testing code and the different ways to do so.

What Is Testing?

Developers rarely think about the process, or how well the code is written while they are writing it. Sometimes, the people who write code are often the absolute worst folk when it comes to judging the quality of that code and the quality of the functionality of the applications they write. That's why it's important for you to make sure you not only know how to write code, but also know how to test it to make sure it works properly.

The process by which you verify and validate your applications is called *testing*, and those who perform the process for a living are called *testers*. You may also hear the process referred to as *quality assurance (QA)*, which is a similar kind of thing.

It is not only the job of the tester to verify that code works properly. When working on commercial software, you, as a developer, should not turn over code to the testing group that doesn't work or that you haven't tried out to a reasonable level of satisfaction. Instead, it is the job of the testing group to verify things that are exceptional in their nature—problems that may crop up in weird circumstances when the user is using the application.

Different Kinds of Testing

As there are different sorts of developers, there are different kinds of tests and different kinds of testers. As a developer, you will rely on unit and integration tests to check bugs, fix problems, and verify that our changes have not badly influenced the program functionality. On the other hand, testers will do the verification and validation of the requirements and functionality of the tests.

Let's take a look at the various kinds of tests, in the order they are generally done in the real world, and see how they apply in your programming life.

Unit Testing

Unit testing is the most basic form of testing for the developer. When you write a "unit," you write tests that exercise the basic functionality of the unit from both *positive* and *negative aspects*.

⚙ DEFINITION

Positive aspects for a test or for code mean that it does what it is supposed to do. For example, if I write a function that is supposed to take a number and square it, I expect that if I pass it a zero, I get back a zero; if I pass it a two, I get back a four; and so forth. **Negative aspects** test for bad inputs and inputs that make no sense. For example, if I write a square root function and pass it a negative number, I expect to get back an error.

I'll show you examples of positive and negative unit tests soon, but for now, the important thing to realize is that unit tests are the sole purview of the developer. Testers do not write unit tests, as they are not expected to understand the deep level of the code, only the functionality the code provides.

Unit testing is important for two reasons. First of all, it shows the code works or at least handles errors properly. Without this minimum, testers really have nowhere to start, and no confidence in the code they are given. Second, unit tests become the basic documentation for how to use the system for both developers and testers.

When you write code, the only real documentation available you can absolutely trust is the code itself and any test code that uses it. Written documentation can go out of date, with changes to the code not reflected in the pages of text, and documentation in the form of online help files or the like can easily be wrong. The only true measure of how code works is to look at it or to run known tests against it. This is why unit testing is crucial.

Mock Testing

Mock testing is a very interesting concept that generally applies to both developers and testers. When you are developing a complex system, it is not at all uncommon to have some pieces of the code ready while others are not. "Mocking," rather than being some way of insulting developers, is the action of providing fake implementations of code so you can test certain actions within the code.

For example, suppose your code had to read a file and return a value from it. You could create a thousand different files and store the values you need in each one, along with the expected result when that value is fed to the function you are testing. Alternatively, you could write a "mock" function that returns the values you want from the file read each time, along with the expected value. It is a powerful but pretty advanced technique for developers.

Ad-Hoc Testing

Ad-hoc testing is probably the most common form of testing. In this methodology, the tester (or developer; it really applies to both) simply tries the code in various ways without really applying any kind of systematic approach. Basically, ad-hoc testing just tries out the code in ways the developer or tester thinks that the user might use it. Ad-hoc testing is not particularly effective, but it is a good quick way of verifying the code is working.

A simple example of ad-hoc testing might simply be trying to type letters in a numeric field or leaving fields blank on a form. There is no really formal methodology to it; you are just trying things as they occur to you. So if a drop-down box says "Select One" in it and you don't, what happens? That's what you're trying to find out with this testing.

> **PROGRAMMING TIP**
>
> All forms of testing have their purposes, and they tend to run from the least formal (such as ad-hoc testing) to the most formal (such as regression testing). Other forms of testing fall somewhere in between. This is not meant to make you into a tester, but some knowledge of how your software is likely to be tested will aid you in developing better code.

Regression Testing

Regression testing is the effort of verifying a change to the underlying code doesn't affect the overall application. For example, suppose you rewrite a function that inputs data from the user and validates it. That function is likely used all over the place, so it would be good to know if it broke any of the functionality that uses the input function somewhere.

Unit tests are often used as automated regression tests to ensure new changes to code do not break the existing application. Testing is not simply about finding problems; it is also about finding problems as quickly as possible so that they can be fixed and never escape to annoy the end user. Therefore, it is common to run regression tests automatically when you make a change to the system, so you know immediately if something has been broken.

Integration Testing

Integration testing is an interesting subject. To understand it, imagine you are building a car. Now, a car is a pretty big thing to put together, so you have various groups working on various pieces—one group might be working on the transmission, another on the engine, yet another on the body and paint, and so on. Each group does unit testing to make sure their pieces work, that the engine runs and generates power, that the transmission turns and delivers torque, and so forth. But how do you know that the transmission works with the engine and make the wheels turn? That is the integration test level.

Load Testing

Along with stress testing and acceptance testing, load testing (also known as performance testing) is done solely by the testing group to ensure the program does what it is supposed to in a timely fashion. It's done once the program is supposedly ready to go to make sure it will stand up to the expected use by the end users.

Suppose, for example, you were creating a website that was supposed to allow 1,000 concurrent users (that is, 1,000 people on it at the same time at any given time). You might set up a test to hammer at different pages using software to emulate 1,000 or even 5,000 users to see how the system responds.

Usability Testing

Usability testing verifies the program is easy to use and that the user can figure out how to accomplish whatever task they are assigned without undue burden due to the user interface.

Usability testing is something of an art, but some parts of it can be considered scientific. For example, you might test to see if the user can move between the fields in a form properly, from top to bottom, using the keyboard. You might also verify that the same font is used on all pages.

Security Testing

Security testing is a test to verify the system remains securely intact, regardless of the types of attacks that are launched against it.

Security testing is of particular importance in the web world, but it has a lot of meaning in the desktop world as well. Knowing that your data is intact is a big relief to many corporate security officers and users.

Acceptance Testing

Acceptance testing (or end-to-end testing) is normally the final test run on the system. The users, developers, and testers all examine the requirements and needs of the system and agree upon a set of tests that verify all of the needs have been met and that the system behaves properly under normal circumstances. Once the acceptance tests are run, the application is then released to the users.

This doesn't mean, of course, there are no bugs—merely that the bugs found are not in the main body of functionality provided by the program.

ERROR MESSAGE

Testing is important, and should not be overlooked. Never forget to test your code before you turn it over to someone else!

Examples of Testing

If you've never done testing before, it can be hard to know where to start. Therefore, I want to introduce some code to be tested, help you write some tests, and discuss what the test results mean.

Let's test a very simple function and look at the kinds of tests you would write were you a developer working on it. The function you'll be working with is shown in Listing 18.1.

```python
def divideByInteger(i, j):
    if (j == 0):
        raise Exception("Division by zero!")
    if (i == 0):
        return 0
    if (i < 0):
        return -1 * (i / j)
    return i / j
```

Listing 18.1

A function to test in Python.

For this, you can write some ad-hoc tests just to get a sense of what kind of things this function will do when it is provided with information. For example, let's look at the output from some simple data inputs:

```
>>> divideByInteger(1, 2)
0.5
>>> divideByInteger(0, 0)
Traceback (most recent call last):
  File "<pyshell#1>", line 1, in <module>
    divideByInteger(0, 0)
  File "F:/Books/Beginning Programming/Chapter 18/ch18-1.py", line 3, in
  divideByInteger
    raise Exception("Division by zero!")
Exception: Division by zero!
>>> DivideByInteger(-1, 1)
1.0
>>>
```

If all you knew about this function was the code that was shown, you might think all of these tests were valid and returned proper data. On the other hand, if you look at the actual requirements for the function, something else might be revealed.

The requirements that were handed to the developer for this function were as follows:

1. Return the integer division result of two numbers—in other words, the nonfractional part of any divisor (such as 4 ÷ 3 = 1).

2. For any division in which the divisor (the top part of the fraction) is zero, return zero.

3. Check for division by zero and, if found, raise an exception.

4. For negative numbers, return the positive result. For example, for -4 ÷ 2, return 2 rather than -2.

5. For all other results, return the normal integer division result.

Now, if you look at the ad-hoc tests, the code handles several of these cases. However, the results of these cases are not necessarily what you would expect. For example, the very first requirement says the result should be an integer. Looking at the result of the inputs (1, 2), you are getting back ½ or 0.5, which is not an integer. This is clearly a violation of the requirements and a bug in the code.

PROGRAMMING TIP

One of the most important things a programmer can do when testing his own—or someone else's—code is to verify the bare minimum of the requirements is being handled. This is known as the "happy path" in programming. Happy path testing is all positive based; it verifies that if you do things the way they are supposed to be done, the system responds the way it should. This kind of positive testing is something programmers should focus on. Negative, or unhappy path, testing is more the area of the tester.

The next interesting bug is caused by the order of requirements, which were not handled properly by the developer. Note that any input in which the top value is 0 should return 0, regardless of the value of the lower value. That is, 0 ÷ 0 will return 0, even though it is division by zero. This is, admittedly, a poorly written requirement, since it depends on the order of how things are evaluated; however, it is a bug nonetheless. Your input of (0, 0) shows this in the ad-hoc testing.

If you create a matrix or grid of the tests you want to evaluate, along with the results of those tests, it would look something like this:

Input	Expected Result	Actual Result
4, 3	1	1.3333333333333333
0, 0	0	Exception
2, 0	Exception	Exception
-4, 2	2	2.0
4, 2	2	2.0

This matrix, known as a *test result matrix,* shows three things: the values you send to the function, the expected result from the requirements, and the actual result when the inputs are passed to the function. In all cases where the actual result does not match the expected result, the test case fails and you have a bug that needs to be fixed.

You next go back to the developer (you, in this case) and point out the discrepancies in the code. As the developer, you look at the matrix and then fix the code, going through the items one at a time and running your tests each time to verify that not only did you fix any bugs, but you also didn't break anything. You are now doing regression testing using your unit tests. Your new code is shown in Listing 18.2.

```
def divideByInteger(i, j):
    if (i == 0):
        return 0
    if (j == 0):
        raise Exception("Division by zero!")
    if (i < 0):
        return -1 * int((i / j))
    return int(i/j)
```

Listing 18.2

A simple function to divide a number by an integer.

Let's look at the input values from the test matrix and the results that come back when you run those input values as tests to the function:

```
>>> divideByInteger(4, 3)
1
>>> divideByInteger(0, 0)
0
>>> divideByInteger(2, 0)
Traceback (most recent call last):
  File "<pyshell#10>", line 1, in <module>
    divideByInteger(2, 0)
  File "F:/Books/Beginning Programming/Chapter 18/ch18-2.py", line 5, in
  divideByInteger
    raise Exception("Division by zero!")
Exception: Division by zero!
>>> divideByInteger(-4, 2)
2
>>> divideByInteger(4, 2)
2
```

Everything looks okay, doesn't it? Ah, if only things were that simple in the testing world. Sadly, no, the answer is that you are actually missing a test and still have a bug. Consider the case of a negative input. The requirement says that a negative input should be treated as a negative number. What if the bottom divisor is negative?

```
>>> divideByInteger(4, -2)
-2
```

Oops. That isn't correct! So, once again, you go back to the developer (still you, sorry) and point out the problem. You sigh and add yet some more code to fix the problem, as shown in Listing 18.3.

```
def divideByInteger(i, j):
    if (i == 0):
        return 0
    if (j == 0):
        raise Exception("Division by zero!")
    if (i < 0 or j < 0):
        return -1 * int((i / j))
    return int(i / j)
```

Listing 18.3

The fixed version of the function.

Now, when you run the problem test, you see the following:

```
>>> divideByInteger(4, -2)
2
>>> divideByInteger(-4, 2)
2
```

Everything works properly! You now have a working function according to the requirements. You can add this code to the codebase and allow others to use it, confident that the code doesn't have any bugs according to the requirements.

PROGRAMMING TIP

Unit testing is a part of the system, just as documentation is or requirements are. You are responsible for writing unit tests that verify that the code works and keeping those tests up to date when the code changes.

What Does Testing Produce?

You've now written some ad-hoc tests that showed some bugs in the preceding example software. Realistically, what did you get out of the process? The answer is, a lot more than you might imagine. For one thing, you have a list of tests you can use in the future to verify that changes to the code do not cause existing functionality to break. Secondly, you know that certain parts of the code are working properly for the inputs you have identified. That means if you track a different problem down to a call to one of those bits of functionality, you know that the underlying code is not to blame, meaning you need to look at the calling program for problems.

A good example of the latter problem is the exception thrown in the case of division by zero. Imagine you call the function with a zero divisor, but the exception is swallowed up by the code that called it. The result is not defined, so you could end up with almost anything happening after that. Check out this small code snippet to see what I'm talking about:

```
def divideByInteger(i, j):
    if (i == 0):
        return 0
    if (j == 0):
        raise Exception("Division by zero!")
    if (i < 0 or j < 0):
        return -1 * int((i / j))
    return int(i / j)

x = 99 # Initialize the variable to some value
try:
    x = divideByInteger(3,0)
except:
    # Don't do anything.
    pass

print("x = {}".format(x))
```

You would expect that the variable *x* would be assigned the value zero, since it is a division by zero issue. However, you don't assign the variable any value in the code that issues the exception, so it remains whatever it happened to be. You can make the case this is a bug in the function for not initializing the variable, but the real problem is the code that called it simply swallowed the exception, meaning you never know that it happened.

You know the division by zero case works, because you have a regression test suite that is reporting no failures. Therefore, the problem with the variable is either something new in the code or something in the calling code. Examining your code, you can quickly realize it is the latter case that is the problem.

So what do you get from a test suite? Validation that your code works and a regression suite you can use to verify that things work. You also get assurance the code you are calling is correct, meaning any issues you run across are in your own code.

PROGRAMMING TIP

The real reason we do regression testing as programmers is to verify that something hasn't broken. When you think about it, if you have to write 10 tests for each feature and run them, then by the time you reach the fiftieth feature, you are spending all of your time doing testing! To avoid that, programmers create a regression suite of tests so it can verify that all of the old features still work the way they are supposed to.

Complex Testing

Testing is often more complex than calling a single function and getting back a return value to test against a known value. You can also test complex systems, such as classes, where pieces interact and you must be sure that the output is still correct even when multiple pieces interact with valid and invalid inputs.

One of the biggest problems in testing a class is the initialization routines often have serious effects on other pieces of code. Depending on how a class is initialized, methods of that class may return certain values or may cause exceptions to be generated.

For our purposes, I will have you try testing a fairly simple class, just because it makes no real sense to create a hideously complex class with no functionality behind it just to test it. Let's begin by creating a class that implements some very basic statistical functions. The class will accept a list of values (numbers) and then compute simple statistics like the mean, mode, and such.

The class shown in Listing 18.4 is far from a complete statistical package. The purpose of this class is to show how to test classes that have data stored inside of them and manipulate it. Don't be afraid of the size of the class or the number of methods it has. The code for the class really isn't very complex, and you can look at it one piece at a time.

```python
class Statistics:
    """ Statistics module or Python """
    def __init__(self):
        self.values = []
        self.value_count = 0
    def set_values(self, vals):
        self.values = vals
        self.value_count = len(self.values)
    def print_values(self):
        for v in self.values:
            print("Value: {}".format(v))
```

```
def compute_average(self):
    total = 0
    for v in self.values:
        total = total + v
    return total / self.value_count
def compute_median(self):
    newList = sorted(self.values)
    mid = self.value_count / 2
    return newList[int(mid)]
def compute_range(self):
    newList = sorted(self.values)
    # Range is largest - smallest
    return newList[self.value_count - 1] - newList[0]
def compute_standard_deviation(self):
    stddev = 0
    average = 0
    average = self.compute_average()
    diffsquared = 0
    sum_diffsquared = 0
    for val in self.values:
        diffsquared = (val - average) ** 2
        sum_diffsquared = diffsquared + sum_diffsquared
    stddev = (sum_diffsquared / self.value_count) ** (1 / 2)
    return stddev
def add_value(self, val):
    self.values.append(val)
def remove_value(self, val):
    self.values.remove(val)
```

Listing 18.4

The statistics class.

This class has numerous problems and quite a few serious bugs. Before you start looking at test cases and writing code to test the thing, you need to take a look at the code and see how many problems you can find. This is called *manual inspection* and is a real technique for examining and testing code. By having other developers and testers manually inspect the code and the usage of that code, you will find many problems you miss while writing the code in the first place.

Did you find them all? Probably not, since a lot of bugs are hidden in code that looks perfectly fine. So the question is, how do you test a system that has different methods that work together? For example, take a look at the compute_standard_deviation() method. The code itself does a pretty standard computation, but there is a call to the compute_average() method embedded in there. That means if the compute_average() method has a problem, it may or may not show up when trying to find the standard deviation. This is a dependency problem, and you need to identify dependencies to have any hope of finding problems in the code.

> **PROGRAMMING TIP**
>
> One of the most important things about programming is building up complex code from simple code. That is, you have simple functions that perform a single action and use them to build up complex actions. Unless the simple code is well tested and verified to work, you will spend all of your time digging through the code to figure out why the complex case fails.

Creating Test Scripts for Reuse

Up to this point, you've done your testing at the IDLE command problem, typing in the data and calls you want to test. This works, certainly, but it is horribly inefficient. Can you imagine doing this for a hundred different methods each time you want to do a regression test of the system? It would be horrible, time consuming, and error prone. The last thing you need is to find "phantom" errors because what you are looking for is caused by sending data that doesn't match your expected output. That would be like typing in the following and expecting a 2:

```
X = 1 + 1
```

But then, after a long day of testing and exhaustion, you type one run as follows and still expect that 2:

```
X = 1 + 2
```

The code is right and the output is right; however, the input is not what it should be, and you are reporting a bug that doesn't exist. Needless to say, developers are not fond of that sort of problem.

So how do you get around the problem of manually entering the data each time? The answer, of course, is to create your own functions that do a single test and then evaluate the list of tests when you want to. This way, you can not only easily run a list of functions, but you can also divide them into segments. For example, you might have a set of functions that test the __init__() method of the class. You can put them all together and run them together and see if the __init__() function runs without having to run all the rest of the functions in the class.

But enough of all that—let's take a look at how you really do this, because that's what you care about most!

Testing Classes

Taking what you know about testing a single method and what you now understand about writing test scripts, you can approach the problem fairly easily. The first step for testing classes is to test the individual methods of the class.

Your first test is of the __init__() method for the code in Listing 18.4 is shown in Listing 18.5.

```
def test_init():
    testobj = Statistics()
    if len(testobj.values) != 0:
        print("Error in test_init: values should be empty. Instead, has {}".
format(len(testobj.values)))
        return False
    if testobj.value_count != 0:
        print("Error in test_init: value_count should be zero. Instead, has
{}".format(testobj.value_count))
        return False
    # If all went well, return a value to the caller.
    return True
```

Listing 18.5

Testing the __init__() method.

Testing methods that take no arguments are pretty easy. You don't have to worry about permutations of the input data—you just want to make sure the final state of the object is correct. In the case of the code in Listing 18.5, you want to make sure the Statistics object is empty when you are done. If the final state of the object is not correct, you have found a bug, which means you need to fix it.

The next step is testing a method that does take arguments. In this case, there are a lot of possible tests, but you'll just look at two of them. In the set_values() method shown in Listing 18.4, you pass in a list of data. You'll first test an empty data set to verify the method handles the case of data not present. That test is shown in Listing 18.6.

```
def test_set_values_empty():
    testobj = Statistics()
    testobj.set_values([])
    if len(testobj.values) != 0:
        print("Error in test_init: values should be empty. Instead, has {}".
format(len(testobj.values)))
        return False
    if testobj.value_count != 0:
        print("Error in test_init: value_count should be zero. Instead, has
{}".format(testobj.value_count))
        return False
    # If all went well, return a value to the caller.
    return True
```

Listing 18.6

Testing the set_values() method with no data.

Of course, you need to do the same test for setting values with a valid list, which you can see in Listing 18.7.

```
def test_set_values_not_empty():
    testobj = Statistics()
    list = [1, 2, 3, 4, 5]
    testobj.set_values(list)
    if len(testobj.values) != len(list) :
        print("Error in test_init: values should be same as input. Instead,
has {}".format(len(testobj.values)))
        return False
    if testobj.value_count != len(list):
        print("Error in test_init: value_count should be same as input.
Instead, has {}".format(testobj.value_count))
        return False
    # If all went well, return a value to the caller.
    return True
```

Listing 18.7

Testing the set_values() method with data.

Note that you set the list variable containing the data to a variable and then work with the variable. This is a good technique for the beginner to get used to, as it allows you to easily change the values, read them from some input file, or verify them in other ways.

ERROR MESSAGE

Hard coding is when you have actual values in a method instead of variables that are either set from an initialization routine or read from a file. You should never hard code values, if at all possible. You should also avoid "magic numbers," which might be, say, the number of days in a year (365), or the value of pi to 2 digits (3.14). Running across these numbers in the code doesn't mean anything to someone who didn't write it, but seeing something more like the following:

```
Number_of_days_in_the_year = 365
```

And then using the variable later on makes a lot more sense.

The process you are using here can be done with each and every one of the methods in the class shown in Listing 18.4. Hopefully, you can see the process of changing the input values, writing functions to test the class methods, and validating the output of those test functions (known as *test automation*) is a very useful thing in the software world.

However, I did tell you there were some serious problems in the code, so I'd like to take a look at some test functions that show the problems, if you haven't found them already.

Listing 18.8 shows a test of the compute_average() method.

```
def test_compute_average_empty():
    testobj = Statistics()
    testobj.set_values([])
    # Run the average
    avg = testobj.compute_average()
    if avg != 0 :
        print("Error in compute_average: average should be zero for empty set.
  Instead, has {}".format(avg))
        return False

    # If all went well, return a value to the caller.
    return True
```

Listing 18.8

Testing the compute_average() method.

Because the average of an empty set (a set with no values) should be zero, you test for that value. However, when you run the test method, you get a very different result:

```
>>> test_compute_average_empty()
Traceback (most recent call last):
  File "<pyshell#9>", line 1, in <module>
    test_compute_average_empty()
  File "F:\Books\Beginning Programming\Chapter 18\ch18_5.py", line 81, in
  test_compute_average_empty
    avg = testobj.compute_average()
  File "F:\Books\Beginning Programming\Chapter 18\ch18_5.py", line 16, in
  compute_average
    return total / self.value_count
ZeroDivisionError: division by zero
```

Oops! What happened here? You called everything properly, didn't you? Well, kind of. If you look at the test case:

```
def test_compute_average_empty():
    testobj = Statistics()
    testobj.set_values([])
    # Run the average
    avg = testobj.compute_average()
    if avg != 0:
        print("Error in compute_average: average should be zero for empty set.
  Instead, has {}".format(avg))
        return False

    # If all went well, return a value to the caller.
    return True
```

You will see that it first calls the set_values() function with no entries in the list. That means the count of list values is zero. Now, let's take a look at the function that the test code calls, compute_average():

```
def compute_average(self):
    total = 0
    for v in self.values:
        total = total + v
    return total / self.value_count
```

The first part of the code is pretty simple and will work under any circumstances. You loop through the values in the list and total them. If there are no values in the list, the total will be zero, and that's fine. It is the second piece of the function that causes the issue. You take the total of all the values and divide them by the count of values. Uh oh, there's where the problem lies! If there are no values, the count is zero, and you get a division by zero error, as you saw in the test run.

PROGRAMMING TIP

This sort of testing is called *edge case testing*. When you work with a list, for example, that list might contain 10 items on average. However, the smallest case is an empty list. This should always be one of your tests. Likewise, a very large number of items in a list may expose other problems, so test it with that kind of input as well.

This error is based solely on a poor programming practice—not checking to see that the value you are dividing by is zero. You can fix this easily enough by changing the method to read as follows:

```
def compute_average(self):
  if self.value_count == 0 :
     return 0
     total = 0
     for v in self.values:
         total = total + v
     return total / self.value_count
```

Physical vs. Logical Errors

Physical errors in programs are caused by bad programming and poor code. Most of the errors you've looked at from this point, such as the previous one dealing with dividing by zero, are caused directly by physical errors. They aren't all that way, however. For example, consider the following test case:

```
def test_compute_average_add_value():
    testobj = Statistics()
    testobj.set_values([])
    # Add a single value
    testobj.add_value(3)
    # Compute the average
    avg = testobj.compute_average()
    if avg != 3:
        print("Error in compute_average: average should be 3 for a single
value. Instead, has {}".format(avg))
        return False

    # If all went well, return a value to the caller.
    return True
```

This test case is similar to, but slightly different from, the previous case. You do create an empty set of values, but then you add a single value to the list and calculate the average.

You might normally think that would return the value, since the average of a single value is that value. However, when you run this test case in IDLE, you get the following very unexpected result:

```
>>> test_compute_average_add_value()
Traceback (most recent call last):
  File "<pyshell#0>", line 1, in <module>
    test_compute_average_add_value()
  File "F:\Books\Beginning Programming\Chapter 18\ch18_5.py", line 95, in
  test_compute_average_add_value
    avg = testobj.compute_average()
  File "F:\Books\Beginning Programming\Chapter 18\ch18_5.py", line 16, in
  compute_average
    return total / self.value_count
ZeroDivisionError: division by zero
```

Now, how can that be? After all, you added a value to the list, didn't you? Let's take a quick look at the values in the list to verify the value was added properly.

First, you add the code to the test case to print out the value:

```
def test_compute_average_add_value():
    testobj = Statistics()
    testobj.set_values([])
    # Add a single value
    testobj.add_value(3)
    # Print the values
    testobj.print_values()
    # Compute the average
    avg = testobj.compute_average()
    if avg != 3:
        print("Error in compute_average: average should be 3 for a single
    value. Instead, has {}".format(avg))
        return False

    # If all went well, return a value to the caller.
    return True
Next, we run the code:
>>> test_compute_average_add_value()
Value: 3
Traceback (most recent call last):
  File "<pyshell#1>", line 1, in <module>
    test_compute_average_add_value()
```

```
File "F:\Books\Beginning Programming\Chapter 18\ch18_5.py", line 97, in
test_compute_average_add_value
  avg = testobj.compute_average()
File "F:\Books\Beginning Programming\Chapter 18\ch18_5.py", line 16, in
compute_average
  return total / self.value_count
ZeroDivisionError: division by zero
```

PROGRAMMING TIP

Adding print statements and other debugging output to a test routine is very common in the programming world. It allows you to see both the input and output values you are sending into various functions. This can help you pin down problems, so you can quickly and easily debug your programs.

As you can see, the value is there. So why isn't the calculation working? Remember, the compute_average() code first calculates the total of all the values and then divides it by the count of values. The division (and error) occurs here:

```
return total / self.value_count
```

The only way you can get a division by zero error is if the value_count attribute of the object is zero, right? But that can't happen, because you added a value and the count should be one. If you go into the test code and print it out, however, you'll see the value_count attribute is zero. That's why you get a division by zero error. The question is, why is this happening?

This is an example of a logical error, rather than a physical one. You have put data in the list and expect the code will look at the list to see how many values are in it. However, the original design for the code didn't use the length of the list; it chose to create another variable in the class that stored the number of data elements. If you look at the add_value() method of the class:

```
def add_value(self, val):
    self.values.append(val)
```

You can see here that while the data is properly added to the list, the value_count variable is not updated. This means if the list was empty to begin with, it remains at zero and you get the dreaded division by zero error.

Never use more variables than you really need. If you have a list and want the count of it, get the count directly using the length of the list, not some other variable.

As this example shows, most logical errors result from an attempt to be elegant or "cute" when writing code. To fix the problem, you can simply add a single line to the add and remove value methods of the class:

```
def add_value(self, val):
    self.values.append(val)
  self.value_count = len(self.values)
def remove_value(self, val):
    self.values.remove(val)
  self.value_count = len(self.values)
```

This line probably isn't necessary, and you could simply replace the value_count variable with either a direct call to the len() function or write your own function to return the length of the list:

```
def value_count(self):
    return len(self.values)
```

You can then use this method everywhere the value_count variable or len() function was used on the list. By keeping it simple, and you can avoid most logical errors in your code.

While physical errors can be caught by simply throwing random data at methods and seeing whether good data is processed and bad data is handled properly (or ignored properly), logical errors usually require a *white box* approach, where you actually know what the code does and how it does it.

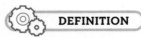

DEFINITION

White box testing requires you to look at the code and see how it works, so you can test individual blocks and choices within the code.

When Have You Done Enough Testing?

Probably the hardest thing to decide when you are writing test code is when you have done "enough." Clearly, if you want to test every single line and every single interaction in your code, you could be writing tests forever. This really isn't very optimal and isn't likely to lead to delivering a product anytime in your lifetime.

In order to avoid testing for life, most test plans include a list of "user acceptance tests." These are tests the testing group or the end users decide are absolutely necessary to use the software. If all of these tests pass, you can at least deliver the code to the user and continue to test the thing for more esoteric problems.

> **PROGRAMMING TIP**
>
> Remember, software is for the end user, not the developer or the tester. It is imperative that you deliver software that works and does the things that were originally agreed upon for the system.

Hopefully, you now have a semi-firm grip on what testing software is and why you need to do it with your own code. End users will put up with a lot in your code, but problems that prevent them from getting their jobs done will not be tolerated. Make sure it does what it is supposed to and, just as importantly, doesn't do what it isn't supposed to.

The Least You Need to know

- Programmers are responsible for basic testing of the code they write.
- There are many different types of testing. Some are solely for programmers, some are solely for testers, and some are for both.
- You can create test scripts for reuse that help you run regression tests to make sure that you didn't break anything.
- There are two different kinds of errors to test for: physical and logical errors. Physical errors are ones that can be caught with simple code, while logical errors require understanding the code.
- In order to avoid testing a program for far too long, just make sure to complete the user acceptance tests. That way, you can release the program to the wild world of users.

The Python Debugger and Debugging

It is inevitable—when writing computer programs, you will introduce defects (or "bugs") into the application. How do you fix them? Debugging helps you find and fix the simplest errors, while software debuggers are essential for more-complex issues. In this chapter, I detail how to debug code.

In This Chapter

- Importing Python's debugger module
- Moving around in code
- Examining and modifying values in the debugger
- Putting in breakpoints
- Using the debugger to evaluate functions
- Exiting the debugger

What Is Debugging?

Code defects were given the cute name "bugs" by Grace Hopper, an operator working on a Harvard computer in 1947. She found that the computer was not working correctly due to a moth that had died on the logic board, causing a short circuit. From that point on, software problems were always blamed on bugs. (Of course, some computer software people prefer to blame gremlins, but we'll leave that to Bugs Bunny.) So the process of finding and removing defects from software has been called *debugging* ever since.

When you are writing very simple programs, such as the ones in this book, it is often enough to simply print out values as you go to see where the problem might be. When the programs get larger and more complex, though, that method begins to break down. For this reason, software debuggers were created early on in the development world. A software debugger allows you to step through your code and examine values and statements to see where a problem occurs.

How to Debug a Python Program

As soon as the language began to gain in respect and use, it was clear that Python would need the kinds of tools other languages have. An interpreted language is considerably easier to write many tools for, because you don't have to do wacky translations from the machine code generated by the compiler to the original source code written by the programmer; instead you can deal with the problem in the code as is.

For example, you might have a statement like this:

```
i = 0
while i < 10:
    print i
```

The code is very straightforward. It simply loops through values and prints them—or does it? In fact, this little code snippet contains a very serious bug—that of the infinite loop.

 ERROR MESSAGE

Many modern programming languages contain warnings in the compiler that will tell you if a value is not changed within a looping structure. Python, alas, does not, requiring you to always double-check to see if the loop terminating condition can be met. A technique known as "code inspection"—whereby someone else looks over your code before it is put into use—can be extremely helpful for tracking down problems like this.

You could look at this code all day and not see the problem, or you could be lucky enough to immediately see it. In this case, of course, the issue is that the value of "i" is never incremented within the loop, so it will simply print the following ad infinitum:

```
0
0
0
...
```

Not exactly what you had in mind, was it?

Now, in this very simple example, finding the problem won't take very long. Realizing that it is printing a zero each time gives you an awfully big clue as to what the underlying defect is. However, in a much-larger program—where this loop might be getting the value of "i" from some function or class method—it might not be nearly as obvious. This is when the debugger really comes in handy.

In Python, the debugger is simply a part of the system called *pdb*. (You might guess the letters stand for "Python debugger," and that would be a lucky guess on your part.) Unlike many other programming environments, the Python debugger actually becomes a part of your program, so it needs to be added and removed when you find a bug and fix it.

Python debugger pdb is implemented as an importable package. To use it, you need to include the following line at the top of any program that is being debugged:

```
Import pdb
```

Instrumenting Code to Be Debugged

Many programming languages allow you to debug a program without doing anything special, because they automatically include the information the debugger needs. For example, the debugger might see a function call in assembler to something called *__add_x()*. This function name would mean absolutely nothing to the developer, who is accustomed to seeing a function that looks more like this:

```
def addX(val):
    global x
     x +=val
```

So, there has to be a translation table somewhere that takes the mangled and strange names that the interpreter or compiler spits out and turns them into the "progammerese" we all know and love. This is how languages like C, C++, and FORTRAN worked. Newer languages like C#, Java, or others use a slightly different approach, whereby the information for the code is stored in an external file. Oddly enough, the extension of that file is quite often pdb, which stands for "program database." It has nothing to do with Python, however.

In the example, the addX() function might be turned into a symbol in the executable called _addX_i_2. To debug the executable, you need to have translation of _addX_i_2 to addX. This functionality is called *instrumenting* the code.

PROGRAMMING TIP

Always try to learn the extensions of the various files in your project so you can easily pick out what is important and what is not. For example, a .py file is a Python source file, while an .ini file is an initialization file that contains program startup information. Databases usually end in a .db or .dbx extension. Knowing what you are looking for makes it considerably easier to pick up existing projects and code and work with them.

Python is again different in how you instrument debugging into your application. In most programming languages, you simply "launch" the debugger, which reads the compiled or interpreted code and the source code and then allows you to merge the two and work with them. With Python, the debugger is an actual source module which you interact with while your program is running.

Take the following example of code:

```
def divide_two_numbers(x, y):
    return x / y

x = int(input("Enter a value for x: "))
y = int(input("Enter a value for y: "))

print("x / y = {}".format(divide_two_numbers(x, y)))
```

This code has a serious bug in it, one that isn't immediately apparent. If you run it as you expect the user to run it—in this case, putting in values for x and y so they can be divided—you get expected output:

```
Enter a value for x: 10
Enter a value for y: 20
x / y = 0.5
```

Whether or not the output should be a floating-point number is up to you; you could easily convert the output to an integer by changing the return statement in your function to read as follows:

```
return int(x/y)
```

Unfortunately, that won't solve the problem. Consider the following input from the user:

```
Enter a value for x: 20
Enter a value for y: 0
Traceback (most recent call last):
  File "M:/Books/Beginning Programming/Chapter 19/ch19_1.py", line 7, in
  <module>
    print("x / y = {}".format(divide_two_numbers(x, y)))
  File "M:/Books/Beginning Programming/Chapter 19/ch19_1.py", line 2, in
  divide_two_numbers
    return x / y
ZeroDivisionError: division by zero
```

Uh oh, that's not good. Now, the traceback is good enough to show you where the error occurred, but what if that was not enough? You would need to debug the program to find the error. If you recall from Chapter 3, you do this by putting in print statements like this:

```
def divide_two_numbers(x, y):
    print("X = {}".format(x))
    print("Y = {}".format(y))
    return x / y

x = int(input("Enter a value for x: "))
y = int(input("Enter a value for y: "))

print("x / y = {}".format(divide_two_numbers(x, y)))
```

The longer that a program gets, the more print statements you need to enter into it to find all of the values—and the easier it is to miss the one that is out of range. So how do you use the debugger to start looking at values as you need them?

As you read earlier, the first step to instrumenting a Python program is to import the pdb module into your application:

```
import pdb

def divide_two_numbers(x, y):
    return x / y

x = int(input("Enter a value for x: "))
y = int(input("Enter a value for y: "))

print("x / y = {}".format(divide_two_numbers(x, y)))
```

This simply loads all of the code for the debugger so it can be used. Now, it's time to use it. This is accomplished by the set_trace() function of the pdb module. You can think of the set_trace() function as "start the debugging from this point on." Because you want to debug the whole program, you add the line to the very top of the entry code:

PROGRAMMING TIP

> Most programming languages use an external program to debug code. Python is special in that it uses the language itself to debug code. The Python debugger (pdb) is written in Python, loaded by the interpreter, and applied to your code at run time.

```
import pdb

def divide_two_numbers( x, y ):
    return x / y

pdb.set_trace()

x = int(input("Enter a value for x: "))
y = int(input("Enter a value for y: "))

print("x / y = {}".format(divide_two_numbers(x, y)))
```

Now, when you run the program, a funny thing happens. It doesn't just show you the prompt to enter the x and y values—it also shows you something completely new:

```
> ch19_1.py(8)<module>()
-> x = int(input("Enter a value for x: "))
(Pdb)
```

As you can see, there's now a brand-new prompt—the debugging prompt. This is here to indicate that you are in the middle of debugging the program. Of course, it does no good to simply launch the debugger—you need to actually use the thing. For that, you need to move about the program.

Moving Through the Code

The easiest way to move through the code is to completely ignore the debugger and just run your program to see what kind of information you might need and where you might need to look at the code. But why would you load the debugger, only to ignore it? The answer is simple: you may have found the problem and simply want to see what the outcome is, or you may have changed something and want to see how the change affects your code.

For these cases, you use the "continue" command, or simply "c" (after all, pdb was written by programmers, so nothing requires more than a single keystroke to accomplish):

```
> ch19_1.py(8)<module>()
-> x = int(input("Enter a value for x: "))
(Pdb) c
Enter a value for x: 20
Enter a value for y: 10
x / y = 2.0
```

This runs the program from the current spot without the debugger interfering.

Stepping Line by Line Through the Code

Of course, you don't always want to just zoom through the entire program and ignore the use of the debugger. Sometimes, you want to step through each line and see what happens when you enter certain values. For this, the debugger provides the next or "n" command to step to the next line of the program.

For example, when the program starts, the next line is the input of the value of x, so you can execute code to that line:

```
> ch19_1.py(8)<module>()
-> x = int(input("Enter a value for x: "))
(Pdb) n
Enter a value for x: 20
> ch19_1.py(9)<module>()
-> y = int(input("Enter a value for y: "))
(Pdb)
```

As you can see, entering n moved you past the input prompt for the x value. You can then input the value of x and look at it, modify it, or do whatever you want with the code before moving on to the input of the y value.

ERROR MESSAGE

One important thing to remember is that the line you are looking at above the Pdb prompt has not yet been executed. Therefore, if you try to look at the value of x before running the input statement, you won't get anything except an error saying the variable name is undefined. You must first step over the line and input the value before you can look at it. This can be a bit confusing at the start, but you will get used to it quickly enough.

One thing you will probably find as you debug is that it is intensely annoying to have to type the n command over and over. For this reason, the debugger provides a shortcut for the last command. If you enter **n** the first time and then press **Enter** at each Pdb prompt, it will repeat the last command you issued to the thing, as you can see here:

```
ch19_1.py(8)<module>()
-> x = int(input("Enter a value for x: "))
(Pdb) n
Enter a value for x: 20
> ch19_1.py(9)<module>()
-> y = int(input("Enter a value for y: "))
(Pdb)
Enter a value for y: 10
> ch19_1.py(11)<module>()
-> print("x / y = {}".format(divide_two_numbers(x, y)))
(Pdb)
x / y = 2.0
--Return--
> ch19_1.py(11)<module>()->None
-> print("x / y = {}".format(divide_two_numbers(x, y)))
(Pdb)
```

Notice that I have not entered any command at the Pdb prompt, but it continues to advance to the next line of code to interpret.

Examining Values in the Debugger

If you simply use print() to examine values, you would have to print out each variable to see what it is. Not only does this slow down the execution of your program, but it also clutters the output to the point where you have no idea what you are looking at anymore.

The debugger makes examining values a lot easier. With the debugger, you look at values as they are created or calculated in the program. That way, you only see values when you want to.

PROGRAMMING TIP

> Remember, you can only look at a variable after it has been created. What is nice, however, is that within the debugger, you can examine a variable once and when you are certain it is correct, ignore it from that point on. On the other hand, a print() function call would print out the value each and every time the piece of code it resides in is called.

The print command, p, prints out the value of a variable that has been defined in the program prior to calling print(). In your program, for example, you could look at the value of the x variable as soon as the user inputs it from the console:

```
> ch19_1.py(8)<module>()
-> x = int(input("Enter a value for x: "))
(Pdb) n
Enter a value for x: 20
> ch19_1.py(9)<module>()
-> y = int(input("Enter a value for y: "))
(Pdb) p x
20
(Pdb)
```

Notice that printing out the value immediately shows you what the user entered. Had you somehow messed with that input and made it wrong, you'd know right away from printing out the value of the variable. This is one of the biggest advantages to using the debugger over embedding print statements or other output devices.

You can also do more with the debugger than just print out the static value of a variable; you can call functions using that variable. Suppose you modify your program to look like this:

```
import pdb

def divide_two_numbers( x, y):
    return x / y

def double_value(x):
    return x * 2

pdb.set_trace()

x = int(input("Enter a value for x: "))
y = int(input("Enter a value for y: "))

print("x / y = {}".format(divide_two_numbers(x, y)))
```

Now, you can run the debugger on the program and call the double_value() function even though it is not called in the program itself:

```
> ch19_1.py(11)<module>()
-> x = int(input("Enter a value for x: "))
(Pdb) n
Enter a value for x: 20
> ch19_1.py(12)<module>()
-> y = int(input("Enter a value for y: "))
(Pdb) p x
20
(Pdb) p double_value(x)
40
(Pdb)
```

PROGRAMMING TIP

One thing experienced programmers keep in their little programming toolboxes are functions they can call directly in the debugger that they will never use in the program. For example, we might want to dump the value of a complex data type like a dictionary to a file. We could have a function that you could call in the debugger that would only dump it when we want to look at the data more concisely outside the realm of the program.

So you have learned how to step through a program and look at values in the debugger. What is next? The ability to change values inside of the debugger would be handy, wouldn't it? Let's take a look at that.

Modifying Values in the Debugger

One of the most valuable operations in the debugger is the ability to actually change the value of a variable while the program is still running. For example, in the case of your code, the issue is that the value of the variable y could be zero. Now, you can test what would happen if you set the value to, say, 1 instead and continued the program.

Let's first look at a run of the debugger with this happening, along with the relevant lines highlighted:

```
> ch19_1.py(11)<module>()
-> x = int(input("Enter a value for x: "))
(Pdb) n
Enter a value for x: 20
> ch19_1.py(12)<module>()
-> y = int(input("Enter a value for y: "))
(Pdb) n
Enter a value for y: 0
> ch19_1.py(14)<module>()
-> print("x / y = {}".format(divide_two_numbers(x, y)))
(Pdb) s
--Call--
> ch19_1.py(3)divide_two_numbers()
-> def divide_two_numbers( x, y ) :
(Pdb) n
> ch19_1.py(4)divide_two_numbers()
-> return x / y
(Pdb) p y
0
(Pdb) y=1
(Pdb) p y
1
(Pdb) n
--Return--
> ch19_1.py(4)divide_two_numbers()->20.0
-> return x / y
(Pdb) n
--Call--
> run.py(270)__getattribute__()
-> def __getattribute__(self, name):
(Pdb) n
>__getattribute__()
-> if name in ('rpc', 'write', 'writelines'):
(Pdb) n
> __getattribute__()
-> return io.TextIOBase.__getattribute__(self, name)
(Pdb) c
x / y = 20.0
```

Let's look at each new block of code or instruction and see what is going on here. First, you have this line:

```
(Pdb) s
--Call--
```

The "s" or step command steps into a function. Normally, if you hit "next" while on a function call, the debugger will step over the function and not show you any of the code within the function. The function or method becomes a black box and you just see the output from it. When the problem you are trying to find is inside of a function, however, it is obvious that you can't do that; you have to go down inside the lower-level code and see what is going on.

Next up, you step through the lines of code defining the function and the Python infrastructure behind it and get to the line that does the actual calculation. Remember, the line showing is the next line to be executed, not the one that was previously run. So you get to this line:

```
-> return x / y
(Pdb) p y
0
```

As you can see, you are now looking at the return statement in the function, where your command should print out the value of the variable y. It does, and you can see that the value is zero, which causes a division by zero error—the exact problem you have been trying to track down.

To now change the value of y to 1, you simply assign the local variable a value in the debugger; that value is then carried over into the program itself:

```
(Pdb) y=1
(Pdb) p y
1
```

As you can see, setting the value gives you no feedback. The essence of the debugger is not to tell you anything unless there is something wrong. To verify the value has been changed, you can print it out, as shown in the preceding code.

> **PROGRAMMING TIP**
>
> When you are writing your own code, do not assume the user will accept as a given that any action she takes is correct. Give her some real feedback saying, for example, "File Saved Properly," rather than simply having the program return to its previous state without an error message. It will make you feel better about the code, and the user will be happier to not have to go out to the file system and verify the file was properly saved.

Following the reset of the variable value, you step through a couple lines just to see the debugger is perfectly capable of debugging the actual Python code in which the system is written, as well as the code you yourself wrote. You then let the program run to completion using the c command:

```
(Pdb) c
x / y = 20.0
```

Now, you can argue that the value returned from the program is not correct, and you would be right. Twenty divided by zero is not 20, nor any other valid number. But changing y to 1 lets you know what the problem is, so you can fix it in the code. Listing 19.1 shows you how to fix it.

```
import pdb

def divide_two_numbers(x, y):
    return x / y

def double_value(x):
    return x * 2

pdb.set_trace()

x = int(input("Enter a value for x: "))
y = int(input("Enter a value for y: "))

if y == 0:
    print("invalid attempt to divide by zero.")
else :
    print("x / y = {}".format(divide_two_numbers(x, y)))
```

Listing 19.1

The updated division program.

There is only one thing wrong with this listing—can you see what it is? Try running it in IDLE and see. When you launch the application in IDLE, you'll see the following:

```
> ch19_2.py(11)<module>()
-> x = int(input("Enter a value for x: "))
(Pdb) c
Enter a value for x: 20
Enter a value for y: 0
invalid attempt to divide by zero.
```

As you can see, the debugger is still running! Not exactly the way you want to deliver the code to the customer. Of course, you can just remove the line that says "pdb.set_trace()," and the whole thing will go back to running the way it was supposed to. However, what if you need to debug the code in the future? You'd have to go back and reinstrument the code and put the set_trace() call back.

Fortunately, you don't have to do that. Within your little program, you can set a single variable that indicates whether you are supposed to be using the debugger or not. I call mine do_debug, but you can call yours whatever you like. The code that shows you how to do this is shown in Listing 19.2.

```python
import pdb
import sys

def divide_two_numbers(x, y):
    return x / y

def double_value(x):
    return x * 2

do_debug = 0
if do_debug == 1 :
    pdb.set_trace()

x = int(input("Enter a value for x: "))
y = int(input("Enter a value for y: "))

if y == 0:
    print("invalid attempt to divide by zero.")
else :
    print("x / y = {}".format(divide_two_numbers(x, y)))
```

Listing 19.2

The conditional debug code.

As you can see, the trace code is only set if the do_debug flag is set to a nonzero or true value. Try setting it to both zero and 1 and see what the difference is. Assuming all the code was entered properly, you should get an output that looks like this for a debug equal to zero:

```
Enter a value for x: 20
Enter a value for y: 10
x / y = 2.0
When you set the debug value to one (do_debug=1), you should see something
   that looks a lot more like this:
> ch19_3.py(14)<module>()
-> x = int(input("Enter a value for x: "))
(Pdb)
```

This indicates the debugger is up and running properly.

Believe it or not, that does cover most of the major functionality of the debugger. But, as with all programs that have utility, there are quite a few other things you can use that are built into the debugger. Let's look at some of them.

Where Am I?

Sometimes, when working with particularly complicated code, it can be useful to know how you got to a given spot. This is most often used with breakpoints (I will talk about this more later in this chapter)—you know where a problem exists in the code, but you don't know how the program got to that precise spot.

The "l" or list command is made to order for this situation. The list command shows what is known as the *stack trace* to indicate where you are in the program. You can issue a list command at any time and it has no impact on the running program.

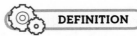
DEFINITION

The term **stack trace** comes from the fact that as each call to a function is made, the name and address of that function is "pushed" onto the stack so that it can be "unwound." This means the program keeps track of where it has been so it can return along the same path that it took, but in reverse. So if a program does this:

```
Func1()
Func2()
Func3()
...
```

The stack trace will look like the same list, but backward:

```
Func3()
Func2()
Func1()
```

And the program will return from func3() to func2() and so forth.

Imagine, for example, that you have code that looked like Listing 19.3 in your application.

```
def func1(level, str):
    print("Level: {} = {}".format(level, str))

def func2(str):
    func1(func2, str)

def func3(str, str2):
    func2(str2 + str)

def func4( str1, str2, str3 ):
    func3("func3", str1+str2+str3)

func4("Hello", "world", "here")
```

Listing 19.3

A complicated program.

I'm not saying you should ever write code like this—simply that you might end up inheriting something like it. Anyway, you run the program to see what it is doing, and it outputs something intensely useful like this:

```
>>>
Level: <function func2 at 0x0237CFA8> = Helloworldherefunc3
```

Oh, well, that helps. Why is this happening? Imagine, then, that you fire up your trusty debugger and step down into the code until you reach the only print statement call in the code. You then issue a list command to see how you got there. Here's what you will see in the debugging session:

```
> chapter 19\ch19_4.py(17)<module>()
-> func4("Hello", "world", "here")
(Pdb) s>>>
Level: <function func2 at 0x0237CFA8> = Helloworldherefunc3
>>>
--Call--
> chapter 19\ch19_4.py(12)func4()
-> def func4( str1, str2, str3 ):
(Pdb) s
> chapter 19\ch19_4.py(13)func4()
-> func3("func3", str1+str2+str3)
(Pdb) s
--Call--
> chapter 19\ch19_4.py(9)func3()
-> def func3(str, str2):
(Pdb) s
> chapter 19\ch19_4.py(10)func3()
-> func2(str2 + str)
(Pdb) s
--Call--
> chapter 19\ch19_4.py(6)func2()
-> def func2(str):
(Pdb) s
> chapter 19\ch19_4.py(7)func2()
-> func1(func2, str)
(Pdb) s
--Call--
> chapter 19\ch19_4.py(3)func1()
-> def func1(level, str):
(Pdb) s
> chapter 19\ch19_4.py(4)func1()
-> print("Level: {} = {}".format(level, str))
(Pdb) n
Level: <function func2 at 0x02370930> = Helloworldherefunc3
--Return--
> chapter 19\ch19_4.py(4)func1()->None
-> print("Level: {} = {}".format(level, str))
(Pdb) p level
<function func2 at 0x02370930>
(Pdb) list
  1     import pdb
  2
  3     def func1(level, str):
  4  ->     print("Level: {} = {}".format(level, str))
```

```
 5
 6    def func2(str):
 7        func1(func2, str)
 8
 9    def func3(str, str2):
10        func2(str2 + str)
```

Okay, the code is very confusing, I'll grant you that. But the one thing you can see is the set of lines that looks like this:

```
-> print("Level: {} = {}".format(level, str))
(Pdb) p level
<function func2 at 0x02370930>
```

It is very hard to believe that the programmer meant to print out the name of the function by calling the lowest-level function. The odds seem higher that she was using some sort of indentation code and meant to show where you were in the system. The listing of the stack trace shows how you got there in the actual code that was run, thereby helping you pinpoint the issue.

Dealing with Functions

Earlier, I talked a little bit about debugging functions when looking at the "s" or step command. This command allows you to enter a function rather than stepping over it. You might have code that looks like this, for example:

```
def func(x, y):
    x = x + 1
    y = y + 1
    return x + y
func(1,2)
```

PROGRAMMING TIP

Debugging is something of a science and something of an art. If you learn the commands of the debugger and then start to use them when writing code, you will learn much more about how things work than by simply trying to read the code or look at the output.

If the debugger is sitting on the line func(1,2) and you enter the command "n" for next, it will just jump over the code in func. If, on the other hand, you enter "s" for step, it will go into the code and begin the next debugging step at the definition of the function.

There is one more command that is not commonly used but may help you in the future—the "r" or return statement. This command will run to the end of a given function or method and will wait until you hit "n" to return to the calling program.

For example, if you are in the middle of a very complicated function and find the problem you are looking for, the "r" command can save you a lot of keystrokes. You don't have to continue to step over or into code to look at what is going on—you can simply move to the end of the function and see what the problem causes in the code that calls it.

Breakpoints

The term *breakpoint* comes from the idea that you are "breaking" into the code to stop execution at a given location or point. When you set a breakpoint, it will stay set for as long as you are debugging the program, so you can wait and try different things within the program to see how it gets to your chosen spot.

For example, suppose you have a reasonably simple program like the one shown in Listing 19.4. This program consists only of a single function and a single call to that function.

```
import pdb

def func(x, y, z, a):
    x = y + z + a
    y = x + a + 1
    z = 34
    return x + y + z

pdb.set_trace()

func(1,2,3,4)
```

Listing 19.4

A simple Python program.

Clearly, it would be easy enough to step into and through this program using the debugger and examine the various variables and their values. But what if this piece of code was embedded in a much larger program and did all sorts of other things? You still just want to look at what happens in the func() routine, but to get to it, you may have to step over hundreds of lines of code. This is clearly not an optimal solution!

A much better solution is to tell the program where you want to begin debugging and let it simply run until you get to that point—this is a breakpoint. It is kind of the inverse of the list command; rather than asking it how you got here, you simply tell it to go there however it likes and to stop when it has reached the point you are interested in.

The format of the breakpoint command is "b location," where "location" is the name of a function or method in which you want to *break* the execution of the program.

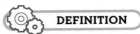 **DEFINITION**

Note that in this case, the term **break** means "stop," rather than "destroy."

Breakpoints are very useful in complex programs, so they're something you may want to learn how to use before you write your own large-scale Python programs.

Using the Debugger to Evaluate Functions

It may seem a bit strange, but you can use the debugger in "immediate" mode to evaluate anything you want. Immediate mode simply evaluates an expression, whether it be an arithmetic (math) expression or a program expression. For example:

```
(Pdb) 1+2+3
6
```

This is immediate mode, because the debugger accepts anything you type into it and tries to evaluate it immediately.

You can also call a function within Python if you are unsure of what it really ought to be returning:

```
(Pdb) str = "This is a test"
(Pdb) p str
'This is a test'
(Pdb) p str[3:]
's is a test'
```

If you notice, in this example, I even created a new local variable: str. It would exist within the program if I wanted it to, but in this case, I simply wanted to see what the rightmost characters of the string were, so I used the debugger to print them out.

Changing a Variable in the Debugger

What if you want to change a variable in the debugger? No problem—just set it to a value. If you modify your little calculation program from Listing 19.4 like this:

```
import pdb

def func(x, y, z, a):
    x = y + z + a
    y = x + a + 1
    z = 34
    return x + y + z

pdb.set_trace()

val = func(1,2,3,4)
print("Val = {}".format(val))
```

You can run the program and look at the output:

```
> ch19_5.py(11)<module>()
-> val = func(1,2,3,4)
(Pdb) c
Val = 57
```

In the preceding lines, you set the value of your variable "val" to the return value of the call to the function func(). This will then be used for the remainder of the program execution. You then tell the debugger to continue using the "c" command and print out the final result of val.

But now, let's set a breakpoint in the function and modify one of the variables. You can see what happens in Listing 19.5.

```
> ch19_5.py(11)<module>()
-> val = func(1,2,3,4)
(Pdb) s
--Call--
> chapter 19\ch19_5.py(3)func()
-> def func(x, y, z, a):
(Pdb) n
> chapter 19\ch19_5.py(4)func()
-> x = y + z + a
(Pdb) n
> chapter 19\ch19_5.py(5)func()
-> y = x + a + 1
(Pdb) p x
```

```
9
(Pdb) x = 1
(Pdb) p x
1
(Pdb) c
Val = 41
```

Listing 19.5

The result of a debugging session changing a variable.

As you can see, you've modified the value of x, changing it from the calculated value of 9 to the set value of 1. As you might guess, this modifies the end calculation to now be 41 instead of 57. So, yes, you can change the program while it is running in the debugger!

Exiting the Debugger

Once you are done debugging your program, there are really two ways to exit the program:

- **Run the "c" or continue command until the program naturally exits on its own.** This works fine as long as the program does not encounter an error or exception, which could lead it to get caught in some sort of loop waiting for the debugger to fix the problem.

- **Run the "q" or quit command to immediately exit the program by calling the exit() method.** If your program simply calculates things or prints out values the user enters, it is safe to use this at any time. Otherwise, you may want to exit the program in a more natural fashion.

 ERROR MESSAGE

The "q" command is a bad ending to a program and may cause open files to lose their data, or connections to be lost to databases and other machines.

Final Thoughts on Programming

So here we are, at the end of the book, looking back on all that you have read and thought about. There are some things I'd like you to keep in mind when you go forward—things that will really help you to get a jump on being a programmer.

First, never be afraid to try new things. That applies to life in general, but programming specifically. Don't say "I can't do that" when talking about a webpage, a system service, an application, or anything else. Try it and see if you can make some headway. You learn so much more by trying and failing than you ever do by watching someone who already knows how to do something do it over again.

Next, think before you code. I can't really stress this enough. Too many programmers leap into writing the complex code for an application without thinking the problem through. Then, when they have discovered that a new wrinkle causes all their pretty code to not work anymore, they "hack" it to work around the issues instead of redesigning it. Always know what you are going to do before you start.

Finally, don't be overawed by those "hot shot" programmers who know how to do everything. They didn't know it all to begin with, and neither do you. Life is about learning, learning is about experience, and only time can bring you the experience you need.

So good luck, good coding, and enjoy yourself. Programming is one of the few things you can do for yourself *and* for others and still make yourself happy.

The Least You Need to Know

- The debugger is a package built into Python that allows you to analyze your program while it is running and make changes as necessary.
- Unlike many other programming languages, code must be instrumented, or modified, in Python in order to use the debugger.
- The debugger can be used to examine and modify values within the program, and can even call built-in functions in Python using those variables.
- Breakpoints allow you to wait until a specific piece of code is loaded and interpreted before beginning the debugging process.

Glossary

accessibility   Refers to whether functions or classes outside of a given class can access the data within the class. Data can be either privately or publicly accessible.

agile programming   A methodology that works directly with users, delivering workable software as quickly as possible.

aliasing   Creating a name that can be used in place of another—usually longer—name.

argument   A variable passed to a program or function that allows it to customize its behavior.

array   A group of variables stored under a single name.

assignment   This simply means putting something on the right side of the equals sign.

binary   Base-2 math, made up of zeroes and ones. This is how machine code used to be written.

Boolean   A true or false value.

break   When referring to a breakpoint, this means "stop," rather than "destroy."

Central Processing Unit (CPU)   Considered the "brains" of a computer, this can add and subtract, save little bits of memory, and retrieve information.

class   The encapsulation of a set of functions and data that model a real-world object. Creating a class is like creating a blueprint for a bunch of objects of a given type.

code by comment   This refers to writing out a series of comments indicating what you plan to do, and then filling in the code between them as you implement it.

coding   The process of creating an application program. *See also* programming.

command prompt   A simple text-based screen allowing you to enter commands and have them directly executed by the computer.

comment   A textual entry in a program that helps other programmers understand the code. Comments are not read or used by the interpreter or compiler.

compiled application   An application that has been translated from human-readable form into code a computer can understand directly.

concatenation   A sequential link of two or more pieces of information.

conditional   An if, else, or elif statement that branches the code based on the value of an expression.

constant   A value that can't be changed, such as the number of days in a month.

data types   Classifications that identify a type or types of data (such as integer), which determines the possible values for that type.

debugger   A program that aids in finding and fixing problems in an application.

declaration   Defining the name and type of a variable.

decomposition   The process of breaking down a big problem into smaller problems.

default   The program setting if the user does not select anything for that value. It is the programmer's responsibility to make sure that all persistent settings for a given value have a default value.

edge case   This refers to a condition that isn't normally encountered but could be.

editor   Similar to a word processor, an editor helps programmers write programs by formatting and checking the text for syntax.

enumerate   To go through a list or set and process each element in some way. An enumeration might be the three colors of a traffic light, such as Red, Yellow, and Green.

epoch   The start of time from the viewpoint of a computer. Normally, the epoch is January 1, 1970.

exception   An error that prevents the program from continuing unless handled by the software.

extensible   In terms of a programming language, this means the language itself can be built upon to create new modules that other programmers can use.

firmware   The software provided by the computer manufacturer to run the hardware in the computer.

fixed format   When each line in the file has data that appears at a specific position.

floating-point number   A number that contains a decimal point. Computers have trouble representing floating-point numbers.

function   A single block of code that accomplishes a single task and can be reused.

graphical user interface (GUI)   A type of user interface that relies on icons, menus, and a mouse, but not typing in commands.

hard coded   Refers to something written directly into a program, potentially in multiple places, where it can't be easily modified.

homogenous   When referring to data, it is data that is all of the same type.

IDLE   The built-in editor and interpreter for Python. *See also* programming editor.

immutable   Unable to be changed. An immutable data structure has data that stays the same forever.

import   To use an external source of code in your own application.

inheritance   Building a class from the basic functionality of an existing class and then adding new functions.

input devices   These provide information to the computer from the user. Other examples of input devices are scanners and card readers, which are common add-ons to computers these days.

installer   An application that puts a program on your computer and configures it.

interpreted application   An application read line by line by a third program (called an *interpreter*), which then executes the code in those lines.

iteration   The repetition of a block of statements within a program. Multiple iterations mean multiple times through the loop.

literal   A constant value, such as 1 or "Hello, world." Constants can be used to describe how to do something or as a prompt for inputting data.

loop   An interactive construct that allows you to repeat a given set of instructions more than once.

module   A set of related functions that accomplish a single task.

mutable   A variable that can have its value changed. A mutable data structure can be changed at any time.

negative aspects   When testing, this refers to looking for bad inputs and inputs that make no sense.

Network Interface Card (NIC)   This allows a computer to talk to networks, such as the internet.

object-oriented programming   A programming method that tries to model real-world entities as programming objects or classes.

persistent storage   Data that remains even after the computer is turned off. Normally, persistent storage is on a device, such as a hard drive or cloud.

pointer (file)   The current position in a file from which all reading and writing will be done.

positive aspects   When testing, this refers to finding out if things do what they're supposed to do.

programming   The science of producing software from requirements using specialized languages.

programming editor   Something like a word processor for programmers. The programming editor helps programmers create the text that will make up a program. *See also* IDLE.

Python   A program created by Guido von Rossum as an interpreted language for writing programming scripts.

requirements   A set of rules and functionality a program is intended to follow.

scope   The lifetime of a variable or function within a program.

set   A unique list of values.

signed value   This type allows for both positive and negative values (for example, -1 or 1).

single point of responsibility   An important rule in programming that says a function or class should do only one thing.

slicing   Extracting a portion of an array or a set.

stack trace   As each call to a function is made, the name and address of that function is "pushed" onto the stack so that it can be "unwound." This means the program keeps track of where it has been so it can return along the same path that it took, but in reverse.

structure   An assemblage of data elements grouped under a single name. A structure contains other objects that can be simple (such as numbers, strings, and so on) or complex (such as other structure objects).

tab stops   The points to which you can advance the printing of letters. These are often used to align text.

tarball   A UNIX compressed file that contains all the stuff you need to run a programming language, such as Python.

testing   Verifying that a program does what it is supposed to do—and doesn't do what it is not supposed to do.

tick   The smallest unit of time that a computer uses, measured by a single iteration of the computer CPU.

traceback   A list of functions that were called previous to the traceback being dumped to the user console. This is Python's way of indicating there's an error in the code.

tuple   A variable array in Python that holds multiple values. Tuples are the only way to return multiple values.

type   A set of rules that applies to a given element (such as time) and defines the set of allowable values and actions that can be used with that type.

unicode   A character set that allows for foreign languages.

unsigned value   This type allows only for positive values.

usability   A multifaceted term that refers to how easy it is for users to accomplish whatever task they need to do.

value   A typed element that can be assigned to a variable or used by a function.

variable   A programming element that contains values of various types and can be modified by the programmer.

white box   This kind of testing requires you to look at the code and see how it works, so you can test individual blocks and choices within the code.

Resources

One of the hallmarks of a good programmer is always wanting to learn, always striving to improve, and always having curiosity about how others do things and whether they are better than how you do them.

The internet is a vast place filled with information, both good and bad, about programming. Likewise, there are software products that can help—or hinder—your programming career. There are even books that can help with specific issues—or with answers to problems you might encounter along the way. In this appendix, I show you some of the places you might go to find answers, learn new ways to do things, or enhance your knowledge of the Python programming language or the basics of programming.

The information you learn about here isn't specific to a way of programming—rather, it focuses on how people choose to do things, how the language can be manipulated, and how you can improve your own coding style by looking at others.

IDE Resources

As a programmer, your first natural instinct is going to be to look for software to help you write code. I've touched on this subject briefly in the book, but right now, I'd like to talk about the kinds of software you are going to need to move your programming forward to professional levels.

An Integrated Development Environment (IDE) allows you not only to write and edit code, but also to compile and run it within the environment. Up to this point, you have been using IDLE, but it is really a very poor man's solution to the problem. Although you can search the web for Python IDEs, I'd like to recommend a few that have been used in the past with much success:

Komodo (komodoide.com/komodo-edit): This is a commercial IDE that supports multiple languages and multiple versions of those languages. It has most of the functionality you would expect in any editor, with the addition of code completion, code debugging, syntax highlighting, and others.

Monkey Studio (monkeystudio.org): This is an interesting cross-breed between a visual designer and an IDE for writing, compiling, and running code. It is different because it allows you to design GUI (Graphical User Interfaces) using the cross-platform QT library, which is not a part of Python. You can drag and drop elements on to a page to your heart's content, write all of the code in the background with your Python editor, compile it all, and run it on multiple platforms (Windows, Mac, and so on).

Ninja-IDE (ninja-ide.org/downloads): This stands for "Ninja is not just another IDE," a programmer's idea of a joke. It has all of the standard functionality, as well as debugging, integrated editing and compiling, and syntax highlighting. Ninja-IDE also has the big advantage in that it is free.

I'm quite sure that by the time this book comes out there will be hundreds of new ones. Just do a web search for "Python IDE" and see which one strikes your fancy. It may be that some work better for you now but aren't as good for you later. That's okay; learning new stuff is always good!

Websites

While websites come and go on the internet, some of them are worth keeping track of. As a beginning programmer, you should pay attention to three types of websites:

- Standards and requirements for code

- Websites offering sample code and techniques for working with the language you are using

- Websites that have people willing to examine your code and help you out with it or simply explain how something works

The following are the websites I think are the best of each type.

Python (python.org): The clear winner in the standards race is Python's website, which is the main repository for all of the documentation and standards for the Python programming languages. It can not only tell you what is in a given version, but also what has been deprecated, added, or removed for that version. The website is very simple, with very few bells and whistles, and lets you do what you need to do with a minimum of effort.

ActiveState Code (http://code.activestate.com): This site is a great resource for sample code and techniques. It contains many "recipes," as the site calls them, of how to do specific actions in Python (such as sending email or writing XML to a file and reading it back). The site is populated by Python programmers, many of whom started out just like you.

Stack Overflow (stackoverflow.com): For answers to your questions or just hints on how to proceed from other people's questions, check out this website. It is run and posted to by programmers that range from beginners, to hackers, to professionals, so you are sure to find your answer there. The site has a list of the most recent questions, answers, and comments, as well as room for you to enter your own. You can also search to see if anyone has asked your question—or something like it—before.

Books

The following are some books that can help you learn more about programming and the Python language.

Beazley, David, and Brian K. Jones. *Python Cookbook,* 3rd ed. Sebastopol, CA: O'Reilly Media, Inc., 2013.

This book provides excellent examples of Python code and algorithms.

Lutz, Mark. *Learning Python,* 5th ed. Sebastopol, CA: O'Reilly Media, Inc., 2013.

This is a good book on the basics of Python.

McConnell, Steve. *Code Complete: A Practical Handbook of Software Construction,* 2nd ed. Redmond, WA: Microsoft Press, 2004.

This is one of the best books ever written about the software development process.

Telles, Matt. *Python Power!: The Comprehensive Guide.* Boston: Thomson Course Technology, 2008.

This Python development book covers all of the various aspects of Python programming by a master programmer.

Index

Symbols

A

B

C

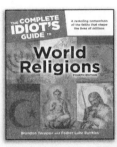

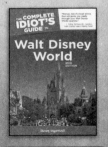